Walt Whitman & the Earth

The IOWA WHITMAN *Series*

Ed Folsom, series editor

A STUDY IN ECOPOETICS

by M. JIMMIE KILLINGSWORTH

University of Iowa Press   Iowa City

Walt Whitman & the Earth

Library of Congress
Cataloging-in-Publication Data
Killingsworth, M. Jimmie.
Walt Whitman and the earth: a study in ecopoetics /
by M. Jimmie Killingsworth.
p. cm.—(The Iowa Whitman series)
Includes bibliographical references and index.
ISBN 0-87745-903-7 (cloth)
1. Whitman, Walt, 1819–1892—Knowledge—Natural
history. 2. Ecology in literature. 3. Nature in
literature. I. Title. II. Series.
PS3242.N2K57 2004
811'.3—dc22   2004047990

04 05 06 07 08 C 5 4 3 2 1

Smile O voluptuous coolbreathed earth!

Earth of the slumbering and liquid trees!

Earth of departed sunset! Earth of the mountains misty-topt!

Earth of the vitreous pour of the full moon just tinged with blue!

Earth of shine and dark mottling the tide of the river!

Earth of the limpid gray of clouds brighter and clearer for my sake!

Far-swooping elbowed earth! Rich apple-blossomed earth!

Smile, for your lover comes!

    —*Leaves of Grass*, 1855

Now I am terrified at the Earth[. . .]

    —"This Compost," 1856

What is this earth to our affections? (unloving earth, without a throb to
    answer ours,

Cold earth, the place of graves.)

    —"Passage to India," 1871

Contents

Acknowledgments *ix*

Introduction: Why Whitman? *1*

ONE. Things of the Earth *15*

TWO. The Fall of the Redwood Tree *48*

THREE. Global and Local, Nature and Earth *74*

FOUR. The Island Poet and the Sacred Shore *98*

FIVE. Urbanization and War *132*

SIX. Life Review *164*

Notes *185*

Bibliography *203*

Index *215*

Acknowledgments

This book seeks a double audience of ecocritics and Whitman scholars, a goal that has required me to draw upon the resources of a wide and generous community. An anonymous reviewer at the University of Iowa Press and my own energetic students and colleagues in the study of American nature writing and environmental rhetoric have provided the impetus and good suggestions I needed to apply the new perspective and methods of ecological criticism to Whitman's poetry for the first time in a book-length work. As for Whitman studies, I have been very lucky in having the attentive guidance of the two leading scholars alive today — the editor of the Whitman Series at Iowa, Ed Folsom, and my dear colleague Whitman biographer Jerome Loving, both of whom read drafts at every stage of the work and gave good suggestions and strong encouragement. I lack the words to thank them sufficiently. Holly Carver of the University of Iowa Press joined Ed Folsom in encouraging me to submit my manuscript, for which I thank her. Sherry Ceniza and the students in her Whitman seminar at Texas Tech also read early chapter drafts and discussed the work with me. My graduate students at Texas A&M provided readings and assistance throughout the project. I owe special appreciation to Soojin Ahn, Lynda Ely, Georgina Kennedy, Steve Marsden, Paul McCann, Amy Montz, Dave Pruett, Matt Sherwood, and Lindsay Sloan. I thank Larry Mitchell, head of the English department at Texas A&M, Dean Charles Johnson and Associate Deans Larry Oliver and Ben Crouch of the College of Liberal Arts, and James Rosenheim of the Glasscock Center for Humanities Research for providing crucial support, both moral and monetary. I thank my daughter, Myrth Killingsworth, an ecocritic in her own right, for being my writing companion throughout the process. In the notes to the text, I try to acknowledge other debts and to show every chance I get that I mean what I say in the introduction: Every scholarly work proceeds as much from a community as it does from the efforts of a solitary individual.

I dedicate this work to my wife and frequent coauthor, Jacqueline S. Palmer, who has but little interest in the interpretation of poetry but knows the value of creative living and how it depends upon the influx of earthly energies. Thank you, Jackie, for showing me the way.

Walt Whitman & the Earth

INTRODUCTION

Why Whitman?

I started college in 1970, the year we celebrated the first Earth Day, two years after Congress passed the National Environmental Policy Act. In my junior year, 1973, the Endangered Species Act was passed. One of the first big test cases was enacted not far from the University of Tennessee where I went to school. The law posed a problem for the plans of the Tennessee Valley Authority (TVA) to dam the Little Tennessee River at a place called Tellico. In fact, TVA had already done substantial work on the dam when the new law was invoked by wildlife biologists working with people we learned to call "environmentalists," a word whose origin dates from my college years. The *Oxford English Dictionary* (1972 supplement) gives 1970 as the earliest instance of the term as used to mean "one who is concerned with the preservation of the environment (from pollution, etc.)" (Killingsworth and Palmer, *Ecospeak* 41). It may seem that environmentalists have been with us forever, but they were a relatively new breed, or were traveling under a new name, when they enlisted the help of a rare little fish called the snail darter, which demanded free-flowing water for spawning and whose presence at Tellico stymied the mighty TVA.

At the time, I was an avid hiker and bird-watcher and an English major with a special interest in Romantic nature poetry. I had been brought up with a love for outdoor life and respect for wild things. But like many young people of the day, I began to feel a deeper identity with nature, a politically charged identity in the early 1970s. My peers and I felt threatened by the same forces that endangered the snail darter. In our minds, these forces coalesced to form what we called "the system," or "the machine," as in "the war machine." As the war in Vietnam lurched toward its chaotic conclusion in 1975, the attention of a mobilized activist youth turned to the war against nature, as we saw it, a war carried out by agents like TVA, the pesticide industry, the oil giants, all part of a pervasive power born during the massive technological mobilization that never wound down after firing up for World War II. President Eisenhower had called it the "military-industrial complex," a system that only grew stronger in our nation's stand-off with the Communist powers in the cold war years.

Like many causes during those formative years of environmentalism, the opposition to the Tellico Dam depended partly on scientific investigation and partly on a web of political identity reinforced by metaphors and myths. The famous nature writer Peter Matthiessen invoked the war metaphor when he traveled to east Tennessee in 1979 to write an article on Tellico for the *New York Review of Books*. He crafted a compelling image of the green and flowing nature of Appalachia cut and partitioned by TVA's concrete and barbed wire, patrolled by armed guards whose presence made the old farms and forests seem like a war zone. Matthiessen spoke of the opposition to the project not only by environmentalists with their snail darter but also by a much older endangered species in the region, the Cherokee Indians. The proposed dam would flood a burial ground and the site of an ancient city that the Cherokees held sacred. In Matthiessen's view, TVA was an irresistible power of government and industry victimizing a peaceful Native people who only wanted to maintain their traditions and honor their ancestors, as well as the tiny snail darter that needed the river to live and propagate its kind, a fetish in those days for the burgeoning movements of political ecology.

The opposition to the Tellico Dam reenacted a grand myth of the conservation movement, stirring the century-old roots of environmentalism with the memory of early efforts to preserve nature in the face of industrial expansion and urban growth. At the center of the myth was the legendary John Muir, the father of conservation. Muir, who entered adulthood as a talented mechanic and inventor, devoted body and mind to the culture of the machine. But a factory accident blinded him temporarily and left him to reconsider his place in the world. When his sight returned, like Paul, he was transformed. Vowing to devote his life to studying not the creations of humankind but those of God, he left his home in the northern Midwest and tramped across the continent, settling finally in the Sierra Nevada, where he formed a bone-deep identification with the high mountains and the great Sequoia trees (trees named, incidentally, for the Cherokee chief Sequoya, whose birthplace was Tellico). Muir wrote volumes of poetic prose extolling the beauty and wisdom of nature, he entertained poets and presidents from Emerson to Theodore Roosevelt in his beloved mountains, he founded the Sierra Club to work for conservation, and he enjoyed many successes in wilderness protection, including the preservation of the Yosemite Valley as a national park. But when he lost the battle to save the Hetch-Hetchy Valley in the late 1890s, his energy failed and he died. It was a dam, built to ensure water for the fast-growing urban population of San Francisco, that did him in. Muir's identification with the land was so complete that his own life seemed to depend upon the preservation of the living waters and the open valley.

By the time TVA finally got to build its dam at Tellico, after hired scientists successfully transplanted snail darters in other rivers, the course of my own environmentalism was firmly established. The sense that something valuable had been lost in the Tellico Valley with its little river and fertile farms led me to join the Sierra Club and to identify with its founder.

My deepening awareness of environmental issues during the years of the Tellico dispute overlapped exactly with my years as a graduate student in English, 1974–1979. On hikes in the Smoky Mountains, one of my regular companions was my friend and major professor F. DeWolfe Miller, who had among other distinguished accomplishments edited a fine edition of Whitman's *Drum-Taps* and was an authority on Whitman's wartime experience. Professor Miller directed my dissertation, which ultimately led to my first book, *Whitman's Poetry of the Body: Sexuality, Politics, and the Text*. As I plodded toward completion of the book, which was finally published in 1989, I worked on a side project involving the language of environmentalism. I had begun to keep a big box of articles about the human threat to nature that I collected from random sources. Now and again I would dip into the box and write an essay about the rhetoric of the environmentalists and their opponents. In 1985 I met Jacqueline Palmer, who also had a box of articles. We decided to merge boxes and work on a book together. The result appeared in 1992, *Ecospeak: Rhetoric and Environmental Politics in America*.

The first article in my box was Matthiessen's essay on Tellico, "How to Kill a Valley," which I saved just as I was saying good-bye to DeWolfe Miller and my friends in Tennessee and heading west where my job search led me. At the time, it never occurred to me to think about my work on Whitman and the body as a project strongly connected to my political and scholarly interest in environmentalism. Considering all the time that Professor Miller and I spent mulling over lines from *Leaves of Grass* as we walked mountain paths through the occasional virgin stand of hemlocks among acres of towering forest regrown in the perpetually wet Appalachian earth after years of logging gave way to national park protection, and considering that I wrote the first chapter of my dissertation while encamped on one of South Carolina's sea islands where the very plants and animals as well as the music of the great ocean resonated with Whitman's experience as the island poet of the New York coastline, I can now only feel obtuse at missing the connection.

But perhaps there are good reasons for my having missed it. Critical consciousness is a communal process, and intellectual culture like any other tends to create blind spots along with its insights in the process of delimiting topics or points of focus for study. For one thing, I was cautioned to keep my work in rhetoric separate from my work in poetics, following the tradition that comes down from Aristotle. A reader of an early draft of *Whitman's Poetry of the Body* urged me to delete every mention of the word *rhetoric* from my pages. Though people like Paul de Man were using the word regularly at the time to describe their criticism of poetic tropes, rhetoric was mainly associated in the American academy of the 1970s and 1980s with practical work in composition (which occupied much of my time as a teacher) and with political prose. I found that my earliest colleagues in the study of environmental rhetoric came from departments of speech communication. Even when the first works of self-proclaimed ecocriticism began to appear in American literary studies in the 1990s, the focus fell primarily upon nonfiction prose in the tradition of Emerson, Thoreau, and Muir. The work I did myself centered on Rachel Carson, Aldo Leopold, and other naturalists who wrote lovely prose with a keen political edge.[1]

The political edge was important. In the early days of environmental rhetoric and ecocriticism, we gravitated toward writers who were overtly political in their engagement with nature. Our chief aim was to "evaluate texts and ideas in terms of their coherence and usefulness as responses to environmental crisis" (Kerridge 5).[2] This approach limited the field nicely as far as nineteenth-century authors were concerned. In England, Wordsworth, Byron, and Shelley, who caught something of the Luddite spirit, could be profitably studied as early influences on environmentalist consciousness.[3] In America, nature poetry seemed tame by comparison to both the English Romantics and our own authors of fiery transcendental prose. Until recently, it did not occur to me to ask why.

I was led back to Whitman and his contemporaries in American poetry through my study of conceptual metaphors in ecology, a study that gradually morphed into a preoccupation with "ecopoetics." Instead of looking for influences and forerunners of environmentalism in literature from various periods, I gravitated toward a form of study that attempted a more radical investigation into the possibilities and limits of human creativity, a study of how we use language to figure out our relationship to the earth, the study of *poiesis* as a kind of making that honors the search for beauty and meaning in human exchanges with nature. As I began to see that the appeal of scientific and activist prose depended upon metaphorical links with topics considered outside the circle of environmentalist concern — Rachel Carson's linking of pesticide abuse with nuclear weaponry and with advances in medical research, for example — I kept remembering my work on Whitman's wild personifications of the earth, his borrowings from medical science, his use of everything from bees and flowers to machines and electricity in celebrations of human productivity and sexual experience. When I decided it was time to choose a site for a scholarly treatment of American ecopoetics, I kept finding myself on the familiar ground of Whitman's poetry. After finally accepting it as my point of departure, I have found the old ground rich enough to generate another book, which amounts to a reconsideration of Whitman's language in light of an ecological understanding of the world and a reconsideration of that world through the lens of Whitman's mighty language.

In this thinking, I find myself part of a communal shift in ecocriticism. I follow the British scholar Jonathan Bate, for example, who has suggested that *ecopoetics* may be an ascendant term in the field: "Ecopoetics asks in what respects a poem may be a making (Greek *poiesis*) of the dwelling-place — the prefix eco- is derived from Greek *oikos*, 'the home or place of dwelling'" (*Song of the Earth* 75) — and the terms "making" and "place of dwelling" recall Martin Heidegger's famous essays "The Question Concerning Technology" and "Building, Dwelling, Thinking," which have been widely cited in environmental rhetoric, philosophy, and politics if not in ecocriticism before Bate. Heidegger's "Question Concerning Technology" illustrates how German Green thinking links back to Muir's experience and anticipates the episode of the snail darter by focusing on a dam — this time a hydroelectric project on the Rhine River — as an example of technology that not only uses the resources of nature for human purposes (a necessary and inevitable requirement of life) but actually alters nature at the level of being. Unlike a boat or even a bridge, the dam interferes with the very "riverness" of the Rhine. Heidegger's distinctions among crafts that are in varying degrees purely instrumental in their negligence of nonhuman being or creative in their concern for enhancing both sides of the interaction become for Bate the foundation of an ecopoetical hermeneutics, which for me suggests a way of questioning the interplay of human language and the objects of nature, paralleling the interplay of authors and readers. Both forms of engagement — from author and nature to author and reader — are matters of give and take that may involve mutual betterment, harmful neglect, or a struggle for domination and manipulation. As Kenneth Burke says in *A Rhetoric of Motives*, the process of identification, which I see at the heart of both environmental rhetoric and ecopoetics, is traditionally associated with overcoming division in a setting of discord and domination (Burke famously invokes the barnyard) but also includes the kinds of appeals associated with the lover, the peacemaker, and the apostle.

While Bate insists that the ecopoetical turn he pursues does not deny the political import of nature writing and ecological criticism, it does suggest for him the simplemindedness of beginning and ending critical work with "a set of assumptions or proposals about particular environmental issues"; instead, he argues, ecopoetics should seek "a way of reflecting upon what it might mean to dwell upon the earth" (*Song of the Earth* 266). And while the field should not be confined to poetry as traditionally defined, or even imaginative literature broadly defined — *poiesis* being an aspect of creativity that touches all parts of life and all genres of writing — it should recognize that poetry deserves special attention: "the rhythmic, syntactic and linguistic intensifications that are characteristic of verse-writing frequently give a peculiar force to the *poiesis*" so that poetry may well offer "the language's most direct path of return to the *oikos*, the place of dwelling" (75–76). Metered writing offers "a quiet but persistent music, a recurring cycle, a heartbeat," the hum of the body that echoes the song of the earth (76).

For me, ecopoetics remains a tributary of ecocriticism, not a separate stream as Bate sometimes suggests. My study favors ecopoetics but also goes with the mainstream of ecocriticism at times. Roughly speaking, I use the term *ecopoetics* when my readings aim for a primarily phenomenological significance and *ecocriticism* when they take a sharply political turn, invoking issues on the current environmentalist agenda. The perspectives shift here and there to show the multifaceted qualities of my subject.

As for my choice of subject in particular — Walt Whitman's poetry — Bate's search into the canon of high Romanticism and its philosophical heritage for the roots of ecopoetics certainly hints toward a rationale for exploring American versions of Romantic and post-Romantic writing.[4] But we can also see an eccopoetical treatment of poets like Whitman as part of an expansion of the canon that dominated early ecocriticism now under way on other fronts as well. Ecocritics are pursuing their themes in ever wider circles of international literature and in a greater variety of genres and modes. They are attending more closely to women writers and underrepresented ethnic groups who have their own versions of environmentalism — ecofeminism, the environmental justice movement, and postcolonial concerns with globalization.[5] Recent critics have gone so far as to suggest that since all writing is concerned with place at some level, any text may yield to the methods and may advance the favored themes of ecocriticism (see Dobrin). Yet some seasoned authors draw back at this suggestion. Patrick D. Murphy, for example, whose work champions ecofeminists and writers of color, suggests in his book *Farther Afield in the Study of Nature-Oriented Literature* that ecocriticism must be careful to distinguish among different levels of engagement with the earth.[6] Struggling to keep Lawrence Buell's concept of the "environmental imagination" alive (when even Buell in his current work seems to be moving on), Murphy argues that "nature-oriented" literature keeps the nonhuman Other as a central concern, refusing to treat the environment as a mere setting for human actions. While his category of "environmental literature" (as distinct from "nature writing," "environmental writing," and "nature literature") is wide enough to admit Walt Whitman — largely because of Whitman's willingness to "encounter the other" in nature, a feature of "environmental" poetry in this scheme (Murphy 11) — I would argue that Whitman's poetry and prose also participate in the other categories of Murphy's taxonomy and that we can sometimes see shifts from category to category within the same text. Failing to find the value in categories that bleed so heavily into one another, I would prefer the widest possible opening of the field and say that ecopoetics has as much to offer to a study of cereal boxes or technical reports as it does to canonical American poetry.[7] In this position, I join Cheryll Glotfelty, among others, in claiming for ecocriticism a field as wide as that claimed by feminism, Marxism, postcolonial studies, and any other critical school. It is not the literature we study but ecocriticism itself that is bound to keep the earthly other in sharp focus.

As the scope of ecocriticism has expanded, so have the theoretical underpinnings of the field grown more complex and sophisticated. Writers such as Bate, who strives powerfully (and in my view successfully) to establish a theoretical foundation for ecopoetics that extends (even as it questions) the hermeneutics of Paul Ricoeur and Martin Heidegger, admits the difficult position of ecocriticism in the current critical climate. Because the "'crisis of representation' or 'hermeneutics of suspicion' is at the core of 'postmodern' literary theory" (or any other version of theory that begins with the prefix *post-*), "[e]cology, with its affirmation of not only the existence, but also the sacredness, of the-things-of-nature-in-themselves seems naïve in comparison" (*Song of the Earth* 247). However, if ecocriticism and environmental rhetoric emerged under the sign of a "naive" realism, which views "nature" as an object that can be brought seamlessly into the language of those who would defend, promote, and protect it, recent work has developed along a continuum whose opposite pole is a radical social constructionist position, which says that nature is always only a construct of language that has more to say about human desire and political ideology than it does about earthly objects themselves.[8] Between these two poles of naive empiricism and social construction we find a variety of positions. On one side, realism has developed into a more complex viewpoint that, while granting the complexity and difficulty of representation, retains some faith in the factuality and reality of the solid earth. At the other pole, one step back from pure social constructionism, we find phenomenological positions such as those of Bate and Buell, who adopt "a more dialectical model for understanding the relationship between social ideologies and the actual dynamics of natural systems and processes" (Levin 175).[9]

Like my subject Walt Whitman, I find myself occupying various points along the continuum in different stages of my thinking and writing. And while I would prefer to see myself in the exact middle, somewhere between the complex realist and the phenomenological positions, it is not my goal to settle the internecine disputes on theory within the field but to reflect and expand upon the theoretical possibilities, adding some neglected or short-changed perspectives, such as new developments in "thing theory" (Brown) and the concept of "resonance" in ecological communication (Luhmann), both of which have powerful implications for a nature-oriented mysticism like Whitman's, even as I hold some of the latest developments at arm's length. I cannot accept, for example, David Mazel's notion that "the supermarket is a complex and instructive nexus of energy flows, as pedagogically sound a window into ecological relations as a pristine forest or wetland" (28), though I admire his critique of environmentalism as a cloak for personal and political agendas on the part of those who claim to "speak for nature."[10] I appreciate Lawrence Buell's blurring of the lines between nature and culture, and between rural and urban life, as a foil for the romanticizing of pristine nature as an alternative to human folly, an earthly force to replace the heavenly gods as the object of our appeals and hope, but I resist going too far in that direction either. The environmental historian William Cronon, on whom Buell relies, is no doubt right in suggesting that the wilderness is more of a myth than a reality in modern life, but the reason for that condition is that human beings have remade the earth on a scale and with powers that our human ancestors, who also walked every part of this land, could not have managed. In her introductory essay "Ecocriticism," Kate Rigby thus argues that it is "precisely the imperilment of the biosphere wrought by [human alteration] which impels the ecocritical reinstatement of the referent as a matter of legitimate concern" (154). It is still valuable for the environmental imagination to reconstruct an image of wilderness and, while acknowledging that the world has altered under human influence, remember that something resists us.

It has been said that facts are the things that refuse to yield to the human will in thought and language, that remain the same no matter what we think or say (Latour 93; Fleck 98). Along these lines, we might also say that while Nature with a capital N is certainly a product of human thinking, an ideological construct, the earth continues to be one thing that resists. Rigby writes, "to the extent that the ecological crisis pertains to what Lacan terms the 'real,' that which precedes, defies and disrupts symbolic representation, it remains strangely elusive to thought, even while pressing in upon us daily, shifting the literal ground of our being" (152). Ecocriticism attempts to bring the crisis and the real into the foreground against formidable odds: "For at the same time that ecosystems sustaining life on earth have become ever more critically endangered by our growing numbers and levels of consumption, ever more people (above all, those whose ecological debt is the largest) live at an ever greater remove from the natural world, unmindful of their impact upon the earth" (151–152). Looking for beauty and meaning in an increasingly engineered world, ecopoetics has an interest in preserving the concept of nonhuman being, that which exists outside language and culture and which hints at something larger and more lasting than the products of human hubris. This acknowledgment of the other-than-human — or "more-than-human natural world" (Rigby 155) — is one of the key points I take away from my reading of the final chapter in Bate's *The Song of the Earth* — entitled "What Are Poets For?" — which offers a cogent apology for ecopoetics in light of the late-twentieth-century distaste for the concept of representation. What I attempt in the following chapters is an extension of Bate's line of thinking that, in drawing upon American pragmatism, among other sources, points us away from a preoccupation with representation. Pragmatism grows impatient with definition, with Heideggerian and Platonic essentialism, and wants to know not so much what something is but what it *does* and how it *fits* in larger patterns and systems.[11]

Even with the new range and theoretical richness of ecocriticism, few scholars have undertaken monographs that look deeply into the writings of a single author. Indeed, some of the leaders in the field have been criticized for their truncated readings that never seem to go beyond the level of the general survey or introduction.[12] With this work on Whitman, I hope to signal a new trend in the field, the aim of which is not only to read deeply into the work of single authors but also, while acknowledging the authors' participation in larger movements, to go beyond the general categorization of them as "naturalistic," "pastoral," "nature oriented," "bioregional," "environmental," "romantic," "modern," or "postmodern" and capture something of their individuality as people and as poets living in their particular corners of the earth.

My central ecocritical contention is that Whitman's poetry embodies the kinds of conflicted experience and language that continually crop up in the discourse of political ecology. At midcareer, when he was producing his most exuberant celebrations of human potential and natural abundance, Whitman was forced to redefine his life and poetic mission in the face of a great and terrible war. The Civil War became the defining moment for American culture as he knew it. The early poems in *Leaves of Grass*, written and published in the 1850s, anticipated the conflict with frantic calls for democratic union. Then came the poems of *Drum-Taps* and his best-known prose works, which illuminated the experience of living through the war as a witness and worker in the military hospitals. Finally, the later poems surveyed an America devastated by loss but sustaining the hope of a more fully democratic nation for the future. Scholars agree that the poems written after the war diverge sharply from those written before in tone, style, and form even when addressing the same themes, including the theme of nature. The difference in quality and voice has been a matter of much dispute. An ecopoetical reading offers a new perspective on the changes in Whitman's work. The poems reflected upon shifting historical contexts, not only the obvious social and political changes brought on by the war but also geographical upheavals in an age of westward expansion, urbanization, galloping development in industry and technology, and emerging globalization. The poems were also affected by Whitman's own physical life. Mediating between world and text, the poet's body felt the accelerated decline of illness and grief associated with the war and its aftereffects, helping to account in part for the increasing abstraction and distance in the postwar poetry's treatment of natural scenes and phenomena.

In short, Whitman's poetry forms a powerful record of life in an aging body, in a war-torn nation, and in an increasingly troubled landscape. Ecopoetical scholarship traces the patterns of this record and seeks connections to our own times. Studies in environmental rhetoric and ecocriticism have suggested, for example, that the discourse of environmentalism in the 1970s had deep ties to cold war rhetoric and the experience of the Vietnam War and that with the new politics of globalization (and rhetoric about the "end of the cold war"), the old metaphors and myths (such as the "population bomb" and other relics of the atomic age) have grown stale and fail to attract a new generation of activists and scholars in humanistic environmental studies.[13] Concern about the "shelf life" of issues and their representations should make us wary of historical arguments that identify post–World War II cultural representations with nineteenth-century Romanticism, as seen in everything from the popular use of the term *Luddite* to the canonization of Wordsworth and Thoreau in British and American ecocriticism. But the interplay among the discourses of war and nature — the world as a scene of battle enacted repeatedly over many generations in the last two centuries — strikes me as a pattern with ongoing significance. This pattern and many others stand out boldly in Whitman's writing in part because we can see it at a distance.

I suspect that the tendency of early ecocriticism to canonize particular kinds of nature writing arose from a need to seek allies and find heroes in the struggle to save the earth. As we come to see "saving the earth" as one metaphor among many — a metaphor conditioned perhaps by the historical experience of the cold war — our focus can broaden to include a greater diversity of writers, the study of whose work may lead to new ways of understanding the human experience of (and on) the earth. And these new ways, we can hope, will partake of values that have guided poetics since ancient times — the search for beauty and meaning in a warring world and an alternative to discourses whose value is measured by the starkest gauges of utility and material profit.

I take as my point of departure in chapter 1 a poem from the second (1856) edition of *Leaves of Grass* — "This Compost" — in my view, Whitman's greatest contribution to the literature of ecology. The poem begins not with a celebration of identity with the earth but with a dramatic recognition of difference. We see the poet face to face with the earthly other, alienated from the very ground of his daily walk by the "thingishness" of the environment, which forces him toward the recognition of death, disease, and dissolution. Though best known as a poet of imposition — the "imperial self," an ego spreading outward — Whitman appears in "This Compost" and in several poems and passages from the 1855 and 1856 *Leaves* as a poet of limits. This chapter considers particularly the limits of language as the poet understood them. Drawing upon recent ventures in what has somewhat whimsically been called "thing theory," as well as theories of ecological communication, I identify in Whitman's response to the earth three crucial incapacities — cognitive, moral, and metaphysical — associated with knowing the objects of the earth through human language. In readings of such poems as "A Song of the Rolling Earth" and "A Noiseless Patient Spider," I attempt a sketch of Whitman's metaphysics as an emerging mysticism of earthly attachment, anticipating the "deep ecology" of the late twentieth century. In many of the early poems, Whitman prefers resonance and indirection to a more thoroughgoing transcendent knowledge and confident representation as a model for human interaction with the earth.

But Whitman's tendency to see the things of the earth as resonant spirits, available to human consciousness only indirectly, is balanced by the tug of a different poetical impulse, the tendency to see nature as a resource. This impulse informs a venerable tradition of nature poetry in nineteenth-century American literature, which takes an object of nature — a spider, a seashell, a water fowl — as a point of reflection upon some aspect of the human condition. This genre, with its tangled history and its problematical but pervasive central trope of personification, occupies center stage in chapter 2, which shows how, depending upon the context, personification can be allied with any one of three politically rich attitudes toward the natural world: nature as object, nature as resource, and nature as spirit. A study of Whitman's late-career poem "Song of the Redwood-Tree" demonstrates his struggle with these various attitudes and the trouble he had, despite his seemingly confident alignment of his poetic program with the reprehensible politics of manifest destiny, in resolving his doubts about the materialistic development of America's land and people.

Chapter 3 continues the discussion of manifest destiny in an exploration of what I see as the globalizing impulse in Whitman's work. The argument is that, from the ecocritical perspective, Whitman's concept of spiritual power takes on a sinister aspect in poems that try to extend the poet's reach beyond the local to national and global contexts, as in the 1871 poem "Passage to India." The globalizing ambition in *Leaves of Grass*, as in American culture generally, is associated with technological development, imperialist politics, abstraction and distance with respect to the natural world, and a spiritualistic pretension to religious superiority. This chapter follows the recent trend to explore "the larger problems that [both] postcolonialism and ecocriticism grapple with," most especially "problems of identity and representation" (O'Brien 145).

Chapter 4 goes the other way, looking deeper into Whitman's success as a local poet — even a "regional" poet — a term of belittlement in the nationalistic and imperialistic culture of modernity, which distinguishes sharply between poets whose appeal is merely regional and poets whose appeal is "universal." An ecopoetical rethinking of such categories favors the view of Walt Whitman as an island poet of the northeastern coastline of America, a poet belonging to a special location, for him a sacred place. Most of Whitman's masterpieces feature scenes of the shoreline and the wetlands of America — encounters between the poet and his "lover, the sea" in "Song of Myself," "Spontaneous Me," and "This Compost"; the ocean as the powerful death-speaking mother of the boy on the beach in "Out of the Cradle Endlessly Rocking" or the force that threatens the "beautiful gigantic swimmer" in "The Sleepers"; the flood tide of the sea-going river that separates the great cities in "Crossing Brooklyn Ferry"; and the swampy retreat of the mournful "solitary singer" in "When Lilacs Last in the Dooryard Bloom'd." Through readings of scenes where water meets land in *Leaves of Grass*, this chapter reveals the significance of sacred places for ecopoetics in general and for the metaphysics of Whitmanian soulfulness in particular.

Chapter 5 considers the effects of modernization upon Whitman's thinking and poetry, focusing on two dominant forces of modern life — urbanization and war. I begin with a modest revision of the view that sees Whitman as America's first urban poet, considering him instead as an urbanizing poet, a powerful representative of the generations of nineteenth- and twentieth-century Americans who, in ever greater numbers, left homes in country villages and small towns to become city dwellers. His vision of a city life built on natural models and preserving an ecologically rich exchange of natural energies among people and places — a vision celebrated in the 1856 poem "Crossing Brooklyn Ferry" — gradually gave way to doubt about the sanity of urban existence. As early as the 1860 *Leaves*, the poet is inclined to retreat to "paths untrodden" to seek renewal of his energies in communion with the earth and with a select few beloved companions rather than the masses of the great city. In the middle of Whitman's adjustment to city life, the Civil War intervened. The weight of critical opinion suggests that the poems written after the war lack the vitality and power of the poems of the 1850s. Recently, biographical critics have suggested another view: that the war in fact "saved Whitman."[14] Both views acknowledge that the war brought a great change in the poet's work. A corresponding change swept over the whole of American life, the social world and its natural environment. Urbanization, technological advancement, and globalization, in rhetoric and in reality, were bound to leave their mark on poetic life. This chapter considers the curious fact that Whitman's direct treatments of war are nearly always loosely packaged with writings about nature — poems such as "When I Heard the Learn'd Astronomer" and "Give Me the Splendid Silent Sun" placed alongside poems of the battlefield, camp, and hospital in *Drum-Taps* and the prose memoranda of the war included alongside rambling accounts of nature in *Specimen Days*. I argue that the war undermined Whitman's confidence in his earthly mysticism and his faith in the redemptive cycles of nature. The wartime poet added modernism to his repertoire, experimenting with imagistic genres that abandoned the prophetic mode in favor of something closer to a reportorial objectivity. When the prophetic muse did overtake him, he began to write a very different kind of poetry, extending the martial spirit he admired in the young soldiers he met to the nationalistic goals of westward expansion. A poem like "Pioneers! O Pioneers!" — which first appeared in *Drum-Taps*

— foreshadows the political and aesthetic trends of the big poems published in the 1870s, notably "Passage to India" and "Song of the Redwood-Tree."

Chapter 6 shows how, in his final writings, Whitman struggled to recover his soulful connection to the earth and thereby renew his inspiration. But in the practice of life review that he undertakes in works like *Specimen Days*, he tends not to recover so much as to transform his Romanticism, ending up with a perspective ironically closer both to earlier poets like Wordsworth and Emerson and also to the later environmentalists whose political program depends upon a strong sense of humanity's alienation from nature. Now Whitman appears to us in layers, his profoundly original experiment with dramatizing poetically the resonant and indirect communion with nature still active but competing for attention with a more modern realism that suggests the objectivity of a scientific observer or the photographic gaze of the ecotourist, an aggressive view of nature as a resource for humanity's development, and a Romantic outlook that in passive states sees nature as a retreat from urban mania and a benchmark for human development and in its activist version uses nature as a perspective for critiquing the human world.

In his many moods, Whitman appears, in the reading I offer here, not only as one of our most powerfully creative poetic experimenters but also as a representative figure in American culture. His difficulty in sustaining a vision of nature is not so much a personal failure as an indicator of the immensity and difficulty of the task he set for himself. We continue to struggle with the same issues, above all how to create a discourse worthy of the earth — our home, our mother, our what? And we can continue to profit from retracing the steps of our poetic forebears, none of whom is more problematic, or more rewarding, than Walt Whitman.

CHAPTER ONE

Things of the Earth

Troubles in the relationships among physical objects, people, and abstractions haunt American ecopoetics from the nineteenth century down to the present time. For his part, Whitman follows Wordsworth in resisting the personification of abstractions — treating ideas as if they were people.[1] And like Marx, he resists the treatment of people as if they were objects — the property of slave owners or cogs in the industrial machine — as well as the treatment of abstractions as reified objects.

But problems arise in *Leaves of Grass* with the status of natural objects. The poet's inclination to see himself reflected in nature frequently leads him into an Anglo-American poetic tradition in which the status of an object appears to depend upon its metaphysical or psychological value. The spider of Jonathan Edwards, the waterfall of Henry Vaughan, the waterfowl of William Cullen Bryant, the marsh hen of Sidney Lanier stand as signs of God's power, glory, and grace. Their standing as earthly beings is sacrificed on the altar of allegory and metaphor. Even Wordsworth's daffodils, the bees of Emerson and Dickinson, Oliver Wendell Holmes's chambered nautilus, Marianne Moore's paper nautilus, and Theodore Roethke's rose ultimately serve as grist for the metaphysical mill, representing some aspect of the poet's identity, some imposition of ego upon the face of nature. Notwithstanding strictures against the pathetic fallacy in literary theory and against anthropomorphism in science, personification and other tropes of imposition persist not only in twentieth-century poetry but even in scientifically informed nonfiction prose, in such influential works as Aldo Leopold's *Sand County Almanac* and Rachel Carson's *Silent Spring*, for which the central metaphors of the earth's body and the health of the landscape are keys to an activist rhetoric (see Killingsworth and Palmer, *Ecospeak*, chapter 2).

Such tropes no doubt reinforce human identity with the earth, but we might do well to recall that the etymology of the word *trope* suggests "a turning" and that turning away is the characteristic action of hysteria, according to Freud, a neurosis in which something is denied that eventually comes to haunt the hysterical subject. What may be denied here is that in extracting personal meaning from earthly objects or treating them as poetic property upon which to build the "more stately mansions" of metaphysics, nature poetry turns away from the earth. It aligns ideologically with the extractive industries that overexploit precious minerals, water, and soil, only to find the "environmental problems" of toxicity and scarcity cropping up later like the return of the repressed in the psychoanalytic model (see Killingsworth and Palmer, "The Discourse of 'Environmentalist Hysteria'").

To some extent, as a human art poetry cannot avoid participating in this kind of extractive or acquisitive discourse. Perhaps the most we can ask is that ecopoetics seek a heightened consciousness, a reconsideration of verbal practices that involve categorizing, naming, or identifying with natural objects. At several moments in the first two editions of *Leaves of Grass* (1855 and 1856), Whitman arrives at this point, pausing to consider his relationship to the earth as a poet and a human being. He comes face to face with certain phenomena in nature that cause him to admit his puzzlement and incapacity, even terror. His poetic response anticipates a recent theoretical trend in literary and cultural studies — the consideration of *things* as a category distinct from physical objects, abstractions, and people.

It is the unspeakableness of things that Whitman most commonly dramatizes during these arresting moments. Things suggest the unspeakable in at least two senses that many of us learned directly from our parents. For the unspeakable in the sense of cognitive incapacity, for example, I had in my own household my stepfather's endless stream of fumblings for the right word — the thingamabob, the whatchamacallit, the doohickey — the thing whose name cannot be recalled in the heat of activity, as in "Hand me that thing on the work bench." For the unspeakable in the sense of unfit to be named for fear of moral or social impropriety, I had my mother's usage. For her, as for the parents of many American children, "thing" was a euphemism for the body's "private parts," as in the hesitant instruction to "tell the doctor about your . . . ah . . . thing." The "thingamabob" and the "ah . . . thing" form an ironic pair in a memory I have of my mother stifling a laugh when a woman pulled in next to us at a gas station, the lid of her car's trunk swinging wide open, and complained loudly to the attendant, "I can't get my thing down."

A third sense of the unspeakable thing is one I gleaned not from home but from excursions into Eastern mysticism and Beat poetry. I mean the ineffable, as in "the thing experienced during deep meditation that is beyond words" — the One, according to Hindu metaphysics, "before whom words recoil" (Shankara, qtd. in Huxley 24). In an introduction to the classic of Chinese mysticism, Lao Tzu's *The Way of Life* (*Tao Te Ching*), R. B.

Blakney writes that the mystics of Lao Tzu's time came upon a "problem of communication": "They had discovered, they said, a unique Something for which there was no word or name. It did not belong to the world in which language is born" (17).[2] If you know it, says the Zen master, you can't speak it; if you can speak it, you don't know it. Jack Kerouac provides a fine example in *On the Road*. Recalling the performance of a jazz saxophone player in San Francisco, the ecstatic protagonist Dean Moriarity says, "Now, man, that alto man last night had IT — he held it once he found it; I've never seen a guy who could hold so long." The narrator, Sal Paradise, asks him what he means by this thing, by "IT":

> "Ah well" — Dean laughed — "now you're asking me impon-de-rables — ahem! Here's a guy and everybody's there, right? Up to him to put down what's on everybody's mind. He starts the first chorus, then lines up his ideas, people, yeah, yeah, but get it, and then he rises to his fate and has to blow equal to it. All of a sudden somewhere in the middle of the chorus he *gets it* — everybody looks up and knows; they listen; he picks it up and carries. Time stops. He's filling empty space with the substance of our lives, confessions of his bellybottom strain, remembrance of ideas, rehashes of old blowing. He has to blow across bridges and come back and do it with such infinite feeling and soul-exploratory for the tune of the moment that everybody knows it's not the tune that counts but IT — " Dean could go no further; he was sweating telling about it. (Kerouac 206)

All three of the linguistic limits or incapacities associated with thingish phenomena — the cognitive "thingamabob," the moral "ah . . . thing," and the mystical "It" — intertwine in Whitman's poems. He dramatizes the cognitive incapacity with the frequent use of words like "something" — especially in the early editions of *Leaves of Grass* in which the poet seems eager to get at states of mind, instinctual relationships, and earthly conditions that have no definite name, as in the line "Something I cannot see puts upward libidinous prongs, / Seas of bright juice suffuse heaven" (LG 1855, 30). For the same purpose, he often resorts to the vague demonstrative "this," as in the never-answered question from the 1855 version of "Song of Myself," "Is this then a touch? . . . . quivering me to a new identity" (LG 1855, 32). Compare the first line of Holmes's poem "The Chambered Nautilus" — "This is the ship of pearl" (Holmes, in Ellmann 139) — in which "this" merely connects the name in the title to the first image of the poem in what becomes a virtual slide show of metaphors, the way a lecturer uses a pointer. In contrast, Whitman's "this" hangs like a question mark in the air. Like the pronouns "I" and "you," the demonstrative "this" is what the linguists call a shifter, or deictic. It shifts attention or points to a context, which in this case is unspecified and thus leaves the reader searching (see Benveniste; see also Jakobson).

As for the unspeakable in the sense of morally unfit to be mentioned in public, we need only remember that a contemporary reviewer of *Leaves of Grass* invoked the old legal formula for sodomy as the crime too horrible to be named among Christians. "In our allusion to this book," wrote Rufus Griswold in the *New York Criterion* of November 10, 1855, "we have found it impossible to convey . . . our disgust and detestation . . . without employing language that cannot be pleasing to ears polite; but it does seem that some one should . . . undertake a most disagreeable, yet stern duty. The records of crime show that many monsters have gone on in impunity, because the exposure of their vileness was attended with too great indelicacy. *Peccatum illud horribile, inter Christianos non nominandum*" (Hindus 33).[3] Whitman himself hesitated to name the emotion that he felt for other men. In the 1860 version of the notorious *Calamus* poems, the poet wonders "if other men ever have the like, out of the like feelings?" (CRE 596). The word "like" in this context functions as a thing, "a place holder for some future specifying operation" (Brown 4). In *Calamus*, as in conversations with friends like Horace Traubel, Whitman seemed to be guarding a secret, hinting toward his homosexuality without confessing it directly.[4] But he could also have been incapacitated by his uncertainty over the emotional turmoil he felt about other men or about his own sexual "nature." It was a thing he had trouble naming. "Manly love" and "adhesiveness" and "comradeship" never quite covered it. "I often say to myself about *Calamus*," he told Traubel, "perhaps it means more or less than what I thought myself — means different: perhaps I don't know what it all means — perhaps never did know" (Traubel 1:76).[5] Whatever we may think about Whitman's disingenuousness, his "foxiness," we need not discount his struggle over the right language and his worries about the "unspeakable."[6]

At the third point of incapacity, Whitman dramatizes what seems to be a version of the mystical ineffable in metaphors mingling things sexual, sentimental, and metaphysical. "I mind how we lay in June, such a transparent summer morning," says the poet in the 1855 "Song of Myself," ostensibly addressing his soul: "You settled your head athwart my hips and gently turned over upon me, / And parted the shirt from my bosom-bone, and plunged your tongue to my barestript heart" (LG 1855, 15). Losing their ordinary functions and anatomical coordinates, the heart and tongue in this passage become uncannily thingish. The images "hover over the threshold between the nameable and unnameable, the figurable and unfigurable, the identifiable and unidentifiable" (Brown 5).

One of Whitman's most powerful dramatizations of thingish incapacity occurs in the poem "This Compost," which dates from the second (1856) edition of *Leaves of Grass*. The poem stands as perhaps the most remarkable nineteenth-century contribution to the poetry of ecology in America. It gathers up the threads of the rhetorical and poetic tradition known as "the sublime," the expression of awe that inheres in "human beings' encounters with a nonhuman world whose power ultimately exceeds theirs," inspiring a sense of humility and mortality (Hitt 609–610).[7] And it anticipates the conjunction of science, activism, and spirituality that would become known as "deep ecology" in the nuclear age of the late twentieth century, a worldview that aims toward a reintegration of subject and object, human and nonhuman, but begins with an acknowledgment of the intrinsic worth, autonomy, and power of the more-than-human.[8] In my reading of "This Compost," the poem's ecological power depends upon its treatment of earthy thingishness. To capture fully the nature mystic's view of the earth as the "Wholly (and Holy) Other" (Graber 2), the poet must engage the limits of human language and being, understanding the earth not only from the perspective of identity but primarily as a thing unto itself. In thus encountering the "Other" in nature, "This Compost" qualifies as an early instance of both an "environmental poem" as defined by Patrick D. Murphy (11) and a "sustainable poem" as defined by Leonard M. Scigaj; it stands as "the verbal record of an interactive encounter in the world of our sensory experience between the human psyche and nature, where nature retains its autonomy" (Scigaj 80).

The poem begins with a scene in which the poet catches himself in the moment of turning away, confronted with "something" he refuses to name, categorize, or tame with a trope. He starts not with affirmations of identity or kinship, or with abstractions and distance, but with a nearly physical repulsion. Out to refresh himself in fine Romantic form, he is confronted with a thing unspeakably offensive:

SOMETHING startles me where I thought I was safest,
I withdraw from the still woods I loved,
I will not go now on the pastures to walk,
I will not strip the clothes from my body to meet my lover the sea,
I will not touch my flesh to the earth as to other flesh to renew me.

(LG 1891–92, 285)

The implication is that before this "something" intrudes, the poet enjoys a physical intimacy with the earth. He "renews" himself by allowing his naked flesh to touch the land or the sea with a sense of likeness and recognition: "as to other flesh." The phrase "where I thought I was safest" suggests a place like home, a familiarity amounting to a familial relation. Indeed, a manuscript for the poem suggests that Whitman once considered beginning with an invocation of the mother, perhaps Mother Earth: "O Mother, did you think / there could ever be a time / when I might not" — the manuscript breaks off before completing the question (*Faint Clews and Indirections* 9). The likeness of the mother — one's own "flesh and blood" — hints at an intimacy beyond all others that is destroyed in the hysterical moment of turning away from the thing that was once the source of renewal.

What was motherly is now "otherly."⁹ The "something" intervenes to disturb the identity, much as the dirt on a window destroys its transparency. The window becomes something to be reckoned with (to be cleaned or cursed). It emerges from transparency to become a thing. "We begin to confront the thingness of objects when they stop working for us: when the drill breaks, when the car stalls, when the windows get filthy, when their flow within the circuits of production and distribution, consumption and exhibition, has been arrested" (Brown 4). When we have to protect air or buy water in plastic bottles, they become things that have stopped working rather than the transparent media of life.

One thing that stops working for Whitman in "This Compost" is the metaphorical network that mediates his relationship with the earth. The nature lover finds the object of his affection fouled. What was once beautiful and comforting becomes hideous and disturbing; what was familiar, strange. In his revision of the manuscript, he rejects the apostrophe to the mother, refusing kinship with a thing so alien, so toxic. He is left with a crisis of identity, the health of the landscape now suspect, his own confident safety threatened by an obsessive concern with infection in a kind of antipastoral gothic fantasy:

> O how can it be that the ground itself does not sicken?
> How can you be alive you growths of spring?
> How can you furnish health you blood of herbs, roots, orchards, grain?
> Are they not continually putting distemper'd corpses within you?
> Is not every continent work'd over and over with sour dead?
>
> Where have you disposed of their carcasses?
> Those drunkards and gluttons of so many generations?
> Where have you drawn off all the foul liquid and meat?

I do not see any of it upon you to-day, or perhaps I am deceiv'd,
I will run a furrow with my plough, I will press my spade through the
    sod and turn it up underneath,
I am sure I shall expose some of the foul meat. (LG 1891–92, 285–286)

Another thing that has stopped working in this first movement of the poem, which encompasses the entirety of Section 1, is the Romantic or transcendental attitude according to which the poet understands himself as the confident son of the earth. He worries that "perhaps I am deceived" and resorts to the experiment with the plough. If he is "sure" of anything, it is that he will produce a horrifying result.

His doubt ultimately yields to the recovery of confidence in Section 2, which begins with an abrupt shift when the poet realizes that in turning the ground with the plough, no "foul meat" is exposed but rather the rich fertile compost of the living soil. "Behold this compost!" he lectures himself as he recovers his voice, "behold it well!"

Perhaps every mite has once form'd part of a sick person — yet behold!
The grass of spring covers the prairies,
The bean bursts noiselessly through the mould in the garden,
The delicate spear of the onion pierces upward,
The apple-buds cluster together on the apple-branches,
The resurrection of the wheat appears with pale visage out of its graves,
The tinge awakes over the willow-tree and the mulberry-tree,
The he-birds carol mornings and evenings while the she-birds sit on
    their nests,
The young of poultry break through the hatch'd eggs,
The new-born of animals appear, the calf is dropt from the cow, the
    colt from the mare,
Out of its little hill faithfully rise the potato's dark green leaves,
Out of its hill rises the yellow maize-stalk, the lilacs bloom in the
    dooryards,
The summer growth is innocent and disdainful above all those strata
    of sour dead. (LG 1891–92, 286)

"What chemistry!" he goes on to say, completing the poem's second movement with an appreciation of the earth's healing powers and a recovery of his sense of safety: "the winds are really not infectious," he marvels; "this is no cheat, this transparent green-wash of the sea which is so amorous after me, / [. . .] it is safe to allow it to lick my naked body all over with its tongues." The tropes of identity — notably the personification of the earth, which now has a body to respond to the poet's own — signal a return to the safety of belonging, kinship, home.

In the third movement, enacted in the last stanza of the poem, the poet adjusts to his new realization and stands in awe before the mystery of the earth's resurrecting powers:

> Now I am terrified at the Earth, it is that calm and patient,
> It grows such sweet things out of such corruptions,
> It turns harmless and stainless on its axis, with such endless succes-
>   sions of diseas'd corpses,
> It distills such exquisite winds out of such infused fetor,
> It renews with such unwitting looks its prodigal, annual, sumptuous
>   crops,
> It gives such divine materials to men, and accepts such leavings from
>   them at last. (LG 1891–92, 287)

From the initial arresting moment, with its anaphoric negatives ("I will not [. . .] / I will not [. . .]"), to this grand affirmation ("It grows [. . .] / It turns [. . .] / It distills [. . .] / It renews [. . .] / It gives"), one of the finest instances of the Whitmanian sublime, we arrive by way of the quasi-scientific concepts of "compost" and "chemistry." The thing that had disturbed him at the start of the poem, transformed by the processes of composting and chemistry, has virtually vanished, leaving only the beautiful nameable objects of the famil-iar earth — the wheat, the willow, the calf, the colt, the corn, the lilacs. The terror of the initial shock yields to the "terrifying" wonder of the sublime.

And yet the voice of the poet remains tempered by the experience; the confident transcendentalism seems never completely recovered once it is broken. In this sense, the poem differs from other passages in the early edi-tions of *Leaves* that take up similar themes, such as the following lines from the 1855 "Song of Myself":

> And as to you death, and you bitter hug of mortality . . . . it is idle to
>   try to alarm me.
> . . . .
>
> And as to you corpse I think you are good manure, but that does not
>   offend me,
> I smell the white roses sweetscented and growing,
> I reach to the leafy lips . . . . I reach to the polished breasts of melons.
>
> And as to you life, I reckon you are the leavings of many deaths,
> No doubt I have died myself ten thousand times before. (LG 1855, 54)

These brave lines anticipate the "resurrection" theme of "This Compost,"
which in the 1856 edition was titled "Poem of Wonder at The Resurrection
of the Wheat," but they fail to capture the drama of the movement toward
wonder from an initial state of "alarm," the very possibility of which is
denied here. The seemingly easy access of the poet to his lover, the earth
("the leafy lips [. . .] the polished breasts of melons"), gives no hint of the
struggle to grasp and appreciate the powerful processes of compost and
chemistry. The casual encounter with death and corruption in these lines
does not give the poet a moment's pause. The line "as to you corpse I think
you are good manure" sounds something like an anticipatory summation
of the first two movements of "This Compost," but it differs not only in
the lack of dramatic development but also in the use of the word "corpse."
The thing that the poet finds so offensive in the opening lines of "This
Compost" may well be a corpse, but it is never named, and the significance of this studied omission cannot be overstated. By refraining from
naming, the poet suggests a repositioning of natural things just beyond
the reach of human intelligence and control. The Comprehensive Reader's
Edition of *Leaves* points to a similar passage from the "Spring" chapter of
Thoreau's *Walden*: "There was a dead horse in the hollow by the path to
my home which compelled me sometimes to go out of my way, especially
in the night when the air was heavy, but the assurance it gave me of the
strong appetite and inviolable health of Nature was my compensation for
this" (CRE 369n).[10] The idea that the transcendental realization is not free
or easy, that it exacts a cost, is captured here, but the confident tone (along
with the personification of the abstraction Nature as healthily hungry),
more like "Song of Myself," doesn't touch the near hysteria of "This
Compost." The naming of the corpse is tantamount to knowing it and
"getting around" it — literally and figuratively. As long as it remains
unnamed, it remains to a large extent unknown and thus continues to
block the path of the knower, a thing unaccounted for, which persists in
demanding attention.

"We don't apprehend things," writes Bill Brown, the leading exponent
of "thing theory," "except partially or obliquely (as what's beyond our
apprehension)" (Brown 4, n.11). If we think of the verb "apprehend" in the
connotation of "to capture" and "things" as beings that resist capture, then
whole worlds of possibility open for ecopoetics, in the "story of objects
asserting themselves as things," which becomes, as Brown says, "the story
of how the thing really names less an object than a particular subject-object
relation" (4). And that's precisely what we're looking for in ecopoetics: a

new way of confronting the linguistic limits and courting the possibilities involved in thinking about the human relation to the things of the earth.

The poetic act of negation associated with the unspeakableness of things in "This Compost" and dramatized in the act of turning away — "I will not go now on the pastures to walk, / I will not strip the clothes from my body to meet my lover the sea" and so on — thus distinguishes that poem from the more positive approach to the earth in "Song of Myself" and other transcendental texts. The positive approach does not necessarily preclude a treatment of the thingish incapacities, as we will see when we return to the rich and varied world of "Song of Myself" later in this chapter. But first, Whitman's recourse to negative forms in the early editions of *Leaves* deserves fuller attention.

In another work from 1856 — "Poem of The Sayers of The Words of The Earth," which eventually would be titled more elegantly "A Song of the Rolling Earth" — the use of negation figures strongly in a meditation on the possibility of communion, or communication, with nature.[11] Whitman scholars have traditionally associated the poem's interest in the relationship between words and things with the chapter on language in Emerson's *Nature.* "A Song of the Rolling Earth" has even been called "a poetic demonstration of the transcendentalist doctrine" (CRE 219n). Recent criticism, however, schooled in the deconstructionist critique of Romantic "naïveté" in matters linguistic, has shown that, if anything, the poem either radically misreads the Emersonian theory of language or intentionally explodes it.[12] The usual conclusion is that Whitman creates a big problem that he leaves unresolved. I would argue instead that Whitman explores the possibility of an ecological theory of communication that he does not develop systematically. He explores not as a philosopher of language but as an experimental poet, and what we have in this poem is not a treatise on language and nature, not even a "poetic demonstration" of a philosophical thesis, but another dramatization of the limits of human language and an attempt to use language to approach the things of nature "indirectly and obliquely" in Brown's words — or as Whitman himself says, by way of "a few hints, a few diffused faint clews and indirections" (LG 1891–92, 14) — rather than by a confident and direct declaration in the transcendentalist manner, a claim to have gotten once and for all to the bottom of things.

From the center of a long tradition in American semiotic thinking, stretching from Jonathan Edwards's Puritan reading of the book of nature to Charles Sanders Peirce's pragmatist reinvention of the triadic sign,

Emerson transmits the Romantic-transcendentalist party line on language theory in three key claims:

1. Words are signs of natural facts.
2. Particular natural facts are symbols of particular spiritual facts.
3. Nature is the symbol of spirit. (Emerson 20)[13]

Emerson's own development of these claims, as well as the considerable commentary they have inspired, ties into a complex web of philosophical influences and is worthy of closer study than time and space permit here. But one clear implication for ecopoetics is that, used with poetic diligence, language can lead human beings to the discovery of spiritual significance in nature.

The 1856 version of "A Song of the Rolling Earth" undoes the logic of this position in its two opening lines:

> Earth, round, rolling, compact — suns, moons, animals — all these
>   are words,
> Watery, vegetable, sauroid advances — beings, premonitions, lispings
>   of the future — these are vast words. (CRE 218–219n)

Later dropped from the poem, the lines reject the linearity of the Emersonian logic in which human words signify natural objects that in turn signify spirit. Instead, the earth and all the things of the earth past and present are themselves called words. These "substantial words" are more real than their weak human counterparts, as the lines that open the final version of the poem make clear:

> A SONG of the rolling earth, and of words according,
> Were you thinking that those were the words, those upright lines?
>   those curves, angles, dots?
> No, those are not the words, the substantial words are in the ground
>   and sea,
> They are in the air, they are in you.
>
> Were you thinking that those were the words, those delicious sounds
>   out of your friends' mouths?
> No, the real words are more delicious than they. (LG 1891–92, 176)

In this final version, Whitman abbreviated the positive assertion of the original two lines in order to get more quickly to the negation that dominates the poem's logic. He creates a curious effect, something like the negation in his famous 1860 poem "So Long!" which declares to his readers that they are holding in their hands not a book but a man. In both cases, he addresses the reader directly and offers a surprising assertion. In "A Song of the Rolling Earth," a dealer in words, a poet, is telling "you" that written and spoken words are not "the real words," that there are "substantial words" that are "more delicious." One way of reading the assertion is to say that he simply collapses the relationship of sign (the word) and object (the earth), bringing us one step closer to the ultimate referent, which Emerson calls "spirit." But the negation forbids that reading. The poem says that "substantial words" are different from the familiar words of print and speech, are part of a system of communication entirely separate from human language.

What we have then is a metaphor in which the figurative element (the word) is named but the literal referent (something the earth has or does) is left unclear, in the form of a riddle or a mystery. The earth has or does something that corresponds to what people do when they communicate with words, but this something cannot be communicated directly in language. With this riddling approach, Whitman seems to be seeking ways to bring the reader into contact with things and states of being for which there are no adequate words. As Ed Folsom says in *Walt Whitman's Native Representations*, Whitman is calling for "the dictionaries of words that print cannot touch," that will give voice to "the things of the earth that language has not yet named, that we have remained blind and deaf to because our language has not yet expressed them" (20). He denies to the earth's "language" the characteristics classically attributed to successful rhetorical utterances in human speech, such as pathos, organization (arrangement, *dispositio*), persuasion, and discrimination; instead of an eloquent orator (implied in the negated traits), he gives us the strange image of the earth as a "dumb great mother":

> The earth does not argue,
> Is not pathetic, has no arrangements,
> Does not scream, haste, persuade, threaten, promise,
> Makes no discriminations, has no conceivable failures,
> Closes nothing, refuses nothing, shuts none out,
> Of all the powers, objects, states, it notifies, shuts none out.
>
> The earth does not exhibit itself nor refuse to exhibit itself, possesses still underneath,
> Underneath the ostensible sounds, the august chorus of heroes, the wail of slaves,

Persuasions of lovers, curses, gasps of the dying, laughter of young
people, accents of bargainers,
Underneath these possessing words that never fail.

To her children the words of the eloquent dumb great mother never
fail,
· ·
With her ample back towards every beholder,
With the fascinations of youth and the equal fascinations of age,
Sits she whom I too love like the rest, sits undisturb'd,
Holding up in her hand what has the character of a mirror, while her
eyes glance back from it,
Glance as she sits, inviting none, denying none,
Holding a mirror day and night tirelessly before her own face.

(LG 1891–92, 177)

The rambling and uneven development of the poem, a product no doubt
of its method of indirection, makes it difficult to know who the "children"
of the "dumb great mother" are (the poets, those who live close to the
earth?) and how they proceed to know her. But hints throughout the poem
suggest the possibility of a kind of communion. Like the denizens of Plato's
cave, people may know the earth's reality indirectly by catching glances of
her face's reflection in "what has the character of a mirror" (in a figure that
has the character of a metaphor but stops short of a full identification) —
an action that may imply the work of science, which studies effects of the
earth, secondhand signs, brief reflections from which a sense of the whole
may be construed. But mostly, we see only her smooth broad back turned
to us and must wonder at the true nature of the face.

The earth is dumb and yet her words never fail her children. Again we have
the riddle, the conundrum, the paradox. Whitman may well intend to present a broad and rolling surface of language, largely impenetrable like the
earth itself. As in the sayings of mystics and spiritual teachers, he urges us to
understand not with the mind but with the soul. The earth speaks to the soul,
not the ear. "The workmanship of souls is by those inaudible words of the
earth," he says. "The masters know the earth's words and use them more than
audible words" (LG 1891–92, 176). Communion with the earth (which can
never quite amount to communication) requires a strong and healthy soul:
"I swear the earth shall surely be complete to him or her who shall be complete, / The earth remains jagged and broken only to him or her who remains

jagged and broken" (LG 1891–92, 179). The "rolling" earth is never jagged and broken; it offers a smooth and pleasing surface. Like the rolling earth, the healthy soul is "real" and responds to a similar "language," which is again described with negation: "No reasoning, no proof has establish'd it" (LG 1891–92, 180). In an affirmation of the soul's language, Section 4, which closes the poem, begins with the unattached demonstrative "These":

> These to echo the tones of souls and the phrases of souls,
> (If they did not echo the phrases of souls what were they then?
> If they had not reference to you in especial what were they then?)
>
> I swear I will never henceforth have to do with the faith that tells the best,
> I will have to do only with that faith that leaves the best untold.
>
> (LG 1891–92, 180)

The act of leaving "These" without a clear referent dramatizes the poet's commitment to leave the best untold. The implication is clear. The soul shares with the earth a system of language and meaning distinct from what we normally understand to be human language and logic. The one may "echo" or resonate with the other without containing or fully comprehending it. The poet may show the way to the experience of the soul and the earth but can never fully capture ("apprehend") it in written or spoken language. The "song" of the rolling earth communicates as much by resonance as by verbal power, but the "things" of the earth are no less real because of the faintness by which we perceive them:

> The best of the earth cannot be told anyhow, all or any is best,
> It is not what you anticipated, it is cheaper, easier, nearer,
> Things are not dismiss'd from the places they held before,
> The earth is just as positive and direct as it was before,
> Facts, religions, improvements, politics, trades, are as real as before,
> But the soul is also real, it too is positive and direct,
> No reasoning, no proof has establish'd it,
> Undeniable growth has establish'd it. (LG 1891–92, 180)

The subject-object relationship with which Whitman is experimenting in "A Song of the Rolling Earth" thus turns on the idea of the soul, which leads back to the fountainhead of Whitmanian metaphysics, "Song of Myself." In Section 5, as it is known in the final version, in a passage that changed very little from its original 1855 version, the poet affirms his belief in the soul and gives a powerful view of the soul in action. When it is welcomed, the soul does not rise from within but comes over the poet like a demon or a muse, possesses the poet, ravishes the body, taking control of the senses.[14] But this metaphysical experience does not distract the senses away from the earth and the body; rather, it turns them toward the earth and the body's sensitive connection with it. The soul itself is linked to the earth; it is an environmental agent that overtakes the ordinary life of the inspired individual and makes everything strange and new. The body seems as transformed as the earth when the soul descends, anticipating the idea from "A Song of the Rolling Earth" that the body, like the earth itself, communicates by means of "substantial words." Electrified with new feelings and almost painfully aware of the abundance of earthy influences, the poet experiences his body — which here goes unnamed, a thing, "the other I am" — at the center of a web of connections in the earth's lap, an open meadow:

> I believe in you my soul, the other I am must not abase itself to you,
> And you must not be abased to the other.
>
> Loafe with me on the grass, loose the stop from your throat,
> Not words, not music or rhyme I want, not custom or lecture, not
>   even the best,
> Only the lull I like, the hum of your valved voice.
>
> I mind how once we lay such a transparent summer morning,
> How you settled your head athwart my hips and gently turn'd over
>   upon me,
> And parted the shirt from my bosom-bone, and plunged your tongue
>   to my bare-stript heart,
> And reach'd till you felt my beard, and reach'd till you held my feet.
>
> Swiftly arose and spread around me the peace and knowledge that
>   pass all the argument of the earth,
> And I know that the hand of God is the promise of my own,
> And I know that the spirit of God is the brother of my own,
> And that all the men ever born are also my brothers, and the women
>   my sisters and lovers,
> And that a kelson of the creation is love,
> And limitless are leaves stiff or drooping in the fields,
> And brown ants in the little wells beneath them,
> And mossy scabs of the worm fence, heap'd stones, elder, mullein and
>   poke-weed. (LG 1891–92, 32–33)

The soul's tongue, plunged to the bare-stripped heart of the poet, is an organ of speech figured here as the phallic means of impregnating the body with understanding and vision. The heart is the womb of the poet that, inseminated by the soul, delivers the vision of an animated world. The words that pour forth — ironically copious after the poet, following the inclination developed at length in "A Song of the Rolling Earth," denies the need for words of wisdom delivered in their usual form — custom, lecture, rhyme — wrap the world in the shape of an arc, the chief timber (kelson) of which is the poet's love for all things that appear before his enchanted eyes. The vibrations of the smallest leaves drooping in the fields, ants with their miniscule movements, weeds growing and spreading, bring impressions to the poet that seem at once full of meaning and difficult to fathom. Meaning accrues (and with it beauty) when the body is understood as replicating the forms of the earth and is thus bound to the earth. The hair, the penis, the testicles, the pores of the skin find their counterparts in the mossy weeds, the leaves stiff or drooping, the heaped stones, the ants' little wells. The poet's loving words wrap the world in a sympathetic embrace, build an arc to hold the human family (brothers and sisters) and all creatures and things of the earth.

The transformation or defamiliarization of the body defuses what might otherwise be the typical associations of a nineteenth-century Anglo-American man surveying the things of nature. It opens a creative connection full of new resonance. The association of the heart with the womb resonates with Buddhist metaphysics, for example, as these words from the *Lankavatara Sutra* suggest: "The self realized in your inmost consciousness appears in its purity; this is the Tathagata-garbha (literally, Buddha-womb)" (qtd. in Huxley 8). It also recalls Native American ecopoetics. "The love of a mother," according to Pueblo thought, "is not, as is presently supposed, a sentimental attachment. Rather it is a way of saying that a mother is bonded to her offspring through her womb. *Heart* often means 'womb,' except when it means 'vulva.' In its aspect of vulva, it signifies sexual connection or bonding. But this cannot be understood to mean sex as sex; rather sexual connection with woman means connection with the womb, which is the container of power that women carry within their bodies" (P. G. Allen 24). Much the same could be said of Whitman. In these lines, the "heart" is within reach of the tongue when the soul settles "athwart the hips." We modern readers, struck by the heat of the trope suggesting non-reproductive (specifically oral) sex, are sometimes confused by the poet's preoccupation with "procreation." Sexual desire for him becomes "the procreant urge of the world" (LG 1891–92, 30). The generative quality of sexual contact, even homo- or autoerotic contact, concentrates on the result, the outcome of experience. When the phallic tongue of the soul insemi-nates the yonic heart of the poet, the result is the vision that arises and spreads around him and that reaches first from beard to toe, the whole length of the poet's body energized by the experience of integration with the natural environment, and then from heaven (the hand of God) to earth (the ants in the little wells). The great and the small, the significant and the presumed insignificant, are connected by the broad arc-shaped web of the poet's loving words (the kelson of the creation is love), the poet's body vibrating with awareness at the center.

What, then, does Whitman mean by the soul? Just as he was not a philoso-pher of language, he was not a systematic metaphysician, so the question will never have a clear answer. To make it even harder to pin down, his understanding of the soul seems to change over time and is different from poem to poem. In the poems dating from the first two editions of *Leaves of Grass*, the soul frequently appears as it does in the lines I've quoted from "Song of Myself." No doubt, Whitman always owes something to his pri-mary metaphysical source, the essays of Ralph Waldo Emerson. But this 1855 version of the soul is not exactly the Emersonian oversoul, the pool of consciousness that we enter when we seek deep within ourselves and iron-ically find the connection to nature and all conscious beings. In later writ-ings, Whitman seems to become more and more Emersonian, but in the image of the soul with the voice that hums and lulls and the phallic tongue that plunges into the womb-heart of the poet, Whitman gives us a rather different picture. It is easy to grow frustrated with all the soul talk in Whitman and decide that when he uses the word "soul," he does so for rhetorical purposes, to intensify what is primarily a materialist under-standing of his world. In *The Lunar Light of Whitman's Poetry*, for exam-ple, Wynn Thomas complains of Whitman's "prattlings about the soul" (12–13). Thomas sees the recourse to metaphysical language as Whitman's "trick . . . of turning up the volume of his rhetoric in order to drown out the noise of his doubts" (266). This is more or less the position I took myself in *Whitman's Poetry of the Body*, especially in my reading of the 1855 poem that would become "I Sing the Body Electric" in later editions. But if we take the poet at his word when he says "I believe in you my soul," we can-not stop there.

If we cannot say precisely what the Whitmanian soul is, we can at least follow a pragmatic path and say what it does. Above all, the soul integrates human life, both in the sense of granting integrity and allowing connec-tions within the self and with the outer world. It lines up the forces of the individual human being with the forces of heaven and earth. Lewis Hyde attributes a similar function to the trickster figure in classical Greek and West African mythology. "Before a body can come to life," Hyde reminds us, "every

separation, every boundary, must be breached in some way; each organ must have its pores and gateways through which something (lymph, blood, bile, urine, electricity, neurotransmitters) may flow. Unless they can incorporate internal forces of transgression, organic structures are in danger of dying from their own articulation." Much like organs, the gods have a tendency to perfect themselves in certain functions; the goddess of chastity prohibits all licentiousness, the god of reason allows no confusion, and so on. The gods tend to have a problem communicating with each other and with human beings. But trickster opens the flow by moving among different systems and realms. Hyde concludes that these stories remind us what can happen if all hope of communication dries up between articulated systems: "First, there will be spiritual hunger ('the gods were hungry' is the opening problem of the Yoruba story [in which the trickster Eshu finds a way to get human beings to renew their practices of sacrifice]). Second, when articulation becomes fragmentation the gods don't just quarrel, they begin to speak languages so distinct as to need a translator" (*Trickster* 259–260).

The soul serves a trickster function in crossing the boundaries of ordinary life, translating strange tongues, communing with untouchables, queering received categories and prescribed relationships. Like the undammed river, the soul flows and may flood unexpectedly. The person out of touch with the soul feels partial, incomplete, alienated. By contrast, the soulful person, overcoming brokenness and fragmentation, feels the articulated and fragmented elements of being flow together, producing wholeness. As a consequence, awareness expands, inward and outward consciousness joining in a seamless network of information paths. The heart, the seat of emotional life, opens like a womb, receiving influences from without and bringing forth visions from within. Finally, the soul speaks. It is the voice within that animates the world with poetic language. It accomplishes the goal that Whitman sets for the poet in the 1855 Preface: "folks expect of the poet to indicate more than the beauty and dignity which always attach to dumb real objects," he writes, "they expect him to indicate the path between reality and their souls" (LG 1855, v). The soul represents the ability of the human mind to perceive meaning and beauty in "dumb real objects," in things. To those out of touch with the soul, the world seems meaningless and dull, little more than a resource base that serves human utility.

Whitman's concept of the soul, which seems loosely connected to the ancient philosophies of yoga and shamanism as well as modern psychology, is not only a rhetorical device; it is the function of creativity itself, the motive force of Whitman's ecopoetics. When I say "loosely connected," I mean that the Whitmanian soul bears a conceptual and therefore metonymic or metaphorical relationship to those fields of knowledge and practice. I do not mean to suggest that I could never produce good evidence for what we generally count as "influence." Still, I contend that it is worthwhile to pursue these loose connections, the speculative use of which figures strongly in the work of scholars like Lewis Hyde and George Hutchinson. Hyde and Hutchinson practice a form of interpretive criticism that opens up the concept of influence, meaning to flow in, from many directions perhaps. Flow is a key idea in ecopoetics in general and in Whitman's poetry in particular (as the readings of scholars ranging from Roger Asselineau to Michael Moon have made abundantly clear). Loose connections, along with ecopoetical patterns of flow, prevail particularly in the tropes of Section 5 of "Song of Myself." The tropes are riddling; the figurative elements are tangentially connected with literal objects or left unattached entirely. The heart takes on womblike qualities, but the substitution is incomplete; the soul with its tongue is only partially personified or materialized. Contiguous relationships predominate over complete identifications. In a groundbreaking study of Whitman's tropology, C. Carroll Hollis suggests that Whitman tended to favor metonymy over metaphor in the early editions of *Leaves of Grass* and that the tendency in the later poems to fall into more conventional uses of metaphor and personifications signals the failure of his early inspiration. While acknowledging the power of this analysis, I want to demur a bit. In my reading, there are plenty of metaphors and personifications in the early poems. What makes the earlier tropes different is the special combination of metaphysical uncertainty, mystical engagement with the earth, and poetic style that Whitman energetically pursues in the first three editions of *Leaves of Grass*, in short his ecopoetics, one strategy of which is the act of incomplete identification mentioned here. The leaves stiff and drooping, the mossy scabs of worm-fence, the ants' little wells are creatively associated with the human body but are never reduced to human meanings. They maintain an integrity of their own. Energized by the soul, the poet's body is continuous with the earth but not dominant over it.

Coming out of the soul-inspired trance of Section 5, the poet expresses a calm reluctance in Section 6 to specify the meaning of the very thing that appears as the central symbol of his book: "A child said *What is the grass?* fetching it to me with full hands; / How could I answer the child? I do not know what it is any more than he" (LG 1891–92, 33). He proceeds with a

Things of the Earth

disarmingly playful series of guesses, one trope unfolding into another, all designed to show the continuity of individual lives and regional or racial types ("Kanuck, Tuckahoe, Congressman, Cuff"), people and nature, heaven and earth, human language and "substantive words" ("a uniform hieroglyphic," the "uttering tongues of grass") but none claiming the confident authority to interpret things once and for all, and finishing finally with a refusal to overinterpret the "hints" that the grass communicates. Using the grass symbol "tenderly," the poet arrives at his faith that human beings participate in the perennial renewal of life, thus anticipating the position to which he returns in "This Compost." Of the grass, he says,

> I guess it must be the flag of my disposition, out of hopeful green stuff
>   woven.
>
> Or I guess it is the handkerchief of the Lord,
> A scented gift and remembrancer designedly dropt,
> Bearing the owner's name someway in the corners, that we may see
>   and remark, and say *Whose?*
>
> Or I guess the grass is itself a child, the produced babe of the vegeta-
>   tion.
>
> Or I guess it is a uniform hieroglyphic,
> And it means, Sprouting alike in broad zones and narrow zones,
> Growing among black folks as among white,
> Kanuck, Tuckahoe, Congressman, Cuff, I give them the same, I receive
>   them the same.
>
> And now it seems to me the beautiful uncut hair of graves.
>
> Tenderly will I use you curling grass,
> It may be you transpire from the breasts of young men,
> It may be if I had known them I would have loved them,
> It may be you are from old people, or from offspring taken soon out of
>   their mothers' laps,
> And here you are the mothers' laps.
>
> This grass is very dark to be from the white heads of old mothers,
> Darker than the colorless beards of old men,
> Dark to come from under the faint red roofs of mouths.
>
> (LG 1891–92, 33–34)

The grass is a flag, a handkerchief, a child; it is language, hair, lap, tongues; it is life itself. The creative principle, the soul, moves blithely among things, connecting and disconnecting in a wide arc of meaning. And yet integration does not overwhelm the integrity of individual things in the ecopoetics of the 1855 and 1856 *Leaves,* certainly not in the method of negation as used in "A Song of the Rolling Earth" and the first movement of "This Compost" and not always in the affirmative method as used in "Song of Myself" and the second two movements of "This Compost." In chapter 2, I consider some cases that represent more troubling aspects of the poet's wild troping in the affirmative method, especially the use of personification as a means to rhetorical identification, a linguistic analog for the human desire to dominate earthly life.

But before leaving the question of how the metaphysical concept of the soul mediates problems among people, earthly objects, and abstractions in Whitmanian ecopoetics, I want to give a bit more attention to the problem of abstraction. Whenever the poet resists naming and specifying objects too closely, he has certainly resorted to abstraction. *Thing* is a more abstract word than *corpse,* which is in turn a level of abstraction distant from "the corpse of a horse." What is interesting about things, however, is that unlike abstractions such as "love" or "justice" or "destiny," they may well present themselves to our subjective gaze in some detail; they may appeal to the senses. When we persist in refusing to name or specify sensible things, we can only appear to be unwilling to know them intellectually or incapable of placing them in a system of common meaning or utility. When Whitman insists on the integrity of earthly or bodily things, he engages, at least indirectly, in a critique of human knowledge and the use of things as resources. The celebration of things as such represents an acknowledgment of human limits and fallibility. The suggestion is that we can have beauty, communion, and even meaning without having full knowledge and utility.

Utility and knowledge may demand a different level of abstraction, in which the distance between subject and object increases to the point that resonance fails and alienation sets in. If the human being feels too close, the integrity of the object (the other) may be overwhelmed; if the subject feels too distant, sympathy fails and the object loses its animating resonance, its appeal to the senses or its soulfulness. In either case, domination may appear justified. What is fascinating about the poems considered in this chapter is the way Whitman plays with closeness and distance, creating an alternating movement of what he calls "pride" and "sympathy" in the 1855 Preface, by which he means the tendency toward self-absorption or self-distinction (pride) and the contrary or balancing movement toward the integration with other beings, the giving (or disintegration) of the self (sympathy):

The greatest poet does not moralize or make applications of morals ... he knows the soul. The soul has that measureless pride which consists in never acknowledging any lessons but its own. But it has sympathy as measureless as its pride and the one balances the other and neither can stretch too far while it stretches in company with the other. The inmost secrets of art sleep with the twain. The greatest poet has lain close betwixt both and they are vital in his style and thoughts. (LG 1855, vi)

"Mystical" is a good designation for this alternating gestalt not least because of the difficulty the poet had in sustaining it. Like enlightenment, bliss, and inspiration in other mystical traditions, the experience of the soul resonating with the "substantial words" of the body and the earth, pride and sympathy in perfect balance, proves ephemeral for Whitman. The inability to sustain the ecstatic energy of contact accounts at least partly for the "uninspired" quality about which critics have complained in poems written after 1871. Hollis, for example, says that the Whitman of the later poems "covered up his lack of prophetic inspiration by pretensions, by over-'poeticalized' language" (26). From an ecocritical perspective, I would hasten to add that part of the appeal of studying Whitman is to see not only his successes but also his failures in what he called his "language experiment" — his attempt in *Leaves of Grass* "to give the spirit, the body, the man, new words, new potentialities of speech" (Whitman, *American Primer* viii–ix).

I would also argue that nobody was more sensitive to his failures than Whitman himself. In one of his finest postwar poems, "A Noiseless Patient Spider," he dramatizes the difficulty of completing, much less sustaining, the energetic connections that the soul seeks:

A noiseless patient spider,
I mark'd where on a little promontory it stood isolated,
Mark'd how to explore the vacant vast surrounding,
It launched forth filament, filament, filament, out of itself,
Ever unreeling them, ever tirelessly speeding them.

And you O my soul where you stand,
Surrounded, detached, in measureless oceans of space,
Ceaselessly musing, venturing, throwing, seeking the spheres to connect them,
Till the bridge you will need be form'd, till the ductile anchor hold,
Till the gossamer thread you fling catch somewhere, O my soul.

(CRE 450)

The ecopoetical problems implicit in this poem become clear when we consider it within the contexts of literary and mythological tradition and the textual history of *Leaves of Grass*. Traditionally, the spider represents power —the dangerous power of God's judgment in Jonathan Edwards's sermons, for example, or in Native American lore the creative power of language and storytelling. The Pueblo Indians give us the figure of Spider Woman not only as the creator of the world but as the original storyteller who weaves and spins and makes living connections among the organic and inorganic elements of the world, animating the inanimate, enchanting the earth. Also known as Thought Woman, she is said to have "finished everything, thoughts, and the names of all things . . . also all the languages" (P. G. Allen 13). We learn of Spider Woman and her creative ways from the oral tradition that in Native American women's literature comes to be written down, extending though never replacing the old storytelling practices. The web of written words resonates with the stories the people tell. Paula Gunn Allen writes, "Since the coming of the Europeans . . . the fragile web of identity that long held tribal people secure has gradually weakened and torn. But the oral tradition has prevented the complete destruction of the web, the ultimate disruption of tribal ways. The oral tradition is vital; it heals itself and the tribal web by adapting the flow of the present while never relinquishing its connection to the past" (45). In the Cherokee tradition, the spider and its web are also associated with creativity, including the aspects of trickery and deceit. Spider is said to be the figure that brought light to the people's side of the world by stealing the sun from the other side (see Awiakta; Edwards, Thompson, and Ely; and Erodes and Ortiz). The Laguna Pueblo novelist and poet Leslie Marmon Silko begins her book *Ceremony* with this invocation:

> Thought-Woman, the spider,
> named things and
>
> as she named them
> they appeared.
>
> She is sitting in her room
> thinking of a story now
>
> I'm telling you the story
> she is thinking. (1)

In twentieth-century Anglo-American literature, the spider becomes the figure of that modern hero or surrogate god, the artist. Again, the web stands for language, the creative medium of thought and literary art, as we see in the musings of Virginia Woolf in *A Room of One's Own*:[15]

> What were the conditions in which women lived, I asked myself; for fiction, imaginative work that is, is not dropped like a pebble upon the ground, as science may be; fiction is like a spider's web, attached ever so lightly perhaps, but still attached to life at all four corners. Often the attachment is scarcely perceptible; Shakespeare's plays, for instance, seem to hang there complete by themselves. But when the web is pulled askew, hooked up at the edge, torn in the middle, one remembers that these webs are not spun in mid-air by incorporeal creatures, but are the work of suffering human beings, and are attached to grossly material things, like health and money and the houses we live in. (44–45)

A web of words spreading away from but anchored to material life is a concept fit for an ecopoetical model of modern writing, beginning in Shakespeare and culminating in such authors as Woolf, resonating with the ancient stories of the Native American tradition and pointing toward the cybernetic networks and "writing environments" of the World Wide Web. The imagery fits nicely with the "web of life" metaphor in ecology, especially as it is developed in Aldo Leopold's influential *Sand County Almanac*. The hypertextual concept of *linking* within and among communicative systems by means of resonating information — which hints at another aspect of the web metaphor, the fact that the filaments of the web bring not only food but also information to the attentive spider — recalls Whitman's treatment of loose connections in a poetic ecology based on association rather than dominance and complete identification.[16] In "A Noiseless Patient Spider," Whitman shows us that like the creator woman of the Pueblo tradition, the poet sends filaments from the root of his own being, seeking to bridge the empty spaces, creating thereby the path between reality and the soul. Unlike speaking, writing is noiseless and ideally patient, the writer isolated from rather than face to face with the ones addressed. The writer sends the filaments forth, seeking to capture the attention of readers and turn their gaze upward and outward.

What is worrisome about the poem, though, and hints at ecopoetical troubles in the Whitman corpus that foretell problems haunting the twentieth-century discourse on nature, is that here the soul seems lost, not only isolated but detached and surrounded by "measureless oceans of space," suggestive not of the material world at all but of abstract, mystifying space — "measureless" space. The soul's attention turns away from the earth (hysterically?), seeking to connect "the spheres," the outward reaches of the universe. The vision focuses first on the material spider, standing on the "little promontory" of solid earth, but by the second stanza the attention wavers, the focus opening so wide that the picture blurs into abstraction.

If read out of the context of *Leaves of Grass* — the poem was originally published in a magazine, after all, and has become one of the most commonly anthologized of Whitman's works — "A Noiseless Patient Spider" could well come off as a quiet nature poem, the poet with his transcendental work paralleling but heroically surpassing the little spider on its promontory. If we read the poem within the context of the whole book, however, it is a very sad poem. The poet feels himself open outward, perhaps in a moment of inward integration, but can only cast his filaments into empty spaces. Like the spider standing on a promontory or headland at the edge of a sea and throwing filaments into the air with no promise of land for anchoring, the poet has reached the limit of his powers. The abundance celebrated in "Song of Myself" has departed. In the early *Leaves*, the soulfulness of the poet singing in a harvest-rich world contrasts with the images of the poor people who have lost touch with their souls, the sick and weary who fail to join the poet in "Song of the Open Road," for example, or the soulless zombies of "The Sleepers." The poet appears to these lost souls as a healer, offering reintegration and revitalization. In "A Noiseless Patient Spider," a different alternative disturbingly emerges: the energized but isolated soul confronting an empty world.

If we read the poem in the full context of production, a study of Whitman's manuscripts reveals that indeed it originated in a mood of grief and isolation. An early draft of the poem appeared in a notebook from 1862–63, which documents Whitman's visit to the Civil War battlefield near Fredericksburg, Virginia, where his brother George had been wounded. In one note, he sketches a scene that would become one of the most powerful poems in *Drum-Taps*:

> Sight at daybreak in camp in front of the hospital tent Three dead
> men lying, each with a blanket spread over him — I lift up one and
> look at the young man's face, calm and yellow. 'Tis strange!
> (Young man: I think this face of yours the face of my dead Christ.)
> (UPP 2:93)

Apparently another sight in camp, or perhaps in Washington where he worked in the war hospitals, prompted Whitman to write the poem that would become "A Noiseless Patient Spider," but it was a man and not a spider that moved him to write, and the connection he sought was not just any bridge or anchor but human love:

The Soul, reaching, throwing out for love,
As the spider, from some little promontory, throwing out filament
    after filament, tirelessly out of itself, that one at least may catch and
    form a link, a bridge, a connection
O I saw one passing alone, saying hardly a word — yet full of love I
    detected him, by certain signs
O eyes wishfully turning! O silent eyes!
For then I thought of you oer the world
O latent oceans, fathomless oceans of love!
O waiting oceans of love! yearning and fervid! and of you sweet souls
    perhaps in the future, delicious and long:
But Dead, unknown on the earth — ungiven, dark here, unspoken,
    never born:
You fathomless latent souls of love — you pent and unknown oceans
    of love! (UPP 2:93)

In this version, the spider-in-nature is luckier than the spider-poet because the spider-in-nature "at least may catch and form a link," whereas the longing of the spider-poet has nowhere to catch. The desire of the spider-poet faintly sounds a predatory note in this version, a dangerous emotion that is suppressed at the time of the writing and purged by the time the poem is finally published in the years after the war. "Faint clews" come to the poet — "certain signs" — that the man who passes (a lonely soldier perhaps) is "full of love" but remains silent, denying the love within. The image that would later become "measureless oceans of space" appears here as "fathomless oceans of love" — "Yearning and fervid!" but latent, waiting — over which the poet mourns, knowing that in failing to acknowledge the love, in failing to make the connection stick, the love dies unknown, ungiven, unspoken, and the soul itself "fathomless" and "latent" goes "unspoken, never born."

We might say that the later version of the poem is sanitized or censored, the homoeroticism removed, so that what is revealed in comparing the two versions is the progress of Whitman's homophobic response to his own emotional life. Again, this is more or less the position I took in *Whitman's Poetry of the Body* in analyzing the self-censoring emendations that Whitman made over the course of many editions. My focus was primarily rhetorical, based on what I saw as a concern with audience as Whitman changed his image from "one of the roughs" to "Good Gray Poet." Other critics take a psychological approach, notably the editors of the Comprehensive Reader's Edition of *Leaves of Grass*, who compliment

Whitman on the impressive sublimation displayed in his revision of "A Noiseless Patient Spider" (450n). Here I am suggesting a social-psychological element in mentioning Whitman's self-directed homophobia, a response that seems common among avant-garde male writers in American literature (compare Ellis Amburn's *Subterranean Kerouac,* for example). And then there's the poem's drift from physical and particular to metaphysical and abstract language. From an ecopoetical perspective, the poem is not sanitized (cleaned to the point of lifelessness) or censored (erased because of market considerations) so much as it is emptied. A tone of controlled stoicism replaces the fervent emotion, and an abstract and distracted concern with linking "spheres" across "measureless oceans of space" replaces the earthy longing of the spider-poet to capture the "passing one" and explore the "fathomless oceans of love." Could Whitman have known that the spider virtually drinks its prey, melting the solid body by applying digestive juices after inflicting the poisonous bite? If so, the phrase "fathomless oceans of love" suggests the abundant liquid, the bountiful potential of the young lover, which, as Whitman sadly understands, will never flow to himself or to any other. The web brings hints to him (certain signs) but not satisfaction (food).

In *Leaves of Grass,* Whitman regularly linked sexual desire, particularly homoerotic desire, with the processes of the living earth. One *Calamus* poem that dates from 1860, "Earth, My Likeness," foreshadows the manuscript version of the spider poem:

EARTH, my likeness,
Though you look so impassive, ample and spheric there,
I now suspect that is not all;
I now suspect there is something fierce in you eligible to burst forth,
For an athlete is enamour'd of me, and I of him,
But toward him there is something fierce and terrible in me eligible to
    burst forth,
I dare not tell it in words, not even in these songs. (LG 1891–92, 109)

The speaker of the poem dare not tell the person he admires about "the something fierce and terrible in me." He does not even dare to name "it" in an instance of the socially prohibitive incapacity of thingishness (the "ah . . . thing"). But the noiseless and patient writer does tell "it" in words for the benefit of the reader, withholding the full meaning perhaps and with it the lush imagery of earthly life that we find in poems like "Song of Myself." The thing here begins to lose its sensible force. He tells us that the earth is "ample," but he does not show us the amplitude, and now the earth begins to round out abstractly, lacking the wild growth of weeds and bumpy activity of anthills, reaching beyond a "rolling" quality into the cold geometry of the "spheric." Even so, the poet tells us that he suspects the subsurface fierceness of the earth, which gives him the confidence to recklessly confess the volcanic desire within himself.

As Whitman's self-image shifted with the years, a tentativeness that would not allow even this much of a confession came over him. And what is most noteworthy for ecopoetics is that with the onset of the more secretive mood, the connection with the solid earth — insofar as it is indicated by attention to detail — seemed to weaken as well.

In what was probably the earliest version of "A Noiseless Patient Spider" — a notebook entry that likely predates even the draft poem from the Civil War notebook — we see that the poem had roots in Whitman's meditations on the difference between the soul's "language" (feeling or intuition) and the language of the human tongue:[17]

> First I wish you to realize well that our boasted knowledge, precious and manifold as it is, sinks into niches and corners, before the infinite knowledge of the unknown. Of the real world of materials, what, after all, are these specks we call knowledge? — Of the spiritual world I announce to you this — much gibberish will always be offered and for a season obeyed — all lands, all times — the soul will yet feel — but to make a statement eludes us — By curious indirections only can there be any statement of the spiritual world — and they will all be foolish — Have you noticed the [worm] on a twig reaching out in the immense vacancy time and again, trying point after point? Not more helplessly does the tongue or the pen of man, essay out in the spiritual spheres, to state them. In the nature of things nothing less than the special world itself can know itself — (NUPM 6:2051)

The best scholarly view understands the note as looking forward to "A Noiseless Patient Spider" — an interesting perspective for ecopoetics, since it suggests that the composition of the poem started not with an experience of nature so much as a metaphysical musing, the thing at stake being an abstract idea in search of an analogy that appears here as a placeholder, the "[worm]." The brackets are Whitman's own. In this view, the next step in the composition would be the development of the manuscript poem with the spider-poet hungry for the love of the stranger. The third step combines the two drafts, in the process of which the hunger for love gets lost and the theme of the soul searching for anchor points in the "spiritual world" comes to predominate. The transformation is completed when the poem gets published in a London magazine as part of a group of related poems on death and the soul under the single title of "Whispers of Heavenly Death." When it is later extracted as a single lyric with its own title in *Leaves of Grass*, the entire process comes to seem devoted to the progressive isolation of the soul and the abstraction of its activities (Diehl 125, 129).

The overall transformation implies the loss of not only Whitman's theme of love and loneliness (predominant in poems composed in the late 1850s and early 1860s), however, but also the concern with language from the mid-1850s. As well as anticipating the 1868 version of "A Noiseless Patient Spider," the note looks back to the 1856 poem "A Song of the Rolling Earth," whose themes Whitman continued for a time to pursue, searching for a clearer statement of how the soul "feels" the presence of the material world and the spiritual world, the tongue or the pen reaching for a solid connection as the silkworm or the spider sends forth filaments to connect the body with the resonating world. The poet's search for the right analogy — "[worm]" or "noiseless patient spider" — might be seen as a dramatic rendering of the process described, the soul reaching out to the earth, hunting for a natural life form that mirrors its own yearning, knowing full well that the things of the earth can never fully represent or be represented, must remain bracketed. We see in such a movement, in the words of one astute critic, "the heart of Whitman's American poetics — the combination of two forms of the physical connected by resonant spirits" (Diehl 118).

Two concepts revealed here — resonance and indirection — deserve lingering over. Resonance is implied in the worm and spider tropes — in the vibrating filaments that represent the tentative connections with the earth. The considerable theoretical power that the concept holds for ecopoetics is suggested in the work of the sociologist and systems theorist Niklas Luhmann.[18] In his book *Ecological Communication,* Luhmann uses the term *resonance* to describe the faint interactions that occur between a system, such as human society, and its environment. Communication in the fullest sense is only possible within the system, Luhmann argues, because systems, like society, are self-referential or "autopoietic." The key medium of social interaction, language, can only directly refer to previous instances of language in an ongoing process of self-determination. (Think of a dictionary definition.) When we use language to describe impressions we receive from the environment, we inevitably begin to talk about something other than the things that present themselves to us. Language is thus communicative but necessarily reductive. By contrast, resonance suggests the prelinguistic sensory impressions, the data, that once formed into language become information.[19] When we see nature as a resource for human development, as an object for study, or as a spirit — or even when we call the things of the earth "nature," a term with a long and complicated history — we are

already talking about something else.[20] In "A Song of the Rolling Earth," Whitman uses negation to hint at a kind of resonance, the "substantial words" that resist what we normally think of as words.

On the few occasions when Whitman mentions resonance directly, the term signifies something that comes through even when it is held back, some vibration that threatens to burst forth, unexpressed and unspoken but perceptible beneath the surface — like the volcanic power hidden beneath the "spheric" ground, and the analogous desire never told, in "Earth, My Likeness." Likewise, in one of the *Children of Adam* poems, "From Pent-Up Aching Rivers," the poet vows to give voice to the "song of procreation," "the muscular urge and the blending," to make use of his "own voice *resonant*, singing the phallus" (LG 1891–92, 79; emphasis added). And in an interesting passage from "Song of Myself," he suggests that even seemingly inert natural materials (in this case, the stones used to pave a street) absorb the unspoken or neglected vibrations of human joy and pain and echo them back to the sensitive listener, the poet:

> The impassive stones that receive and return so many echoes,
> What groans of over-fed or half-starv'd who fall sunstruck or in fits,
> What exclamations of women taken suddenly who hurry home and
> give birth to babes,
> What living and buried speech is always vibrating here, what howls
> restrain'd by decorum,
> Arrests of criminals, slights, adulterous offers made, acceptances,
> rejections with convex lips,
> I mind them or the show or *resonance* of them — I come and I depart.
> (LG 1891–92, 35; emphasis added)

"Resonance" in this case is an alternative to "show." It is nondiscursive but nevertheless palpable. In a late essay from *November Boughs* about Elias Hicks, Whitman recalls the great Quaker preacher's "resonant, grave, melodious voice." He remembers being moved not by the words or doctrine of the preacher, what he calls "the discourse," but rather being carried away by the "magnetic stream of natural eloquence, before which all minds and natures, all emotions, high or low, gentle or simple, yielded entirely without exception" (CPCP 1233, 1234). This portrait brings to mind the claim in "A Song of the Rolling Earth" that "The masters know the earth's words and use them more than audible words" (LG 1891–92, 176).

A related concept that Whitman uses more commonly than resonance to signify, among other things, this sense of "natural eloquence" (meaning both the eloquence of nature and human eloquence that resembles the natural phenomenon) is "indirection." Like resonance, indirection can mean what is withheld but hinted at. In the *Calamus* poem "Among the Multitude," for example, the poet writes, "Ah lover and perfect equal, / I meant that you should discover me so by faint indirections" (LG 1891–92, 111). Or the word can suggest the incapacities of thingishness, as when, speaking through the persona of a father with his child in "On the Beach at Night," the poet hints at the existence of the immortal soul, dramatizing both the cognitive and the metaphysical incapacity:

> Something there is,
> (With my lips soothing thee, adding I whisper,
> I give thee the first suggestion, the problem and *indirection*,)
> Something there is more immortal even than the stars,
> (Many the burials, many the days and nights, passing away,)
> Something that shall endure longer even than lustrous Jupiter,
> Longer than sun or any revolving satellite,
> Or the radiant sisters the Pleiades. (LG 1891–92, 206; emphasis added)

Indirection appears frequently in statements Whitman makes about his poetics, particularly when he is trying to say what is unique about his own method. In the late poem "Laws for Creation," he declares to other poets and makers (rather forcefully and directly, considering the theme), "There shall be no subject too pronounced — all works shall illustrate the divine law of indirections" (LG 1891–92, 299).

In one sense, an indirection is simply a trope, a figure of speech or thought — an analogy, a metaphor, a parable. Complementary to this positive meaning, however, is the negative implied in the prefix of indirection. In this sense, it is a poetic feature that actively resists the direct, the literal, the conventional, and thus represents an attempt to create or dramatize resonance, to simulate for the reader the experience of the body or interaction with the environment through the use of language while trying to avoid the self-referentiality of language. It is an attempt to extend the linguistic experience beyond its usual limits by calling attention to those very limits. This sense is captured nicely in the late poem "You Tides with Ceaseless Swell":

> YOU tides with ceaseless swell! you power that does this work!
> You unseen force, centripetal, centrifugal, through space's spread,
> Rapport of sun, moon, earth, and all the constellations,

What are the messages by you from distant stars to us? what Sirius'?
    what Capella's?
What central heart — and you the pulse — vivifies all? what bound-
    less aggregate of all?
What subtle *indirection* and significance in you? what clue to all in
    you? what fluid, vast identity,
Holding the universe with all its parts as one — as sailing in a ship?
                              (LG 1891–92, 389; emphasis added)

In *Democratic Vistas*, Whitman writes of the process of striving to attain a "poetry worthy the immortal soul of man" that involves "a freeing, fluidizing, expanding, religious character, exulting with science, fructifying the moral elements, and stimulating aspirations, and meditations on the unknown":

> The process, so far, is *indirect* and peculiar, and though it may be suggested, cannot be defined. Observing, rapport, and with intuition, the shows and forms presented by Nature, the sensuous luxuriance, the beautiful in living men and women, the actual play of passions, in history and life — and, above all, from those developments either in Nature or human personality in which power, (dearest of all to the sense of the artist,) transacts itself — out of these, and seizing what is in them, the poet, the esthetic worker in any field, by the divine magic of his genius, projects them, their analogies, by curious removes, *indirections*, in literature and art. (No useless attempt to repeat the material creation, by daguerreotyping the exact likeness by mortal mental means.) This is the image-making faculty, coping with material creation, and rivaling, almost triumphing over it. This alone, when all the other parts of a specimen of literature or art are ready and waiting, can breathe into it the breath of life, and endow it with identity. (CPCP 986–987; emphasis added)

The image-making faculty, fully engaged, is not mimetic or referential in a positivistic sense; Whitman sees as "useless" the "attempt to repeat the material creative, by daguerreotyping the exact likeness by mortal mental means." Image making instead represents the poet's best attempt to create an energy flow, a poetic ecology, that draws strength from the earth and passes it on to the reader. The ideal reader for much of Whitman's career — certainly in the time between the electric prose of the 1855 Preface and the trenchant critique of American materialism in *Democratic Vistas* (1871) — was the poet of the future. For this would-be aspirant, the 1855 Whitman offers advice on the proper setting for reading his work. The message is, stay close to the earth:

> read these leaves in the open air every season of every year of your life, re-examine all you have been told at school or church or in any book, dismiss whatever insults your own soul, and your very flesh shall be a great poem and have the richest fluency not only in its words but in the silent lines of its lips and face and between the lashes of your eyes and in every motion and joint of your body. . . . . (LG 1855, vi)

CHAPTER TWO

The Fall of the Redwood Tree

Chapter 1 has shown how Whitman's ecopoetical experiments depend largely upon his concept and method of indirection. For Whitman, an indirection in its simplest sense is a trope; in the cases considered thus far — the respect for the terrible thingishness of the earth in "This Compost," the complicated attempt to define the limits and possibilities of communion in "A Song of the Rolling Earth," the externalization of the soul as a resonating component of the environment in "Song of Myself," and the progressive abstraction of spiritual experience in the composition history of "A Noiseless Patient Spider" — we see that indirection also involves resistance to the direct and the literal. Sustaining this resistance often proves troublesome for Whitman. The problem arises with tropes of identity and association — metaphor, metonymy, synecdoche, and allegory — all of which function powerfully in the ecological imagination. Rather than dwelling upon limits and incapacities, such tropes may tend to overwhelm difference, often to the point of insensitivity. For ecopoetics, metaphor is particularly problematical because it is a form of language that identifies two ostensibly unlike things.[1] Modern definitions of nature, despite the troubled survival of a concept like "human nature," begin from a point of difference, nature being designated as the nonhuman realm, the environment. But metaphors appear to have little respect for such boundaries, leaving tension and irony (sometimes unintended irony) where difference had once prevailed.

Perhaps even more problematical is personification, the attribution of human characteristics to nonhuman entities. Personification may be seen as a subcategory of metaphor because of its interest in identity, but it also partakes of metonymy and synecdoche when it involves a looser form of association.[2] In science, personification is known as anthropomorphism and is generally prohibited in descriptive writing. I remember an exercise in zoology lab designed to cure us college sophomores of this form of wit. We were directed to watch a group of white mice in a wire cage and make notes about how they behaved. To torment the lab assistant, who took his work very seriously, we would say things like, "When the mouse rubs his little hands together, he looks just like he's praying." As the voice of judgment, the lab assistant would say, "Those aren't hands, he's not 'little' by mouse standards, he's not praying but preening, and how do you know it's a 'he' anyway?" We would shrug and submit to reason, writing down something like, "In the right front quadrant of the cage, a mouse, weighing approximately 5 grams, gender and age indeterminate, rubbed its forepaws together for one minute and 15 seconds during the observation."

This kind of correction was gaining currency during Whitman's day, when science was professionalizing and expanding its sphere of influence. While, on the one hand, Darwin's theories were bringing the human family closer to the animals, on the other hand, the analytical imagination of modern science was separating organisms from their world. Alienation and division, consonant with the prohibition of anthropomorphism, prevailed over integration and holism. Division, implied in the very word *environment*, signifying that which surrounds, found its way into literary theory and practice as well as science. We see it in Ruskin's concept of the pathetic fallacy — which cautions poets to avoid the age-old practice of seeing their emotions mirrored in nature, in the weeping of the willow and the sagging of the moon in the night sky — and we see it again in literary naturalism's portrayal of nature as a force indifferent to human suffering. Finally, it appears in the work of recent nature writers such as Edward Abbey, who reject personification as a sentimentalist relic that interferes with the Zen-like contemplation of the earth as the wholly other.[3]

Whitman bucked the trend of making clear separations between human beings and nonhuman nature. Though his practice might be seen as another instance of belatedness, a nostalgic drift back into Romantic nature poetry or the elaborate conceits of the English metaphysical poets, his excessiveness, his very wildness, argues against this possibility, as does the complexity of his tropes, some of which defy easy categorization.[4] Certainly no other writer before or after him experimented so widely and warmly with personification. *Leaves of Grass* pushed the limits of this trope, as it did with so many others, especially in the energetic performances of the first three editions. In doing so, it anticipated a number of important conflicts in twentieth-century thinking about the human relationship with the earth. In particular, Whitman's use of personifying tropes showed shifts in his attitudes toward nature that anticipated the conflicts among three dominant perspectives of twentieth-century discourse on the environment — the views of nature as spirit, nature as object, and nature as resource (see Killingsworth and Palmer, *Ecospeak*, 10–18). One of the great ironies of ecopoetics, a sure indication that the study of poetic form must take account of multiple contexts, is that identification with the earth, as represented in personification and other tropes, serves not one but all three of these perspectives depending upon the context and the way the elements of the trope — person and natural object — interact and reflect one upon the other.

Though the 1855 Preface seems to prohibit certain forms of personification — notably the personification of abstractions (see chapter 1, note 1) — there is no shortage of personifying effects in Whitman's early poems. Whitman's notorious poetry of the body, which includes many of his most celebrated poems, makes bold use of the trope, encompassing whole landscapes of life, as in these well-known lines from the 1855 version of "Song of Myself":

Smile O voluptuous coolbreathed earth!

. . . .

Far-swooping elbowed earth! Rich apple-blossomed earth!
Smile, for your lover comes!

Prodigal! you have given me love! . . . . therefore I to you give love!
O unspeakable passionate love!

Thruster holding me tight and that I hold tight!
We hurt each other as the bridegroom and the bride hurt each other.

You sea! I resign myself to you also . . . . I guess what you mean,
I behold from the beach your crooked inviting fingers,
I believe you refuse to go back without feeling of me;
We must have a turn together . . . . I undress . . . . hurry me out of
    sight of the land,
Cushion me soft . . . . rock me in billowy drowse,
Dash me with amorous wet . . . . I can repay you. (LG 1855, 27)

In what is for Whitman a typical move, this passage eroticizes the seemingly innocuous category of nature lover with rhetoric calculated to shock sentimental sensibility as surely as it denies the separation of human from nonhuman.[5] Whitman's earth is neither a mother nor a goddess nor a dead cold rock but a lover. Its dark and inviting moisture resists the old myths of sweet maternity, imperious sublimity, or cool indifference, just as the poet who reads the signs of desire in the crooked fingers of the sea, rushing to undress and exchange amorous wetness with the willing partner, defies the stereotype of the nature poet calmly contemplating a picturesque scene or paralyzed before the sublime vision of an all-powerful nature. In Whitman's poem, both the personified earth and the earthy poet are highly active in their lovemaking — reckless of all possible danger ("out of sight of the land"), excessive or "prodigal" in the old sense of spendthrift. Indeed, the idea of spending and overspending permeates the passage. "I can repay you," boasts the poet-lover to the "rich" and "prodigal" earth-lover, careless of the medical warnings prevalent in his day against overspending — "spending" being a slang expression for orgasm, excessive enjoyment of which was thought to deprive the body of vital fluids. From the excessiveness of the earth itself — the effusive productivity that Thoreau marveled over and that Annie Dillard would come to celebrate in her brilliant 1974 prose work *Pilgrim at Tinker Creek* — Whitman extrapolates a model of loving that refuses to be limited by the penny-pinching standards of the Victorian sexual economy.[6]

But another economy urges caution here. The ecocritical perspective — fully aware of how concepts of the earth's abundance have led to abuse and overuse — leads to questions about the motives behind Whitman's lines. The attractiveness of the imagery — the earth with cool breath and elbows, adorned in apple blossoms — and the humor of the speaker's winkingly self-ironic hyperbole may mask sinister implications. After Annette Kolodny's early ecofeminist critique of the pioneering mentality that treats the land as a woman's body to be possessed and dominated, we may only dare to smile at Whitman's machismo.[7] Our caution may well lead to the general question of how seeing nature as mother or lover, or in any way seeing ourselves reflected in the environment, affects our concept of human responsibilities toward nature. Such questions make even the innocent clichés of personification suspect, much less the wild troping of our groundbreaking poet.

And yet the science and nature writers who have been most influential in twentieth-century political ecology have employed a personifying rhetoric. Rachel Carson's 1962 book *Silent Spring*, the founding text of contemporary environmentalism, couches its most fervent appeals in personifications reminiscent of Whitman's best poems, conceptualizing the earth in terms of the human body.[8] The "health of the landscape," in her words, sustains our own bodies in health; when the land grows sick, human health must decline as well. Surveying the damage from pesticides and industrial pollution, Carson laments the "scars of dead vegetation" and the "weeping appearance" of afflicted trees (69, 70, 71). Each element of her trope, the earth's body and the human body, informs the other. Just as the earth experiences health and illness, she says, "[t]here is also an ecology of the world within our own bodies" (170) — the cycles and chemical interrelations by which we live and die. A precedent for Carson's wide-ranging personifications appears in Aldo Leopold's mid-twentieth-century essay "Thinking Like a Mountain," which urges readers to abandon the short-term thinking of cattlemen who exterminate wolves to protect herds and increase deer populations but ultimately unbalance the ecology of the land, leaving too many deer. The deer then destroy their own food supplies, stripping the mountain of its vegetation and driving themselves into starvation. From the vantage of its mighty stature and the wisdom of its many years, the mountain — quite clearly a personification of ecological consciousness — sees the big picture and understands the whole story that deer and people cannot comprehend (Leopold 129–133). In another essay, "The Land Ethic," Leopold proposes that we extend ethical rights to the land, granting the earth the same ethical status that we grant fellow human beings (201–226). Environmentalist rhetoric thus moves toward literalizing the personification of the earth. As Rene Dubos writes, "The phrase 'health of the environment' is not a literary convention. It has a real biological meaning, because the surface of the earth is truly a living organism" (27). In this literalizing argument, the resistance to the direct and literal that indirection implies tends to dissolve along with the separation of human beings and nature implied in the concepts of system and environment.

The personifying rhetoric of the political ecologists thus departs from the normal practices of two centuries in scientific discourse. Political ecologists personify in spite of the aesthetic and scientific objections to this figurative reintegration and identification with the earth. This calculated rhetorical risk has definite political consequences. Division might actually be politically productive, as any attempt to figure the world in human terms invites the kind of human-centered understanding of existence that can lead to the unwise or immoral treatment of the nonhuman. In anticipating the personifications of holistic ecologists and their rhetorical risks, Whitman's poems embody some of the deepest conflicts of modern globalizing intelligence. We find in *Leaves of Grass* the contradictory impulses to stress, on the one hand, the unity of human and nonhuman nature, which may lead to exploitation through an uncritical assertion of spiritual if not material identity, and, on the other hand, to preserve the integrity of the earth as an environment distinct from human interests and society.

Whitman's poetic practice varies so widely that it is hard to generalize from poem to poem, from period to period in his career, and even from section to section within long poems like "Song of Myself." But one identifiable trend follows a pattern familiar to Whitman scholars. The poems written before the Civil War, for the first three editions of *Leaves of*

Grass, give us great clusters of vivid scenes and images that shock the conventional ear and suggest radically new, close-up perspectives on the world — in the manner of the passage about the "voluptuous earth" and the poetic lover — while the later poems grow more distant, more politically conservative, and more traditionally "poetic" in diction and structure. It is tempting to say that the poems of the early *Leaves* are simply better, that the poet's inspiration failed him after the war, thus repeating a common critical argument in Whitman studies, one that I embraced in my earlier work. But I have listened carefully to the critique of that position, particularly as developed by Robert Leigh Davis and James Perrin Warren. In this chapter and throughout this study, I hope to follow Davis, Warren, and others in developing a more subtle understanding of the differences between Whitman's poems of the 1850s and those that came later, much as writers like Michael Moon and Vivian Pollak have added to our understanding of how Whitman's youthful writings of the 1840s differed from his mature work in *Leaves of Grass*.

One approach to the problem that contributes nicely to an ecopoetics of Whitman's verse comes from Martin K. Doudna. His essay on "Nature" in the Whitman encyclopedia argues that Whitman seems at various times to treat the nonhuman world in two distinct ways — "as the material world of objects and phenomena (*natura naturata*)" and "as the force — usually personified as feminine — that pervades and controls that material world (*natura naturans*)": "In Whitman's pre–Civil War poetry, the *naturata* aspect of nature tends to predominate.... In such later works as *Democratic Vistas* (1871) or his last major poem, 'Passage to India' (1871), the *naturans* aspect predominates and nature becomes largely an abstraction" (451). My argument proceeds along similar lines in this chapter but with more attention to the ecological consequences of the trend toward abstraction.

In yielding to metaphysical abstraction, Whitman's postwar writing follows the poetics associated with his contemporaries from the genteel tradition, the "schoolroom poets" Bryant, Longfellow, Whittier, Lowell, and Holmes, whose taste for abstraction is cited as a major identifying feature in George Arms's now classic study *The Fields Were Green* (3–8). Whitman's "A Noiseless Patient Spider," for example, probably composed during the war and published first in an 1868 number of London's *Broadway Magazine*, echoes one of the most popular nature poems of the day, Oliver Wendell Holmes's "The Chambered Nautilus," which appeared a decade earlier. In using an object of nature as a point of departure for a metaphysical reflection, the two poems resonate within a long tradition of nature poetry, which goes back at least to the seventeenth century among writers in English. In

America, the tradition informs the sermons of Cotton Mather and Jonathan Edwards and the poems of Edward Taylor. In England, the poet Henry Vaughan is perhaps the best seventeenth-century exemplar of the tradition, though any of the "metaphysical poets" might serve. Vaughan's poem "The Waterfall," for example, concludes:

> As this loud brooks incessant fall
> In streaming rings restagnates all,
> Which reach by course the bank, and then
> Are no more seen, just so pass men
> [. . .] Thou art the Channel my soul seeks,
> Not this with Cataracts and Creeks." (344)[9]

Holmes's poem is worth quoting in full and considering closely as an example of a textual web that, like Whitman's final version of "A Noiseless Patient Spider," threatens to come loose from its moorings in nature and history but which, unlike Whitman's, is more forthright in connecting to previously established anchors in literary and religious discourse:

> This is the ship of pearl, which, poets feign,
>   Sails the unshadowed main, —
>   The venturous bark that flings
> On the sweet summer wind its purpled wings
> In gulfs enchanted, where the Siren sings,
>   And coral reefs lie bare,
> Where the cold sea-maids rise to sun their streaming hair.
>
> Its webs of living gauze no more unfurl;
>   Wrecked is the ship of pearl!
>   And every chambered cell,
> Where its dim dreaming life was wont to dwell,
> As the frail tenant shaped his growing shell,
>   Before thee lies revealed, —
> Its irised ceiling rent, its sunless crypt unsealed!
>
> Year after year beheld the silent toil
>   That spread his lustrous coil;
>   Still, as the spiral grew,
> He left the past year's dwelling for the new,
> Stole with soft step its shining archway through,
>   Built up its idle door,
> Stretched in his last-found home, and knew the old no more.

Thanks for the heavenly message brought by thee,
 Child of the wandering sea,
 Cast from her lap, forlorn!
From thy dead lips a clearer note is born
Than ever Triton blew from wreathèd horn!
 While on mine ear it rings,
Through the deep caves of thought I hear a voice that sings: —

Build thee more stately mansions, O my soul,
 As the swift seasons roll!
 Leave thy low-vaulted past!
Let each new temple, nobler than the last,
Shut thee from heaven with a dome more vast,
 Till thou at length art free,
Leaving thine outgrown shell by life's unresting sea!

(Holmes, in Ellmann 139–140)

The apparent occasion of the poem is the poet's observation of a seashell, the washed-up remains of a mollusk known as the chambered or pearly nautilus. But rather than a reflective nature poem in the manner of Wordsworth's "I Wandered Lonely as a Cloud" or Emerson's "Each and All," in which the poet comments on a personal experience in nature with the implied reader looking on sympathetically, Holmes's poem has the feel of a lecture or sermon that takes the shell as its text. He challenges the reader directly to consider the meaning of this phenomenon that "before thee lies revealed." The object of his reflection could not have been found during a walk on the beach. Holmes lived in Boston, on the Atlantic Coast of the United States, and the nautilus is a creature at home in the deep waters of the Pacific and Indian Oceans. If he saw the shell at all — and comments he made to friends about the poem suggest that he may have only read about it and saw pictures in a scientific volume (including a cross section, "Its irised ceiling rent, its sunless crypt unsealed") — he probably saw it in a parlor collection or in a display case of the museum at Harvard where Holmes was a professor of medicine and where his famous colleague Louis Agassiz studied the nautilus. One of the great taxonomists among nineteenth-century scientists, remembered now as an opponent of Darwin (as well as a defender of polygenesis and an exponent of racialist thought), Agassiz is still cited in the scientific literature on the chambered nautilus for correctly identifying it as a distinct species of the mollusks classed as cephalopods, related to the octopus, the squid, and the cuttlefish but the only living mollusk to have a complete external shell. The shell of the so-called paper nautilus (the subject of a later poem by Marianne Moore dedicated to Elizabeth Bishop) is an egg case excreted only by the female. More closely related to the extinct ammonite, the chambered nautilus was known mainly by abandoned shells and fossilized remains during Holmes's day. Science would wait more than a hundred years for photographs of the creature in its natural habitat, which generally lies below a safe depth for human diving. Among the adventurers who first caught the nautilus on film when this "living fossil" came up to feed at night from depths as great as 2,000 feet to the relatively safe diving depth of 200 feet was Captain Jacques Cousteau, the inventor of the aqualung, who published a clear photograph of a living nautilus in 1973 (Cousteau 27).[10]

No wonder, then, that Holmes's poem resists a simple description of the creature and the shell as surely as the poet's wit obscures the scene of observation, preferring instead to turn the chambered nautilus into something other than itself with an extensive use of metaphor. The vagueness could be partly the result of missing information. Scientific texts of the day, such as Agassiz and Gould's textbook *Principles of Zoology*, give only sketchy descriptions of the animal and its habits. Unlike the cuttlefish, which is generously described, the nautilus could not be known through observation or dissection. Only by the title of Holmes's poem can we know that the riddling metaphor of the first line — ship of pearl — refers to a mollusk shell. Within four lines, the ship has become a bird unfurling its sails like wings, and by the end of the first verse the nautilus has been implicitly compared to Ulysses, the hero who heard the Sirens sing. The nautilus's very name and much of the information provided by Holmes depend upon the legend ("poets feign") that it sailed the seas by inflating a membrane to catch the wind and drive it along — a legend fit for life among seaport dwellers like the Boston poet. In fact, a living chambered nautilus never comes near the surface and propels itself by squirting out jets of water collected within an organ specialized for propulsion — so that the jet-setter–scientist Cousteau has greater claim to kinship with the creature that he describes as "jet-propelled" (Cousteau 27).

Holmes may have confused the chambered nautilus with the paper nautilus or argonaut, a surface-exploring octopus with an expandable membrane in one of its tentacles (though also without the fabled power to "sail"). In his letters, Holmes admitted that some readers had noted the mistake. "I have now and then found a naturalist," writes Holmes, "who still worried over the distinction between the Pearly Nautilus and the Paper Nautilus, or Argonauta. As the stories about both are mere fables, attaching to the Physalia, or Portuguese man-of-war, as well as these two mol-

luscs, it seems over-nice to quarrel with the poetic handling of a fiction sufficiently justified by the name commonly applied to the ship of pearl as well
as the ship of paper."[11] Though Holmes justly claims poetic license, the correction of his science clearly rankled, for he mentioned it more than once
in his letters. His irritation is worth noting because it demonstrates the
competing claims for closeness to nature between the literary and scientific discourses of the day. It reminds me of the irritation of a scientist I met
who told me that he resented the criticisms of poets and activists who say
that science distances itself from nature through measurement and objectivity. This scientist, who studied the great saguaro cactus in its natural
Arizona habitat, told me, "No poet or environmentalist ever got as close to
a cactus as I get when I stretch my measuring tape around one."

One of Holmes's sources may hold the key to his injured pride as a
scientist-poet. The reference to Triton's "wreathèd horn" in the penultimate
stanza is a clear allusion to what is arguably the most famous nature poem
in the English Romantic canon, Wordsworth's sonnet "The World Is Too
Much with Us," every line of which is so rich from an ecopoetical perspective that it deserves our close attention:

> The world is too much with us; late and soon,
> Getting and spending, we lay waste our powers:
> Little we see in Nature that is ours;
> We have given our hearts away, a sordid boon!
> This Sea that bares her bosom to the moon;
> The winds that will be howling at all hours,
> And are up-gathered now like sleeping flowers;
> For this, for everything, we are out of tune;
> It moves us not. — Great God! I'd rather be
> A Pagan suckled in a creed outworn;
> So might I, standing on this pleasant lea,
> Have glimpses that would make me less forlorn;
> Have sight of Proteus rising from the sea;
> Or hear old Triton blow his wreathèd horn. (Wordsworth 182)

Wordworth's powerful sense of human loss and alienation from nature resonates with modern environmentalist thinking. In his view, we are so completely possessed by "the world," meaning the materialist society of human
formation, that we cannot see nature as anything more than a resource to
be harvested and sold. Significantly, this theme does not resonate strongly
with Holmes and Whitman. What Whitman may have taken from "The
World Is Too Much with Us" is the erotic personification of nature — "This

Sea that bares her bosom to the moon" — and the sense of the "powers" that we potentially share with nature. What Holmes took away from his reading was the notion that the pagans may have been more completely attuned to nature than are modern people. This notion he rejects even as he alludes to Wordsworth. Whereas the pagan falls in worship before the power of nature, creating gods of the moon and sea, the scientist-poet sees natural objects as sources of information and lessons on life.

Among the poets, we find the three views of nature, which compete, conflict, interact, and overlap in modern ecological discourse — nature as spirit (the dominant view among mystics and many activists), nature as an object of study (the dominant view in science), and nature as resource (the dominant view of business and industry). Wordsworth laments the view of nature as resource and offers the alternative of a romantic revival of the pagan view of nature as a spiritual power that aligns human potential ("our powers"), wasted in the activities of getting and spending, with the fullness of such natural forces as moonlight and wind, which suggest the power to see through darkness and stir the world to motion and sound. The link that Wordsworth seeks to form with the pagan past involves the sense of wonder at nature's majesty, which getting and spending tend to deny in the obsessive pursuits of human power. The Romantic sense of the sublime restores the beauty and meaning of nature (including human nature) in a protest of the disenchanted industrial model of a dead nature reduced to supplying the material needs of human progress.[12]

Holmes strikes a more modern note by invoking the view of nature as an object of study. This view potentially differs from the view of nature as resource in its close attention to the object, the respectful care of the observation, and in the best case, the treatment of the object as a thing in itself, beyond its usefulness for human consumption. The view shares an enthusiasm for the object with the view of nature as spirit but differs in invoking a sense of distanced curiosity instead of the sublime sense of wonder. Under the disenchanting and yet thankful gaze of the scientist-poet, the shell reveals a "clearer note [. . .] Than ever Triton blew from wreathèd horn"; that is, a message that the pagan could not have gathered. The sense of wonder implied in the heroic allusions and metaphors of the opening stanzas gives way to humble modern personifications in verses three and four, the nautilus appearing as a "frail tenant" who occupies cell after ever larger cell much as a dissatisfied householder adds new rooms to contain a growing family or a growing ambition. In another letter, Holmes again dismisses complaints against his confusing the paper and pearl nautiles, this time citing "Roget's *Bridgewater Treatise*," which provides an illustration of the shell in cross section, showing "the series of enlarging compartments successively dwelt in by the animal that inhabits the shell, which is built in a widening spiral."[13] Holmes seeks to divert attention away from objections to the poem's opening metaphors and point to the metaphorical import of the successive chambers of the creature's life, which has a stronger informational foundation in then-contemporary scientific understanding.

And indeed, the enlarging chambered spiral of the shell is the figure that carries the poem to its close, showing the way, to use Whitman's words, between reality and the soul. Holmes's poem suggests that the soul is a sailor on the seas of life but also a householder expanding its dwelling — leaving the "low-vaulted past" for "each new temple, nobler than the last" — until finding all material enclosures too tight, it abandons its impressive shell upon the shores of life and seeks the greater freedom of heaven. Insofar as the poem has a moral, it is that we should expand our souls as fully as we can in earthly life, leaving behind a record of our efforts and preparing ourselves for the last great expansion in heaven, of which Jesus said, "In my Father's house are many mansions" (John 14:2). Significantly, however, Holmes the scientist-Christian leaves the religious message implicit and thus anticipates Whitman's vague suggestions about "measureless oceans of space" into which the spider-soul flings its filaments.

Despite the two poets' increasing secularization, they both retain the framework of a kind of sermonizing poetry that, though employing identity-forming tropes like metaphor and personification, requires a thoroughgoing and dualistic separation of nature and humankind, as well as body and soul. By the time Holmes published "The Chambered Nautilus," the pattern was well established in American nature poetry. It appears, for example, in another famous poem, "To a Waterfowl," by William Cullen Bryant, a poet and journalist on the New York scene whom Whitman greatly admired and may have imitated in his early career. According to Jerome Loving, Bryant was the young Whitman's "favorite poet." It is unlikely that the feeling was mutual, although as editor of the *Evening Post* Bryant did reprint "Blood Money," Whitman's first free-verse poem (Loving, *Walt Whitman* 43, 128–129, 153). In "To a Waterfowl," Bryant begins in the same way that Holmes would end his poem, with an apostrophe. The poet addresses the natural object — in this case, a duck or goose in flight:

> Whither, midst falling dew,
> While glow the heavens with the last steps of day,
> Far, through their rosy depths, dost thou pursue
>   Thy solitary way? (Bryant, in Ellmann 32)

More so than Holmes and Whitman, Bryant follows directly in the tradition of English metaphysical poetry, owing more to the seventeenth century than to Romantics like Wordsworth who lament the loss of natural powers. Here the poet confidently reads in the book of nature the heavenly message that the "Power whose care / Teaches thy way along that pathless coast" will also "lead my steps aright" (32–33). Once again, the observation of nature leads the poet to reflect not on natural objects but on the supernatural. The bird appears only schematically in the early stanzas, a mark barely distinguishable at a great distance, beyond the range of both the hunter's gun ("fowler's eye") and the poet's descriptive gaze. The bulk of the writing concerns the environment of the vast skyscape (the "desert and illimitable air"), contrasted with the reedy wetland toward which the waterfowl wings its way home ("the plashy brink / Of weedy lake, or marge of river wide") (32). Finally, the mind drifts from its connection with the world and seeks some hold in the equivalent of Whitman's "measureless oceans of space." We move from the schematic image of the bird ("darkly seen against the crimson sky, / Thy figure floats along") to the abstraction of providential guidance, the hand of God further abstracted as a "Power" — instinct for the bird, perhaps, and intuition for the poet (32). In contrast to earlier Christian poets, Bryant offers not the consolation of a biblical, doctrinal, or personal God but a more general deific force and thus participates in a progressive secularization of nature poetry, which becomes increasingly humanistic in Holmes and Whitman.[14] In this respect, we can see how the path opens from Protestant responses to nature into scientific reflection, which removes first the religious messages from readings of nature and then, with its prohibition of anthropomorphism, removes human messages, seeking finally to see the natural thing in its own right before applying lessons back to human life.

"The Chambered Nautilus" and "To a Waterfowl" have in large part accounted for Holmes's and Bryant's continued presence in American literature by being among the most frequently anthologized poems from the nineteenth century. Whitman's "A Noiseless Patient Spider," with its tidy length and its tendency to treat traditional themes while still preserving the outward elements of Whitman's free verse, has also become a favorite in recent anthologies. I would argue that its attractiveness also stems from its easy recognition as a nature poem in the old tradition. In this regard, it is not surprising that it seems to allude directly to Holmes's closing apostrophe — "Build thee more stately mansions, O my soul" — which turns on a metaphorical identification of the human spirit with the sea creature and its chambered shell, a partial personification, and a lesson taken from the observation of nature. Compare Whitman's closing lines:

> And you O my soul where you stand,
> Surrounded, detached, in measureless oceans of space,
> Ceaselessly musing, venturing, throwing, seeking the spheres to
>   connect them,
> Till the bridge you will need be form'd, till the ductile anchor hold,
> Till the gossamer thread you fling catch somewhere, O my soul.
>
> (LG, 1891–92, 343)

Metaphor binds the objects it joins — here the spider and the soul — in a web of identity that ideally reveals a third element. In this poem, for example, we could say that the third element is thematic — the heroic will of natural beings to live beyond their limits. A similar theme emerges from "The Chambered Nautilus." But ecology might suggest that what we have here is a human quality — the dissatisfaction of living within limits — imposed upon nonhuman nature whose great lesson in fact may have something more modest to teach: animals adapt within environmental limits while the human drive for transcendence may represent a philosophical instance of the kind of hubris that urges people to overtax an environment with their desire to remake the world according to their own desires. Read in this way, the metaphor imposes the human will for power upon the natural object, the spider or the nautilus, and the poems function ideologically. They substitute history, specifically the drive for human progress that obsessed nineteenth-century Americans, for nature — a characteristic move, according to the leading theorists of ideology. Building upon Marx and Engels's *The German Ideology*, for example, Roland Barthes argues that the "depoliticized speech" of bourgeois rhetoric "transforms history into nature": "The world enters language as a dialectical relation" but "comes out . . . as a harmonious display of essences. A conjuring trick has taken place; it has turned reality inside out, it has emptied it of history and filled it with nature" (129, 142). Raymond Williams makes a similar point, which Wynn Thomas has applied to his readings of Whitman: "[T]he idea of nature contains an extraordinary amount of human history. What is often being argued . . . in the idea of nature is the idea of man, and this not only generally, or in ultimate ways, but the idea of man in society" (qtd. in Thomas, *Lunar Light* 117).

Metaphor often provides the rhetorical means by which ideological ends are enacted. In theory, metaphor functions through a kind of gestalt in which the reader's focus alternates between the two elements of the metaphor, with the third element arising from the alternating pattern. But in practice, one or the other of the two elements may so dominate the trope that the other becomes a mere vehicle for celebrating some aspect of the dominant element. And the convention of nature poetry we are considering tends to reduce nature to a vehicle for the celebration of some human or divine quality. The poems begin with a focus on an object — significantly, an object viewed mainly in isolation, the waterfowl appearing as a dark spot against a backlit sky, the shell of the nautilus deposited out of the sea and taken away from the shore, the spider outlined on a schematic headland against the background of the ocean — decidedly different from the treatment of natural objects in poems like "Song of Myself," which gives us profusive meadows of creatures linked in interactive habitats. Thus decontextualized, brought into the poetic laboratory, the waterfowl, the nautilus shell, and the spider appear first as objects of study but are ultimately abstracted into human lessons. The metaphorical gestalt ceases to alternate; the poet's focus swings entirely away from the objects toward a philosophical point. Abstraction and distance rule the day in the movement we call, somewhat ironically, "reflection," the tendency to move from outward observation to inward exploration, the tendency to forget the resonating earth and build our mansions in the autopoietic comfort of language, the tendency to live inside our minds with decreasing regard for the world outside — a movement reinforced by the increasingly indoor existence favored by air-conditioned urbanization in modern times.

These reflective nature poems share something with the extractive practices of modern industry, treating natural objects as resources consumed for human purposes. In this sense they contrast strongly with Wordsworth's "The World Is Too Much with Us," with its complaint that nature is lost to us through our rush toward "getting and spending." Closer to home, they contrast with Emerson's claim in "Each and All" that nature resists our efforts to accommodate it to our needs or isolate the qualities of natural objects that please the human mind — the bird's song or the seashell's delicate enamel. "Nothing is fair or good alone," he tells us:

> I thought the sparrow's note from heaven,
> Singing at dawn on the alder bough;
> I brought him home, in his nest, at even;
> He sings the song, but it cheers not now,
> For I did not bring home the river and the sky; —
> He sang to my ear, — they sang to my eye.
> The delicate shells lay on the shore;

The bubbles of the latest wave
Fresh pearls to their enamel gave,
And the bellowing of the savage sea
Greeted their safe escape to me.
I wiped away the weeds and foam,
I fetched my sea-born treasures home;
But the poor, unsightly, noisome things
Had left their beauty on the shore
With the sun and the sand and the wild uproar.

(Emerson, in Ellmann 38)

Emerson follows convention in driving toward a lesson at the end of the poem, but it is a lesson that resists abstraction, distance, and division, preferring instead to offer a critique of the human mind that would divide truth from beauty:

Then I said, "I covet truth;
Beauty is unripe childhood's cheat;
I leave it behind with the games of youth:" —
As I spoke, beneath my feet
The ground-pine curled its pretty wreath,
Running over the club-moss burrs;
I inhaled the violet's breath;
Around me stood the oaks and firs;
Pine-cones and acorns lay on the ground;
Over me soared the eternal sky,
Full of light and of deity;
Again I saw, again I heard,
The rolling river, the morning bird; —
Beauty through my senses stole;
I yielded myself to the perfect whole. (Emerson, in Ellmann 38–39)

The clear allusion to Keats's famous "Ode on a Grecian Urn" obscures somewhat the Wordsworthian theme that Emerson draws upon here, the notion that in pursuing an "adult," rationalistic vision of the world, we "lay waste our powers," lose the perceptual link that children, or pagans, have with nature. A precedent for this concept appears in the seventeenth-century English prose work *The Centuries* by Thomas Traherne, who argues that "the barbarous opinions, and monstrous apprehensions, which we nickname civility" make modern people more barbarous than the "rude and barbarous Indians" who "go naked and drink water and live upon roots" but "are like Adam or Angels in comparison to us." "Your barbarous inventions," says Traherne, "spoil your knowledge. They put grubs and worms in men's heads that are enemies to all pure and true apprehensions, and eat out all their happiness. They make it impossible for them, in whom they reign, to believe there is any excellency in the Works of God, or to taste any sweetness in the nobility of Nature" (116–117). A fascinating claim in Traherne is that the Christian experience restores the childlike perception, that the idea of being born again includes the possibility of awakening again the wonder of nature.[15]

Emerson takes the Romantic path that follows from Traherne farther than any other American poet of his time. A textbook approach to Romanticism might focus on the critique of rationalism in "Each and All" — the refusal to divide truth from beauty that may imply a critique of science, which in Wordsworth's famous formula makes us "murder to dissect" or in Poe's view "clips the angel's wings" (see chapter 5 for further discussion). But an ecopoetic approach suggests that Emerson shares science's interest in the specific and particular, right down to the names of the plants that curl about the poet's feet. He virtually sinks into nature. Grounded in this way, the reflections on truth and beauty seem as much an opportunity to allow the poetic sensibility to play over a natural scene as an occasion to assert a philosophical view. Indeed, the metaphysical theme of the poem — the welding of truth and beauty into an organic whole — had become a truism by Emerson's time. What makes the poem deserving of a modern reader's attention is the fond naming of the native plants and the image of the poet-philosopher rooted to his place on earth as surely as are the sparrow and the pearly seashell that retain their beauty only when viewed in their natural context. Emerson's attention to detail keeps the poem from lapsing into the kind of abstraction and distance that allows the nature-as-object view to drift toward the nature-as-resource ideology, eclipsing entirely the view of nature as spirit.

Abstraction and distance — along with the use of reflective verse in the ideological service of the nature-as-resource perspective — certainly predominate in a group of Whitman's poems from the 1870s that I call the globalizing group. Among the most striking of these is "Song of the Redwood-Tree," first published in *Harper's Magazine* in 1873. In linking manifest destiny to a view of nature as a boundless resource base for human expansion, the poem can only offend the sensibilities of modern environmentalists and proponents of environmental justice. In an early venture into ecocriticism, the 1980 essay "How Emerson, Thoreau, and Whitman

Viewed the Frontier," Gay Wilson Allen writes, "I know of no other literary work which so naïvely reveals the American national consciousness of the nineteenth century — though with most of the people it was probably an unconscious drive. But whether conscious or unconscious, it made the plunder of their natural resources inevitable — and tragic, courting hubris, as we can now see" (126). More recently, in the introduction to the short volume *Earth, My Likeness: Nature Poems of Walt Whitman*, editor Howard Nelson opines that "Song of the Redwood-Tree" "combines some of Whitman's least compelling writing, rhetorical in the weak sense, with a pure dose of 19th Century boosterism of modern progress that should make 21st Century readers wince" (5).

From the perspective of environmental justice, the poem hints at the kind of "romantic and racist" language that the ecocritic David Mazel, with only the slightest anachronism and reductiveness, attributes to Whitman's celebration of Custer's bravery at Little Bighorn in the poem "From Far Dakota's Cañons," published in the *New York Tribune* and first added to *Leaves of Grass* in the centennial year of 1876. Like Richard Slotkin, who alludes to the poem, originally titled "A Death Sonnet for Custer," in his 1985 opus *The Fatal Environment: The Myth of the Frontier in the Age of Industrialization*, Mazel uses Whitman's imagery as the point of departure in his discussion of how representations of land and people run together in ideological constructs of nature in general and in the mythic treatment of forces resisting European Americans' ascendancy on the western frontier in particular. Custer appears in the poem as a reminder of the heroic times of the Civil War, a past that Whitman feared was slipping from the hold of American memory. The hero dies surrounded by hostile forces both human and natural. The "wild ravine" and the "dusky Sioux" become "the fatal environment" in one of only two uses of the key word *environment* in all of Whitman's poetry (LG 1891–92, 366). The other appears also in a scene of war, in "The Centenarian" from *Drum-Taps*: "The General watch'd them from this hill, / They made repeated desperate attempts to burst their environment" (LG 1891–92, 233). Whitman uses the word literally to indicate surroundings. In both instances, a seemingly prophetic connotation of danger foretells the modern use of *environment* as a synonym for the nonhuman world. The ascendant race is threatened by the earth and the dusky savage, identified in the environmental mythology as forces threatening civilization, both less than fully human. As Mazel argues, the language of Whitman's poem is "scarcely able to distinguish people from place"; the "wildness and the duskiness seem to function in concert, as parallel markers of what is really important: the very otherness of a grand western environment in which the canyons, the Sioux, and the Sioux's resistance are all of a piece" (xi–xii). In "Song of the Redwood-Tree," Whitman does not mention directly the threat of the western American Indians, but the way he represents the yielding of environmental resistance to what he calls "*a superber race*" strongly anticipates the more direct treatment in the Custer poem.

With its operatic structure and elegiac tone, "Redwood-Tree" also recalls two earlier poems, "Out of the Cradle Endlessly Rocking" and "When Lilacs Last in the Dooryard Bloom'd." Like those poems, it employs a special type of "indirection" that fascinated Whitman, a version of personification in which nonhuman creatures are made to speak. The delivery alternates between the poet's voice in roman type and the voice from nature in italic type. In "Redwood-Tree," the poet ventriloquizes the voice of the great sequoia tree itself, or rather the spirits that inhabit it — dryads and hamadryads, the kind of mythical figures that the poet avoided on principle in the earlier, less conventional elegies, when the mockingbird sings in "Out of the Cradle" or the thrush in "Lilacs." As in the earlier poems, the poet takes comfort in the other's voice after experiencing an initial unquiet. But the unquiet of "Redwood-Tree" is neither as profound nor as arresting as it is in "Out of the Cradle" and "Lilacs," and the resolution is far too rapidly enacted and disturbing in its implications. The great tree is made to submit willingly, and even gladly, to the superior "race" of human beings in their march westward. As Allen puts it: "A Conservationist or a Preservationist must find the logic of this poem maddening. The tree not only accepts annihilation, but glories in being 'absorb'd, assimilated' by these superior creatures who will 'really shape and mould the New World, adjusting it to Time and Space'" (126). Wynn Thomas confesses "sadness about the way Whitman here abuses one of the most potent, imaginative devices of his poetry" — the "song from some natural source, which his soul humbly acknowledges and 'tallies.'" In "Redwood-Tree," the device becomes a "convenient propaganda trick, involving a psychological process of rationalization rather than initiation" (*Lunar Light* 139). And though the poet calls his poem a "prophesy and indirection," he makes no effort to capture the subtle resonances of the earthly environment or to distance himself from the powerful things of nature, preferring instead to translate directly into conventional poetic language and become himself the privileged spokesman for nature. Whitman's use of this device is significant not only because it shows a particular development in his own corpus but also because it is a poetic strategy that remains alive and well, though in modified forms, throughout the twentieth century, as David W. Gilbert shows in *Greening the Lyre: Environmental Poetics and Ethics.* In an argument similar to the one Andrew McMurry makes in his treatment of a nineteenth-century case of the "phonocentric fallacy" ("'In Their Own Language,'" 61), Gilbert argues that "the attempt to represent nonhuman entities as speaking subjects" in late-twentieth-century poetry, "while serving to establish a less hierarchical relationship with the nonhuman by deprivileging human linguistic ability, is appropriately viewed as a colonizing move that remains susceptible to serious epistemological and ethical critique" (6). Gilbert concludes that "the move to recognize the nonhuman subject, though motivated by admirable ethical concerns, is inevitably nagged by epistemological difficulties, which ultimately suggests that an ecocentric ethic is poorly served by such a strategy" (41).

Though Gilbert's position is perhaps overgeneralized — the ventriloquist device proves satisfactory, I would argue, in poems like "Out of the Cradle" and "Lilacs" (see the discussion in chapter 4) — such a critique is fully justified in a poem like "Song of the Redwood-Tree," which begins by establishing the dual voices of poet and tree:

A CALIFORNIA song,
A prophecy and indirection, a thought impalpable to breathe as air,
A chorus of dryads, fading, departing, or hamadryads departing,
A murmuring, fateful, giant voice, out of the earth and sky,
Voice of a mighty dying tree in the redwood forest dense.

Farewell my brethren,
Farewell O earth and sky, farewell ye neighboring waters,
My time has ended, my term has come.

Along the northern coast,
Just back from the rock-bound shore and the caves,
In the saline air from the sea in the Mendocino country,
With the surge for base and accompaniment low and hoarse,
With crackling blows of axes sounding musically driven by strong arms,
Riven deep by the sharp tongues of the axes, there in the redwood
    forest dense,
I heard the mighty tree its death-chant chanting.

                                        (LG 1891–92, 165–166)

The poet occupies a position of privilege, not only in relation to the spirits of the trees but also in relation to the nearly unconscious woodsmen who clear the trees:

The choppers heard not, the camp shanties echoed not,
The quick-ear'd teamsters and chain and jack-screw men heard not,
As the wood-spirits came from their haunts of a thousand years to
    join the refrain,
But in my soul I plainly heard. (LG 1891–92, 166)

Quite different from the boy-poet who finds identity with the mocking-bird to whom he lends his voice in "Out of the Cradle" or the brother-poet who identifies deeply with the solitary singing thrush in "Lilacs," the poet in "Song of the Redwood-Tree" assumes the stance of a reporter. He offers little comment on the death-chant, leaving it to the voice of the tree to explain human progress in prophetic terms:

Murmuring out of its myriad leaves,
Down from its lofty top rising two hundred feet high,
Out of its stalwart trunk and limbs, out of its foot-thick bark,
That chant of the seasons and time, chant not of the past only but
    the future.

You untold life of me,
And all you venerable and innocent joys,
Perennial hardy life of me with joys 'mid rain and many a summer sun,
And the white snows and night and the wild winds;
O the great patient rugged joys, my soul's strong joys unreck'd by man,
(For know I bear the soul befitting me, I too have consciousness, identity,
And all the rocks and mountains have, and all the earth,)
Joys of the life befitting me and brothers mine,
Our time, our term has come.

Nor yield we mournfully majestic brothers,
We who have grandly fill'd our time,
With Nature's calm content, with tacit huge delight,
We welcome what we wrought for through the past,
And leave the field for them.

For them predicted long,
For a superber race, they too to grandly fill their time,
For them we abdicate, in them ourselves ye forest kings!
In them these skies and airs, these mountain peaks, Shasta, Nevadas,
These huge precipitous cliffs, this amplitude, these valleys, far Yosemite,
To be in them absorb'd, assimilated. (LG 1891–92, 166–167)

From an ecopoetical perspective, the troubles with the poem begin in its reliance on not only old mythological conventions but also traditional poetic language — "myriad leaves," "stalwart trunk and limbs," and "lofty top" — to portray the disappearance of one of the most distinctive natural features of North America. Whitman's tree appears as an abstraction, a nonbeing, an idea that the poet inhabits in order to justify the ways of humans to nature. Admittedly, we hear of the forest "rising two hundred feet high" and of the "foot-thick bark," but the poet's imagination seems far more attentive to the tools and operations of the logging camp. Whitman, who had never seen a redwood tree in the wild, retreats from his early commitment not to make poems distilled of other poems, as if lacking the experience or the energy to celebrate the redwoods with the evocative and suggestive images of his greatest poetry. In a fascinating analysis of the cultural context of the poem, Diane Kirk observes that "Song of the Redwood-Tree" is "notably lacking in description of the visible features of the trees." The emphasis on the "foot-thick bark" and the height of "two hundred feet" may well be traced, as Kirk argues, to an exhibit in New York in the early 1850s called "Mother of the Forest." The bark of a giant sequoia was removed up to 116 feet and reassembled in the New York exhibit. Samuel Clemens saw a similar exhibit in Philadelphia in the early 1850s. Whitman makes no mention of the exhibit, but it is just the kind of event he relished, and the features of the bark and the impressive height could well have lodged in his memory and resurfaced in 1873 when the poem was written, a time when redwoods were the frequent subject of scientific writing, as Kirk shows.[16]

Worse yet, the language of the poem — the mention of superior races and assimilation, for example — nods toward the darker side of manifest destiny, the racist logic that at the time Whitman wrote the poem was used to uproot indigenous peoples from their land so that white settlements could grow and dominate the western United States. What amounted to the systematic extermination of tribal life during this era gives the celebration of "the new culminating man" that Whitman attributes to the voice of the redwood tree a chilling note:

> Not wan from Asia's fetiches,
> Nor red from Europe's old dynastic slaughter-house,
> (Area of murder-plots of thrones, with scent left yet of wars and scaffolds
>   everywhere,)
> But come from Nature's long and harmless throes, peacefully builded
>   thence,
> These virgin lands, lands of the Western shore,

To the new culminating man, to you, the empire new,
You promis'd long, we pledge, we dedicate. (LG 1891–92, 167)

It is this clear substitution of nature for history in the portrayal of the pioneers as nature's offspring that Whitman picks up as his theme when the
song of the redwood fades and the voice of the poet returns. In an obvious
instance of social Darwinism, he confidently asserts the "naturalness" of
westward expansion and finally globalization — the ultimate completion
of "the New arriving, assuming taking possession":

> The flashing and golden pageant of California,
> The sudden and gorgeous drama, the sunny and ample lands,
> The long and varied stretch from Puget sound to Colorado south,
> Lands bathed in sweeter, rarer, healthier air, valleys and mountain cliffs,
> The fields of Nature long prepared and fallow, the silent, cyclic
>   chemistry,
> The slow and steady ages plodding, the unoccupied surface ripening,
>   the rich ores forming beneath;
> At last the New arriving, assuming, taking possession,
> A swarming and busy race settling and organizing everywhere,
> Ships coming in from the whole round world, and going out to the
>   whole world,
> To India and China and Australia and the thousand island paradises
>   of the Pacific,
> Populous cities, the latest inventions, the steamers on the rivers, the
>   railroads, with many a thrifty farm, with machinery,
> And wool and wheat and the grape, and diggings of yellow gold.
>
> (LG 1891–92, 168)

Whitman's very treatment of the redwood's voice as emanating from a
ghostly entity already departed from the scene of present-day life invokes
a pattern that has been conventionally applied to Native peoples from colonial days down to modern times. As Renée L. Bergland argues in *The
National Uncanny: Indian Ghosts and American Subjects,* American Indians
— as well as black slaves and other figures with a problematically sketchy
history — appear with surprising frequency in the literature of European
Americans not as realistic characters (like the loggers in Whitman's poem)
but as the vanishing Americans, the ghosts of a former time replaced by the
flesh and blood of new and vigorous men and women. Bergland writes, "In
American letters, and in the American imagination, Native American
ghosts function both as representations of national guilt and as triumphant

agents of Americanization" — representations conjured obsessively over the full span of American national history in a "dynamic of unsuccessful repression" (4–5). In *God Is Red*, American Indian social critic and philosopher Vine Deloria Jr. calls upon similar themes in a trenchant critique of white authors' obsession with the archaeology and distant history of American Indians and almost total neglect of present-day American Indians — another instance of the rhetoric of ghostliness in the service of racial politics.

In Whitman's poem, the all too easy substitution of redwoods for red people in the ghostly discourse suggests the nationalizing or globalizing impulse and the environmental racism against which contemporary protesters raise their voices.[17] True to the "national uncanny" thesis of Bergland, the rhetoric of national pride in "Redwood-Tree" is accompanied by what seems to be an undercurrent of guilt or grieving. The note of resignation in the redwood tree's song rings oddly true, partly perhaps as a signal of unsuccessful repression, or rather the return of the repressed. In the chapter "Whitman and American Indians" in *Walt Whitman's Native Representations*, Ed Folsom documents Whitman's difficulty in dealing with the presence and disappearance of American Indians. Folsom shows how Whitman tried but failed to compose a complete poem celebrating Native peoples in North America and also how he attempted, in the manner of the white nativist movement of his times, to co-opt the concept of the "savage" for his own purposes — in the passage about "the free and flowing savage" in "Song of Myself," for example. Folsom deploys the ghostly discourse himself in discussing Whitman's dilemma: "Whitman's haunting lines in 'Song of Myself' . . . capture the cultural ambivalence of a country that was at once destroying and honoring the 'savage,' that was denigrating savagery in the Indians while celebrating it in whites" (58–59). We hear vaguely the hint of doubt that Whitman may have felt — a remnant of the American Indian perspective? — in the description of the pioneers as a "swarming and busy race" in "Song of the Redwood-Tree."

Another explanation arises from an analysis of personification as a trope of identity. Certainly ideology drives Whitman's decision to allow the spirit of the redwood to speak in human language only long enough to bless the people who destroy the very life of the forests. But the note of resignation issuing from the old trees martyred to the march of progress may have an autobiographical source as well. Whitman composed the poem in the autumn of 1873 during what seems to have been a spell of depression. He had suffered a stroke in January of that year that left him paralyzed on his left side and forced him to leave his government job in Washington, D.C., and move into the Camden, New Jersey, home of his younger brother

George, the war hero and successful businessman. Whitman's writing was not going well, he was troubled by the state of the Union in postwar times, and he continued to be disappointed in the public reception of his work.

He complained of dizziness and continued lameness in his left leg. He was lonely in Camden, away from Peter Doyle, Ellen O'Connor, and his other friends in Washington. The redwood poem resonates with the emotion and duplicates the poetics of identity that we find in another poem, "Prayer of Columbus," written about the same time and published in *Harper's Magazine* in March 1874, a month after "Redwood-Tree" appeared in the same venue. In a letter to Doyle, Whitman admitted that "Prayer of Columbus" was "colored [. . .] with thoughts of myself" (*Correspondence* 2:278). The poem gives us the great explorer as "A BATTER'D, wreck'd old man / Thrown on this savage shore, far, far from home" who after "Venting a heavy heart" at some length receives a kind of shallow comfort in a vision of the future as he prays to God, his only true companion:

> And these things I see suddenly, what mean they?
> As if some miracle, some hand divine unseal'd my eyes,
> Shadowy vast shapes smile through the air and sky,
> And on the distant waves sail countless ships,
> And anthems in new tongues I hear saluting me. (LG 1891–92, 323, 325)

The autobiographical echoes, though less striking in "Song of the Redwood-Tree," are sufficient to make it a fit companion piece for "Prayer of Columbus." Like the forest giant, whose spirit departs and leaves the field to the energetic pioneers, Whitman was on the verge of giving up his ambitions when he wrote the two poems.[18]

Whitman's identification with the redwoods, then, stemmed from his own feeling of being overrun and left behind in the postwar years as the agents of material progress (such as his brother George) took charge of the national identity. In this respect, his writing in the 1870s foreshadowed the work of critics like Aldo Leopold and Rachel Carson who built an ecopolitical sensibility on the foundation of a profound identity with the land and its creatures in an era of massive industrialization. For Whitman, the identification with the redwoods was not strong enough to override his faith in material progress — a faith that he had committed himself to celebrating as the poet of America. With these conflicting identities — the kind of conflict that would keep the American public in the years to come alternately attracted to and suspicious of environmentalist politics — the poet could not find the energy to allow the ambivalence hinted in the poem to mature into a full-scale critique. Ironically, his lack of critical energy may have resulted from the same resignation and the same illness that permitted his identity with the redwoods in the first place.

Only a few years before the publication of this poem, in *Democratic Vistas* (1871) Whitman had forcefully warned that the focus on material development threatened to destroy the inherent spirituality of America, and this theme echoes, albeit weakly, in "Song of the Redwood-Tree" to suggest what amounts to the ghost of a protoenvironmentalist critique. The spirit of the redwoods departing as the dull-witted ("unconscious") agents of material development enter the scene suggests an allegory for the shift of human attitudes toward the natural world. The perspective of nature as resource overwhelms the perspective of nature as spirit. The latter departs, replaced in the public mind by a soulless materialism in which the earth is a dead thing to be exploited by a swarming and busy human race.

CHAPTER THREE

Global and Local, Nature and Earth

A manuscript draft of a never-used preface for "Song of the Redwood-Tree" that Whitman sketched for possible inclusion in the 1876 *Leaves of Grass* shows not only that he was very much aware of the geographical element of his poetic program but also that he felt some anxiety about drifting too far away from the places he knew best — the sea islands, villages, and cities of his homeland on the Atlantic Shore:[1]

> Song of the Redwood Tree
> Preface.
> Without deprecating at all
> the magnificent accomplishment
> & boundless promise of the Older
> > and which where I was born and grew
> States flanking the ∧ Atlantic Shore,
> I see at least just as much
> [cause? course? corpse?] that the real America is to
> > expand and take definite
> loom up and take ∧ shape
> with immensely added population, products & originality
> in the States drained by the Mississippi
> and in those flanking the Pacific.
> > facing

The argument I will pursue in this chapter is that Whitman's worry over the location of the "real America" and the relationship of his own "accomplishment" and "promise" to locales near and far was well founded. His poetic reach was hardly "boundless." Much as businesses and nations often go to pieces when they stretch their resources too far, Whitman's poetry generally suffers from overextension. He is at his best as a local poet, a loyal son of the New York islands. When he tries to expand to global proportions, or even when he strives for continental and national coverage, his rhetoric appears falsely inflated, a great balloon floating over a landscape he cannot touch but can only see abstracted at a distance, like a map with dots for cities and random-seeming names. In this mode, he tends to treat nature as an abstraction — Nature with a capital letter; the idea of Nature rather than the things, patterns, and processes of the material earth; Nature emptied of its earthy contents and filled with human politics and history. When he globalizes, he happily celebrates the accomplishments of technological progress, some of which in fact may have been troublesome for him when they cropped up in his own backyard. He crowed with praise for the engineering achievement of the Mississippi River bridge in St. Louis, for example, but as Arthur Geffen shows in an insightful essay, "Silence and Denial: Walt Whitman and the Brooklyn Bridge," the poet remained curiously quiet about the equally great feat of engineering in his own hometown. Very likely he was torn between his commitment to the ideology of technological progress and the sad reality that the bridge of bridges made his beloved Fulton Ferry obsolete and destroyed the neighborhood upon which it depended, a site that Whitman considered "almost a holy place" (Geffen 2). The idea of sacred places, which I consider more fully in chapter 4, proves to be a key concept in ecopoetics, indicating not only a personal commitment to geographic loyalty but also a sense of limits. As people stray from their own bioregion, they retain something of its character even when the journey is primarily imaginative. The creative spirit, which Whitman addresses as his soul, thrives best and inspires most fully when it arises like a local deity from the ground where the poet has lived and walked and loved. In Whitman's case, when he strives for the global vision, what he calls his soul comes to seem more and more derivative or conventional and less a matter of direct and even sensual experience.

In "Passage to India" — a poem published in 1871, only three years before "Song of the Redwood-Tree" and composed during the time Whitman was weakened by his wartime service but not yet debilitated as he was after the 1873 stroke — the poet inaugurated the global vision that he would always thereafter identify with technological progress. Industry surged in the years following the Civil War, riding the crest of wartime engineering and foreshadowing the runaway technological expansion in the years following World War II, which was also advanced by military research and development, the cold war feeding what President Eisenhower called the military-industrial complex, the dominance of which ultimately led to the series of political reactions we now know as the environmentalist movement.

While the New England transcendentalists balked at technological progress and global expansion — witness Thoreau's comments on the railroad or Emerson's famous critique of travel — Whitman's self-concept as a poet of the people (rather than a man of the woods like Thoreau or a high-minded moralist like Emerson) led him to view grand-scale technological progress as an opportunity for extending human spirituality as well as realizing a new level of material comfort for an ever larger percentage of the population. As a New Yorker, Whitman would have been particularly sensitive to the development of transportation and communication technology. By 1860, New York City was not only a great port served by extensive international and local systems of transport (including the ferries and omnibuses that Whitman loved), it was also the hub of the nation's information network. Thanks to steam-powered travel and the telegraph, messages arrived from Europe in about a week and a half, as opposed to the month and a half required a hundred years earlier. More messages were sent to and received from New York than from any other city in the United States. New York boasted seven daily newspapers, a hundred weeklies, and more than fifty monthlies. The seventeen publishing companies produced a third of the books printed in the United States. And advertising was evolving from a simple product-information business into the persuasive (and pervasive) force we know today, flooding people with words and images against which to measure their material status and accomplishments.[2] As a newspaperman, printer, and professional poet (as well as a consummate self-promoter), Whitman came of age in this dynamic and expanding informational web.

Whitman's world was well on its way to becoming what Marshall McLuhan a century later would call "the global village," a world brought closer and to some degree homogenized by rapid transport and communication, and "Passage to India" is a hymn for the global tribe, celebrating the grand connections — the opening of the Suez Canal, the building of the transcontinental railroad, and the laying of telegraph cables across the oceans:

> Our modern wonders, (the antique ponderous Seven outvied,)
> In the Old World the east the Suez canal,
> The New by its mighty railroad spann'd,
> The seas inlaid with eloquent gentle wires. (LG 1891–92, 315)

In his appreciation for the beauty and wonder of human creativity, figured here as a version of the technological sublime, Whitman invokes the soul, ostensibly reversing the pattern that would inform "Song of the Redwood-Tree," in which the spirits of the forest depart at the advance of human progress, leaving a reduced version of nature, a dead resource base for the use of pioneering people. By contrast, "Passage to India" invites the soul to

realize the animating possibilities implied in technological progress, justified as a natural outcome of the divine plan:

> Passage to India!
> Lo, soul, seest thou not God's purpose from the first?
> The earth to be spann'd, connected by network,
> The races, neighbors, to marry and be given in marriage,
> The oceans to be cross'd, the distant brought near,
> The lands to be welded together. (LG 1891–92, 316)

In one sense, "Passage to India" is a web-making poem, offering poetic reinforcement for the great network that spans the earth, strengthening the
links among the farthest outposts of humanity. The globalizing Whitman
longs to see the completion of Columbus's voyage of discovery as a journey of the human spirit rather than a materialist fulfillment.

But despite the focus on peace and cross-cultural tolerance in this passage, which countenances even the possibility of interracial marriage —
"The races, neighbors, to marry and be given in marriage" — the poem's
prophetic vision, "impell'd by the past" and headed toward a certain future,
opens the door to the kind of thinking all too easily enrolled in the service
of political imperialism.[3] Within the space of a few lines, the delicate language of the web, with its metaphorical sources in nature and simple craft
— "the eloquent gentle wires" of the transoceanic cables that span the earth
with a "network" — yields to the more mechanical and sinister image of
the "lands to be welded together." The web suggests living high and light,
but welding implies a more forcible, rigid joining. Such accomplishments
as the "strong light works of engineers" mentioned in the third line of the
poem seem suddenly heavy.

The suggestion of a divine plan — "God's purpose from the first" — adds
a further ideological burden by suggesting the exact version of manifest destiny that a hundred years later would trouble Vine Deloria Jr., whose 1972
book *God Is Red* was reissued in 1992 as a counterweight to the commemo-
rative celebrations of Columbus's voyages 500 years earlier. "Western history
is written," writes Deloria, "as if the torch of enlightenment was fated to
march from the Mediterranean to the San Francisco Bay. But reaching the
western edge of North America, history must inexorably move to Japan, and
it has appeared to do so, stripping the American experience of its cosmic
validity" (69). According to this view, the imperialist march of technology
becomes not a saving grace for the poor and scattered members of the human
family but a means of asserting racial superiority: "A variant of manifest destiny," writes Deloria, "is the propensity to judge a society or civilization by

its technology and to see in society's effort to subdue and control nature the fulfillment of divine intent." This ideology "adopts the secular doctrine of cultural evolution and attaches it to theological language" but "falls flat" when confronted with the environmental record of large-scale technological development: "In less than two and a half centuries American whites have virtually destroyed a whole continent and large areas of the United States are now almost uninhabitable" (69). Communication technology, a "light" work of engineering if ever there was one, only contributes to the problem, in Deloria's view, by disregarding differences with a universalism fueled by manifest destiny. "The world . . . is not a global village," Deloria insists, "so much as a series of nonhomogeneous pockets of identity that must eventually come into conflict because they represent different historical arrangements of emotional energy" (65). Whitman's prophetic commitment to the technological version of manifest destiny finds reinforcement in the prose work *Democratic Vistas*, also published in 1871 and in many ways a prose companion to "Passage to India." The emphasis on spirituality in that work again appears alternately as a rationale and a critique of materialism. He connects communication technology, including literature it would seem, directly to the imperialist spirit in this passage, for example:

> Long ere the second centennial arrives, there will be some forty to fifty great States, among them Canada and Cuba. When the present century closes, our population will be sixty or seventy millions. The Pacific will be ours, and the Atlantic mainly ours. There will be daily electric communication with every part of the globe. What an age! What a land! Where, elsewhere, one so great? The individuality of one nation must then, as always, lead the world. Can there be any doubt who the leader ought to be? Bear in mind, though, that nothing less than the mightiest original non-subordinated SOUL has ever really, gloriously led, or can ever lead. (This Soul—its other name, in these Vistas, is LITERATURE.). (CPCP 981)[4]

But Whitman's propagandistic commitment to the full sweep of manifest destiny nowhere sounds more loudly than it does in "Passage to India." By the same token, nowhere do we find a better instance of the poet's "turning up the volume of his rhetoric in order to drown out the noise of his doubts" (Thomas, *Lunar Light* 266). The doubts that whisper beneath the rhetoric in "Song of the Redwood-Tree" virtually shout at the reader in "Passage to India." The earth itself seems to resist the poet's sweeping claims, as we see in a curious segment of the poem that breaks the optimistic mood, if only for a moment. Whitman questions the human connection with the earth, wondering whether modern people, these "feverish children" with their "restless explorations," can count on the affections of the "great mother":

> Who speak the secret of the impassive earth?
> Who bind it to us? what is this separate Nature so unnatural?
> What is this earth to our affections? (unloving earth, without a throb
>   to answer ours,
> Cold earth, the place of graves.) (LG 1891–92, 318)

In this key passage, Whitman conceptually divides the material earth from abstract Nature. The "voluptuous" earth to whom the poet vowed his love in the 1855 version of "Song of Myself" now appears unyielding and cold, the place of graves. Though the poet is clearly setting up a rhetorical conflict that he will quickly resolve, the sense of abandonment in his portrayal of the "unloving earth, without a throb to answer ours" ultimately sounds more convincing than the solution that he offers. It is a note that will sound again in "Prayer of Columbus" and "Song of the Redwood-Tree," poems published only two years later, after Whitman suffered the paralytic stroke that left him feeling that the world was passing him by, a feeling that gave him a weak sense of identity with the spirits of the earth driven into oblivion by the inexorable material march of modern life.

In "Passage to India," Whitman can only address his doubts through an aggrandizement of the poet's role, a strategy undertaken with the bombastic tone usually associated with psychological overcompensation. A hint of something like professional jealousy leads him to insist upon the importance of the poet in the creation of the modern technological wonders. Engineers and scientists work with mere materials, he suggests, but the poet makes the final connection in the world's web by linking with the spirit and realigning the world of humankind with Nature and with God:

> After the seas are all cross'd, (as they seem already cross'd,)
> After the great captains and engineers have accomplish'd their work,
> After the noble inventors, after the scientists, the chemist, the geolo-
>   gist, ethnologist,
> Finally shall come the poet worthy that name,
> The true son of God shall come singing his songs. (LG 1891–92, 318)

The "true son of God, the poet" will justify the earth to humankind: "Nature and Man shall be disjoin'd and diffused no more," we are told, "The true son of God shall absolutely fuse them" (LG 1891–92, 319). The poet of the people — the shaman who shows the way between reality and the soul —

now seems more concerned with calming the anxieties of the restless (as well as his own anxieties) with a paternal hand, subduing resistance to the workings of the social order. His insistence that the poet will fuse "Nature" and "Man" remains more of a declaration than a poetic act. The fusing is not dramatized, as it is in the energetic tropes of poems like "Song of Myself," nor is it narrated, as it is in poems like "Out of the Cradle Endlessly Rocking." It is displaced into an ideal future, a kind of second coming, the glorious age when "the poet worthy that name / The true son of God shall come singing his songs."

Compared to Whitman's earlier statements of his poetics and his own claims to have arrived as the singer of the New World, "Passage to India" gives us a view of the poet that is at once newly inflated and newly depleted. On the one hand, the poet is equated with the Christian savior, the Son of God. With its capitalized abstractions "Nature," "Man," and "God," these lines seem a far cry from the 1855 expressions of the poet's love for the earth in "Song of Myself," in which humility in the face of the earth's power often intervenes into expansive celebrations of selfhood. "The press of my foot to the earth springs a hundred affections," the 1855 poet boasts, but he adds a respectful qualification and an acknowledgment of incapacity: "They scorn the best I can do to relate them" (LG 1855, 21). On the other hand, the coming of this god-poet as conceived in "Passage to India" is delayed for the moment, leaving us with the curiously diminished prophet-poet who actually appears onstage in the poem. The god-poet, we are told, will reclaim the dead earth as a resource to be refined into transcendental Nature fit for nurturing the human soul. But for the present, the earth must remain under the dominion of the engineers and materialists, who master its challenges with their powerful tools and look upon it as a resource base to satisfy human appetites and ambitions.

The concept of the soul also changes in this poem. Rather than the creative communing animus, the invited soul that resonates with the earth, by means of which poetry realizes connections and aligns the body and mind with heaven and earth, the soul takes on the qualities normally attributed to it in the dominant Protestant theological tradition, the means by which human consciousness is elevated above the material earth and its nonhuman creatures. The soul grows haughty:

O sun and moon and all you stars! Sirius and Jupiter!
Passage to you!

Passage, immediate passage! the blood burns in my veins!
Away O soul! hoist instantly the anchor!

Cut the hawsers — haul out — shake out every sail!
Have we not stood here like trees in the ground long enough?
Have we not grovel'd here long enough, eating and drinking like mere
    brutes? (LG 1891–92, 322–323)

The command "hoist instantly the anchor" betrays an unintended irony
when placed within the ecopoetic model of reading, which celebrates the
links, the anchors, that ground linguistic and spiritual practice in an awareness of the human dependence upon the earth. Reaching above the level of
"trees" and "brutes," now mere objects without value, used and discarded
resources, the soul grows greedy as well as haughty. The very stars and planets stir the desire for new territory, new frontiers.[5] The flavor of these lines,
and the poem as a whole, oddly foreshadows the words of the notorious
British imperialist Cecil Rhodes, who once said, "To think of the stars that
you see overhead at night, these vast worlds which we can never reach. I
would annex the planets if I could."[6]

How different are these closing lines of "Passage to India" even from "A
Noiseless Patient Spider," which may have been composed about the same
time and was published only a few years earlier. The concept of the soul as
a lonely spider reaching for distant spheres with an untiring but uncertain
spinning of light filaments yields to the concept of the soul as a brave
explorer confidently setting sail for the stars, repressing all doubts and urged
forward by the questing imperialist thunder of the national poet. And how
the ambitions of the poet for his soul have expanded from the simple desires
of 1855, when it took only the press of human intimacy to please the soul
well, as he says in the earliest version of "I Sing the Body Electric," with its
strong sense of what is "enough" for the soul:[7]

I have perceived that to be with those I like is enough,
To stop in company with the rest at evening is enough,
To be surrounded by beautiful curious breathing laughing flesh is
    enough,
To pass among them . . . to touch any one . . . . to rest my arm ever so
    lightly round his neck or her neck for a moment . . . . what is this then?
I do not ask any more delight . . . . I swim in it as in a sea.

There is something in staying close to men and women and looking on
    them and in the contact and odor of them that pleases the soul well,
All things please the soul, but these please the soul well. (LG 1855, 79)

I do not want to overstate the differences between the prewar and postwar poems. No doubt there are continuities. The structural movement in

"Passage to India," for example — using the suspicion that the earth is indifferent to and separated from human purposes to question the sense of kinship and belonging — is also enacted in the rhetoric of "This Compost" in 1856. But the mood of that remarkable earlier poem is far more welcoming to the modern ecological intelligence. There the earth, after the moment of alienation passes, appears to him as a great compost heap, its marvelous chemistry yielding miracles of rebirth. Out of the putrid rot of death comes nourishment for the human body (resources to be consumed and enjoyed), for the mind (objects full of meaning and interest), and for the spirit (objects full of beauty and models for creativity). The poem itself is a compost heap, the images of rot and death ultimately setting up a stronger commitment to the earth's body (and the human body as well):

> What chemistry!
> That the winds are really not infectious,
> That this is no cheat, this transparent green-wash of the sea which is
>   so amorous after me,
> That it is safe to allow it to lick my naked body all over with its
>   tongues,
> That it will not endanger me with the fevers that have deposited them-
>   selves in it,
> That all is clean forever and forever,
> That the cool drink from the well tastes so good,
> That blackberries are so flavorous and juicy,
> That the fruits of the apple-orchard and the orange-orchard, that mel-
>   ons, grapes, peaches, plums, will none of them poison me,
> That when I recline on the grass I do not catch any disease,
> Though probably every spear of grass rises out of what was once
>   catching disease. (LG 1891–92, 286)

The poem depends upon the gestalt of the alternating trope. The earth is alternately "myself" and the wholly other. It can never be entirely one or the other without some form of self-deception or inflated rhetoric, usually a claim of total identity with the earth or a full transcendence of it, both of which signal an imposition of ideology, a transformation in which the earth is overwhelmed by the social and psychological needs of the poet or in which the social or psychological reality is denied and the illusion of a pure earth poetry is offered to the (rightly skeptical) reader.

Another crucial feature of the catalog of images in Section 2 of "This Compost" is its local quality, which recalls Emerson's "Each and All." The pastoral scene comes straight from the late summer fields, orchards, and wood margins of the eastern United States — wild things like blackberries, willows, and mulberry trees; farm products like apples and wheat; cows calving and horses foaling. There is nothing comparable to the imagistic power of this passage in a poem like "Passage to India," in which Whitman maintains his characteristic enumerative style only by creating encyclopedic lists of cultural and geographical features, no doubt drawn from reading. By contrast, "This Compost" grounds its reflections in close attention to the objects that are close at hand and most familiar to the poet.[8] By attending closely to these homely objects (in every sense of "homely" — unattractive to conventional taste, the familiar that is said to breed contempt but that attracts the eye of the earth-loving poet), Whitman steps toward his more general pronouncements. As with the movement between the human and the earthly in the personifying tropes, the movement between specific and general develops here as an alternating gestalt, culminating in the final lines of the poem with a celebration of the capitalized Earth (the poet still resisting the more abstract Nature):

> Now I am terrified at the Earth, it is that calm and patient,
> It grows such sweet things out of such corruptions,
> It turns harmless and stainless on its axis, with such endless successions of diseas'd corpses,
> It distills such exquisite winds out of such infused fetor,
> It renews with such unwitting looks its prodigal, annual, sumptuous crops,
> It gives such divine materials to men, and accepts such leavings from them at last. (LG 1891–92, 287)

Faith in the earth's bounty — expressed in the last line with its questionable hint that do what we will, the earth will reward us — is based in this poem not upon the pioneer's sense of the world as an inexhaustible storehouse for human exploitation but upon respect for the power of the earth's processes to restore health and complete its mighty cycles. The theme of respect takes the form of sublime wonder in "This Compost." As a celebration of the landscape in health, the poem stands as an able experiment in the special version of personification that reappears in Leopold's "Thinking Like a Mountain" and Carson's Silent Spring, both of which also bear the marks of local experience.[9] The alternating consciousness of the poet (and later the scientific activists) embraces the earth with signs of kinship and even identity but retains enough distance to keep the idea of environment alive, as a realm of being distinct from human interests. "This Compost" shows how the discursive counterpart of using good judgment in protecting the environment may well be the act of keeping the personifying impulse in check — modeling an alternating form of consciousness that refuses to allow human imagination to fully possess the earth and reduce it to a mere reflection of self-serving desires.

Not all of Whitman's prewar poems are so free as "This Compost" from the globalist aspiration that informs "Passage to India." Moreover, the invocation of a specific local identity hardly represents a poetic inoculation against the globalizing motive and imperialist ideology. Ironically, the prewar poem that leans heaviest in the direction of manifest destiny and its poetic counterpart of sweeping abstraction bears the American Indian name of Whitman's childhood home on Long Island, "Paumanok." "Starting from Paumanok," which dates from 1860 when it appeared as "Proto-Leaf," set the tone for the third edition of *Leaves of Grass*. It was clearly conceived as a thematic overture intended to direct the reading of the whole book, the composition of which Whitman began in the late 1850s to understand as "the Great Construction of the New Bible" (qtd. in Bowers 45). In its depiction of "Spirituality," the "flame of materials," and its "mistress, the Soul" (Blue Book 1:9), "Proto-Leaf" hints toward, on the one hand, an alternating movement that closely integrates the material and the spiritual and, on the other hand, a version of spirituality more hierarchical and transcendental than any that had appeared in earlier editions of *Leaves*. In his integrating mood, the poet wonders, "Was somebody asking to see the Soul?" As an answer, he challenges the reader to look no farther than "your own shape and countenance — persons, substances, beasts, the trees, the running rivers, the rocks and sands," all of which, he says, "hold spiritual joys" (Blue Book 1:16). Anticipating the theme of "Enfans D'Adam 3" (later "I Sing the Body Electric"), a poem dating from 1855, "Proto-Leaf" declares (somewhat prosaically) that "the body includes and is the meaning, the main concern — and includes and is the Soul": "Whoever you are! how superb and how divine is your body, or any part of it" (Blue Book 1:17). These themes, mainly drawn from the earlier poems that "Proto-Leaf" introduces in their new arrangement for the third edition, rub up awkwardly against the newly intensified transcendental and dualistic conception of spirituality and soulfulness. In his transcendental mood, the poet celebrates "The Soul! / Forever and forever — Longer than soil is brown and solid — Longer than water ebbs and flows" (Blue Book 1:9), a view that suggests a hierarchy of value with the soul transcendent over the objects of material nature. No doubt Whitman remains firm in his commitment to be the poet of the body. "And sexual organs and acts!" he writes, "do you concentrate in me — For I am determined to tell you with courageous clear voice, to prove you illustrious" (Blue Book 1:10). And more than ever, anticipating the unveiling of his homoerotic *Calamus* poems in the new edition, he commits himself to "the song of companionship" and the "ideal of manly love": "I will therefore let flame from me the burning fires that were threatening to consume me," he declares: "I will write the evangel-poem of comrades and of love" (Blue Book 1:10–11). But as a counterbalance, he voices a new commitment to "inaugurate a Religion" and goes on to say that "the whole earth, and all the stars in the sky, are for Religion's sake" and that "the real and permanent grandeur of These States must be their Religion" (Blue Book 1:11–12).

In the space of three pages in "Proto-Leaf," Whitman uses the word *religion* seven times, more than the total number of times the word appears in the entire text of the 1855 *Leaves of Grass* (including the Preface). Ten instances appear in the final version of "Starting from Paumanok" compared to only six in the 1855 *Leaves*. Not only the quantity but also the character of the usage changes. Nowhere in the 1855 poems does Whitman use *religion* — a term usually associated with formal practices and institutions — to describe his own project as he does in 1860. In 1855 he more commonly mentions religion as something to be overcome or at best tolerated by the all-accepting personality, as in the following lines:

> We consider the bibles and religions divine . . . . I do not say they are
>   not divine,
> I say they have all grown out of you and may grow out of you still,
> It is not they who give the life . . . . it is you who give the life [. . .]
>
> (LG 1855, 60)

In 1860, though, by calling his book a bible and giving the name of religion to his program of self-realization, Whitman assumes the vestments of priesthood, a rather different persona from the one of 1855, who comes before the reader "hankering, gross, mystical, nude" (LG 1855, 25).

The intensification of the religious motive in 1860 may have opened the door to an enhanced enthusiasm for manifest destiny, the divine plan for the new "race" of Americans celebrated later in "Passage to India" and "Song of the Redwood-Tree." The fully developed theme is strongly anticipated in the closing passages of "Starting from Paumanok." It was already present in the 1860 "Proto-Leaf" and underwent very few changes in subsequent editions. In the final version, the most unsettling passage appears in Section 16:

> On my way a moment I pause,
> Here for you! and here for America!

Still the present I raise aloft, still the future of the States I harbinge
glad and sublime,
And for the past I pronounce what the air holds of the red aborigines.

The red aborigines,
Leaving natural breaths, sounds of rain and winds, calls as of birds
and animals in the woods, syllabled to us for names,
Okonee, Koosa, Ottawa, Monongahela, Sauk, Natchez,
Chattahoochee, Kaqueta, Oronoco,
Wabash, Miami, Saginaw, Chippewa, Oshkosh, Walla-Walla,
Leaving such to the States they melt, they depart, charging the water
and the land with names. (LG 1891–92, 27)

In these lines, which appeared late in the manuscript history of the poem
and may have originally been part of a failed effort to write an entire poem
devoted to American Indians (Folsom, *Native Representations* 93), the poet
depicts Native peoples much as he depicts the great trees in "Song of the
Redwood-Tree" — as "departing" from the American landscape (see
Bergland and chapter 2). They become as insubstantial as breath. But unlike
the ephemeral sounds of the wind and rain and the cries of animals in the
forest, Indian breath has formed words that have attached to places and
natural features such as rivers and mountains. The words retain a place in
the new culture after Native peoples depart. By leaving the sounds of their
breath upon the places they have occupied and held sacred, Indians "melt"
into the cultural memory and the land itself, "charging the water and the
land with names." The verb *charge* is part of the soul vocabulary Whitman
developed for *Leaves of Grass*. In the poem that would become "I Sing the
Body Electric" in 1867, the poet says of his friends and lovers (or metaphorically, his readers), "they will not let me off, nor I them, till I go with them
. . . and charge them with the charge of the Soul" (Blue Book 1:291). The
suggestion, then, is that unlike the departing redwoods, which depend upon
the poet to hear them and give them voice, the souls of Indians remain in
the places they have inhabited, living on in indigenous languages used as
place names. Whitman always wanted to expand the use of Indian names
— preferring "Mannahatta" to New York and "Paumanok" to Long Island,
for example — and in his poems to honor the souls of the departed Indians
with catalogs of the names reconnected to their "aboriginal" sources so that
future generations would remember their origins.

As for the living American Indians of his time, however, Whitman could
see no future. In "Starting from Paumanok" and elsewhere, he follows the
trend of Anglo-American literature in treating Native peoples as already

departed, as ghostly figures on the current scene. He adds a material element to this component of what Renee Bergland calls the "national uncanny," assuaging the collective guilt associated with the systematic removal and killing of the Indians by honoring the very breath patterns captured in their languages. In focusing on language, the naming power of the Native peoples, Whitman suggests a hierarchical chain of being. Though close to nature, and like natural objects such as trees and animals subject to transformation and removal in the face of the progressive march westward, the Indians have the human power to mark the historical record with their languages, unlike the redwoods and other beings of the forest who would "depart" silently were it not for the good graces of the poet. But in Section 17, Whitman hints at his view of Indians as an inferior people who must stand aside (or be removed by force) to make way for the "new race dominating previous ones and grander far, with new contests, / New politics, new literatures and religions, new inventions and arts" (LG 1891–92, 28).

Following again the logic that European Americans' superiority is revealed by their technological achievement, Whitman envisions the old West transformed by the progressive march of the new race with their mighty tools:

See, steamers steaming through my poems,
See, in my poems immigrants continually coming and landing,
See, in arriere, the wigwam, the trail, the hunter's hut, the flat-boat, the
   maize-leaf, the claim, the rude fence, and the backwoods village,
See, on the one side the Western Sea and on the other the Eastern Sea,
   how they advance and retreat upon my poems as upon their own
   shores,
See, pastures and forests in my poems — see, animals wild and tame
   — see, beyond the Kaw, countless herds of buffalo feeding on short
   curly grass,
See, in my poems, cities, solid, vast, inland, with paved streets, with
   iron and stone edifices, ceaseless vehicles, and commerce,
See, the many-cylinder'd steam printing-press — see, the electric telegraph stretching across the continent,
See, through Atlantica's depths pulses American Europe reaching,
   pulses of Europe duly return'd,
See, the strong and quick locomotive as it departs, panting, blowing
   the steam-whistle,
See, ploughmen ploughing farms — see, miners digging mines — see,
   the numberless factories,

See, mechanics busy at their benches with tools — see from among
　　them superior judges, philosophs, Presidents, emerge, drest in
　　working dresses,
See, lounging through the shops and fields of the States, me well-
　　belov'd, close-held by day and night,
Hear the loud echoes of my songs there — read the hints come at last.

(LG 1891–92, 28)

As thoroughly as any other in *Leaves of Grass*, this extraordinary passage shows how the poet's globalizing mentality arises from the imposition of local experiences and values upon far-ranging peoples and landscapes. The vision here gives us the great American West, the buffalo and wigwam and backwoods villages left behind, transformed into a sprawling nineteenth-century version of New York City with its powerful technologies of transportation and communication, its shops and factories, its working people elevated to high offices and occupations, and of course its beloved poet enjoying the echoes of his songs in every corner of the transformed world. In many ways, the passage embodies the modern mentality lamented in Wordsworth's "The World Is Too Much with Us." The world — the human-made world of human city-dwellers, that is — so dominates our minds that we can no longer see the natural world or the possibility of a different way of life.

Like "Passage to India," "Starting from Paumanok" contains hints of inner conflict beneath the brash progressive rhetoric — if not exactly guilt, then some other form of emotional turbulence dating from the composition of the poem in the late 1850s. The word that Whitman often used for inner conflict was *perturbation*. Among other biographers, Gay Wilson Allen has shown how by the 1860s the poet associated the word particularly with the turmoil he felt over homosexual desires that occasionally threatened to boil to the surface in ways he must have deemed inappropriate (*Solitary Singer* 339). Whitman often represented perturbation as an unquenchable heat or inner fire and resorted particularly to the image of flame with its phallic suggestiveness. The imagery appears fully realized in an 1881 poem, "Thou Orb Aloft Full-Dazzling," which employs a striking instance of the pathetic fallacy in an apostrophe to the sun: "As for thy throes, thy perturbations, sudden breaks and shafts of flame gigantic, / I understand them, I know those flames, those perturbations well" (LG 1891–92, 352). As early as 1855 the poet would identify flames with a passion that threatened to overcome him with intensity, as in the famous lines that would remain unchanged in every edition of *Leaves of Grass*, finally appearing in Section 28 of "Song of Myself" — "Flames and ether making a rush for my veins, / Treacherous tip of me reaching and crowding to help them" (LG 1891–92, 52).[10] The code emerges most strongly in 1860 as part of *Calamus*, the cluster of poems that not only focused modern readers' attention on Whitman's homoerotic themes but also allowed for a darkening of the poet's predominant optimism, an admission of doubts, guilt, and depression. In his discussion of *Calamus*, Allen picks up Whitman's own code, referring to the "smoldering fires" of the poems (222). At one point Whitman considered naming the poems "Flames of Confession." Roger Asselineau invokes the connection to Baudelaire. The *Calamus* poems, he says, "are 'Fleurs du Mal.' Whitman felt this so strongly that for a time he thought of a similar title . . . . He jotted down . . . 'Flames of Confession,' 'Drops of My Blood' . . . , 'Drops of Evil,' 'Flames of Evil,' 'Verses of Evil'" (*Evolution*, 2:119). In "Calamus 14," the poet tells of "the flames of me, consuming, burning for his love whom I love!" (Blue Book 1:360). This poem, like the later performance "Thou Orb Aloft Full-Dazzling," features a tortured syntax that seems itself to reflect the poet's "perturbations."

The same code appears to inform the 1860 version of "Starting from Paumanok," which as part of its overture function introduces the *Calamus* theme, complete with flame imagery and odd syntax — including the unattached demonstrative "These," which we have seen in the account of thingish incapacity in chapter 1, in this case a possible sign of the moral or social incapacity (the "ah . . . thing"):

> I will sing the song of companionship,
> I will show what alone must compact These,
> I believe These are to found their own ideal of manly love, indicating
>   it in me;
> I will therefore let flame from me the burning fires that were threaten-
>   ing to consume me,
> I will lift what has too long kept down those smouldering fires,
> I will give them complete abandonment,
> I will write the evangel-poem of comrades and of love,
> (For who but I should understand love, with all its sorrow and joy?
> And who but I should be the poet of comrades?) (Blue Book 1:10–11)

Continuing a few lines later in the confessional vein — which suggests a general trend in the nineteenth-century discourse on sexuality, as Michel Foucault has suggested, and which recalls the "dark patches" section of the 1856 poem "Crossing Brooklyn Ferry" (see Killingsworth, *Whitman's Poetry of the Body* 48–54) — Whitman admits his participation in "evil," though he quickly moves to put the very concept in question:

> Let others ignore what they may,
> I make the poem of evil also — I commemorate that part also,
> I am myself just as much evil as good — And I say there is in fact no evil,
> Or if there is, I say it is just as important to you, to the earth, or to me,
>   as anything else. (Blue Book 1:11)

If *Calamus* is an early version of the "coming out" story in the history of gay consciousness, we must acknowledge that however much Whitman longed to be the heroic poet of comradeship, he struggled mightily with his confession and felt at least ambivalent if not ashamed or guilty about his passion for young men. We have already seen him transform the spider metaphor to eliminate the predatory aspect and censor the homoerotic element. He would also revise an early manuscript version of *Calamus* (originally called "Live Oak, with Moss") so that the narrative (or "sonnet sequence") of a homosexual love affair would be pushed into the background of the group, making the cluster of poems primarily a celebration of comradeship as the foundation of democracy and following the trend of abstraction and distancing we have seen in the nature poems. (For more on *Calamus*, see chapter 5.)

Many scholars influenced by New Criticism and Freudian psychoanalysis have proposed that Whitman achieved an admirable sublimation, an artistic achievement that transcended the passions tormenting him, as he became increasingly aware of his own consuming and exclusively homosexual passion. "His art saved him, by purifying his passions," Asselineau argues, for example (*Evolution* 2:119). Whitman's own language seems to support such a view, at least partially. He says he will turn the flames that threaten to consume him outward, releasing them to the world as poetry. In seeming defiance of the sublimation thesis, however, he does not deny the more direct outlet of love and sexual experience. He will realize his love for what it is, and he will encourage others to do so, such as the generic "young man" he addresses in "Proto-Leaf." If you are "so earnest — so given up to literature, science, art, amours," he says, or "burnt up for Religion's sake," do not be "pensive and silent" but rather "Proceed, comrade": "It is a painful thing to love a man or woman to excess — yet it satisfies — it is great" (Blue Book 1:12). Still, he refuses to rest easy with unalloyed material satisfaction or even emotional satisfaction: "there is something else very great," he tells the young man, "it makes the whole coincide, / It, magnificent, beyond materials, with continuous hands, sweeps and provides for all" (Blue Book 1:12–13). If passion is a flame that burns within, spirituality is the flame of the world. It consumes materials as passion consumes people. The psychological and metaphysical trend of the poem, confused and incompletely articulated though it is, leans toward an interpretation of spiritual passion as a sublimation in which passion may switch from one object to another; it may start as erotic stimulation and end up as religion. Or it may go in the other direction; it may seem to be religious fervor and end up being expressed as love for another person. Passion has many outlets and may shift from one stream to another in the process of flaming out.

But Whitman's hierarchy sets the realization of spirituality — the "something else" that "makes the whole coincide" — above the mere living of material life. There is a good possibility that by the 1860s Whitman had come to see his candid celebration of the body in direct language as a failure. His attempt to construct the new American bible could thus represent an effort to give his radical poetry of the body a more conventional garb — the language of spirituality. The result is that the 1860 poems seem to drift from one mode to the other, a sign of Whitman's own ambivalence.

The hierarchy emerging in the 1860s has disturbing ecological implications. Spirituality, he says, is the "flame of materials" (Blue Book 1:9). Set free in nature, spirit consumes the earth. It refines and purifies materials. In this sense, Whitman is right to say that "evil" is just as important "to the earth" as to anything else. The suggestion is that strong passions driven forth into the world free the individual but consume the earth. The earth becomes a burned sacrifice. The soul, rather than being the silk-spinning organ of a spider reaching out for connections, takes on the qualities of the internal combustion engine, transforming the world with the flames of its passion. The earth provides material resources for the soul's consumption. The hungry soul consumes even the body's passions and produces spiritual products, such as poems:

> I will make the poem of materials, for I think they are to be the most
> spiritual poems,
> And I will make poems out of my body and of mortality,
> For I think I shall then supply myself with the poems of my Soul and
> of immortality. (Blue Book 1:9–10)

The language of consumption dominates the poet's thinking about the earth in such passages, with only his obvious fear of being "consumed" himself by passion as a counterweight to the rationalization of commodification and domination, the rights to which he claims through transcendent spirituality and its political cousin, manifest destiny.

Along with the new emphasis on religion and manifest destiny in "Starting from Paumanok" comes a new, somewhat more abstract treatment of nature, a version of the concept that ultimately plays a limited role in *Leaves of Grass*, yielding finally to a yet more distanced and abstract version, such as we have seen in "Passage to India." While the earth with its power to attract, repel, and reflect takes a leading role in all stages of the poet's career, Nature as an abstraction comes rather late to *Leaves of Grass*. Indeed, according to the reading of his friend, the celebrated nature writer John Burroughs, Nature as such has little, if any, place in *Leaves of Grass*. Writing in his 1867 *Notes on Walt Whitman as Poet and Person*, Burroughs says, "no modern book of poems says so little about Nature, or contains so few compliments to her" (41). One of the finest observers of the natural world in the history of American letters and a pioneering ecocritic who figures prominently among the nineteenth-century figures in David Mazel's collection *A Century of Early Ecocriticism*, Burroughs sees Whitman as something entirely different from the standard nature poet: He "is not merely an observer of Nature, but is immersed in her." In the work of earlier poets, "Nature [is] talked of and discussed," but Whitman's poems "approximate to a direct utterance of Nature herself." Burroughs is particularly adamant about Whitman's engagement with things and avoidance of abstraction: "He no sooner starts a principle than he surrounds it and clothes it with a living texture of things and doings, redeeming it from all appearance of an abstraction . . . so that the effect upon the mind is not the effect of gems or crystals, or their analogues in poetry, but of living organisms." "The poet, like Nature," he concludes, "seems best pleased when his meaning is well folded up, put away, and surrounded by a curious array of diverting attributes and objects. . . . But the word or phrase is always an electric one. He never stops to elaborate, never explains" (Burroughs, *Notes* 41, 43–44; see also Warren, "Whitman Land").

Burroughs's insights wear well with the early poems, but even by the time his book was published just after the war, when his friendship with Whitman was still fresh and growing, abstraction had come to play a larger part in *Leaves of Grass*. In the 1855 *Leaves*, nature appears to be defined as the special character of a person or thing, that which makes it most itself, or as a synonym for the earth (*natura naturata*). Nature defined as a godlike force moving within all creation, the mystical Other (*natura naturans*), which Burroughs appears to take as the normative definition (drawing probably upon Wordsworth and Emerson), does not begin to appear until 1860 both in new poems and in revisions of old ones (a little earlier than Martin Doudna has suggested in his Whitman encyclopedia entry, which sets the line of demarcation at the Civil War). The poem that had been "Bunch Poem" in 1856 (referring to Whitman's strange metaphor for semen as "this bunch plucked at random from myself" [Blue Book 1:307]), for example, got a splendid new Emersonian first line in 1860 — "Spontaneous me, Nature" (Blue Book 1:304) — and would be titled "Spontaneous Me" from 1867 on (CRE 102n, 103). The new line adds a thin layer of metaphysical abstraction over what is one of Whitman's most forthright and joyous celebrations of the human body's earthiness, a rhapsodic outpouring of metaphors with a strongly alternating gestalt reminiscent of "Song of Myself" and "This Compost." The experience of identity with the earth begins with a contemplation of the body, particularly the penis, metaphorically conceived as the "poem" that "all men carry" in a scene of autoerotic fantasy:

> Beautiful dripping fragments — the negligent list of one after another,
>   as I happen to call them to me, or think of them,
> The real poems, (what we call poems being merely pictures,)
> The poems of the privacy of night, and of men like me,
> This poem, drooping shy and unseen, that I always carry, and that all
>   men carry,
> (Know, once for all, avowed on purpose, wherever are men like me,
>   are our lusty, lurking, masculine poems,)
> Love-thoughts, love-juice, love-odor, love-yielding, love-climbers, and
>   the climbing sap,
> Arms and hands of love — lips of love — phallic thumb of love —
>   breasts of love — bellies pressed and glued together with love,
> Earth of chaste love — life that is only life after love,
> The body of my love — the body of the woman I love — the body of
>   the man — the body of the earth,
> Soft forenoon airs that blow from the south-west,
> The hairy wild-bee that murmurs and hankers up and down — that
>   gripes the full-grown lady-flower, curves upon her with amorous
>   firm legs, takes his will of her, and holds himself tremulous and
>   tight upon her till he is satisfied. (Blue Book 1:305)

From the image of the bee upon the flower, a trope that conflates feeding and sex — the suggestiveness of which has become a convention in American ecopoetics, among writers as different as Emily Dickinson and Zora Neale Hurston — the catalog of images continues through a number of earthy scenes, arriving finally back where it began, at the poet's contemplation of his own genitals ("The sensitive, orbic, underlapped brothers, that only privileged feelers may be intimate where they are") (Blue Book 1:306). Swearing the "oath of procreation," the poet links himself to Nature, which can be conceived as the Other only in the sense of the Other within, the Spontaneous Me, the identity of the self with something like instinct, the "greed that eats me day and night with hungry gnaw," the erotic impulse to connect and reproduce (Blue Book 1:307). The attitude of the loafer — the "careless" and "random" character — prevails in this poem despite the "greediness" of the passion that drives him. The particularity of the imagery makes the abstraction appealing and credible, if largely superfluous.

The overture of "Proto-Leaf" captures this version of Nature in some of Whitman's most frequently quoted lines, a passage revised and moved to "Song of Myself" in later editions:

> Creeds and schools in abeyance,
> Retiring back a while, sufficed at what they are, but never forgotten,
> With accumulations, now coming forward in front,
> Arrived again, I harbor, for good or bad — I permit to speak,
> Nature, without check, with original energy. (Blue Book 1:8)

What Whitman calls Nature in this passage and in the 1860 version of "Spontaneous Me" — the primeval part of him that speaks unchecked and connects him to the world — bears a strong resemblance to what he calls the soul in poems dating from 1855 and 1856. It is the means by which he realizes the sources of his self, both in his body and in external nature. The lines immediately preceding the passage in its final position in "Song of Myself" suggest the deep connection to the earth stretching many generations, creating a settled feeling of being at home with the earth: "My tongue, every atom of my blood, form'd from this soil, this air, / Born here of parents born here from parents the same, and their parents the same" (CRE 29). The autoerotic experience of the body in the "hairy wild-bee" passage of "Spontaneous Me" — the realization of the body's identity with the things, processes, and creatures of the earth — leads the poet to the same kind of peace and understanding, the "wholesome relief, repose, content" (Blue Book 1:307) portrayed in Section 5 of "Song of Myself" in the passage that begins with his "inviting the soul," passes through an experience with the intensity of sexual orgasm, and ends with his vision of webbed unity with all living things and the knowledge that a "kelson of the creation is love" (see chapter 1).

Clearly the 1860 version of Nature retains from 1855 and 1856 the concern with integration and oneness with the earth. The alienation that must be overcome by a scientifically recharged view of the earth in "This

Compost" and that requires the upgrading of the poetic function in "Passage to India" is granted in "Spontaneous Me" to the creative capacity in all people, signified by the universality of sexual desire, the penis as a poem that all men carry. Here we have the foundation for a democratic conception of ecopoetics and human creativity that recalls the words of the 1855 Preface:

> The land and sea, the animals fishes and birds, the sky of heaven and the orbs, the forests mountains and rivers, are not small themes ... but folks expect of the poet to indicate more than the beauty and dignity which always attach to dumb real objects .... they expect him to indicate the path between reality and their souls. Men and women perceive the beauty well enough ... probably as well as he. The passionate tenacity of hunters, woodmen, early risers, cultivators of gardens and orchards and fields, the love of healthy women for the manly form, sea-faring persons, drivers of horses, the passion for light and the open air, all is an old varied sign of the unfailing perception of beauty and of a residence of the poetic in outdoor people. They can never be assisted by poets to perceive ... some may but they never can. The poetic quality is not marshalled in rhyme or uniformity or abstract addresses to things nor in melancholy complaints or good precepts, but is the life of these and much else and is in the soul[....] [P]erfect poems show the free growth of metrical laws and bud from them as unerringly and loosely as lilacs or roses on a bush, and take shapes as compact as the shapes of chestnuts and oranges and melons and pears, and shed the perfume impalpable to form. The fluency and ornaments of the finest poems or music or orations or recitations are not independent but dependent. All beauty comes from beautiful blood and a beautiful brain. If the greatnesses are in conjunction in a man or woman it is enough .... the fact will prevail through the universe .... but the gaggery and gilt of a million years will not prevail. Who troubles himself about his ornaments or fluency is lost.
>
> (LG 1855, v)

The implication is that men and women who live close to the earth already enjoy a complete integration, a soulful life.[11] The function of the poet is to "show," not to create anew (the human genitalia being the "real" poem, "what we call poems being merely pictures," as he says in "Spontaneous Me"). The poet cannot exceed people's capacity for creativity or create a poem beautiful enough to compete with nature but must be content with reminding people of their close connections among themselves and with the earth, or reinforcing natural trends. Again, the metaphor of the poem as a web comes to mind, a light overlay of reality resonating with implied meaning and providing a higher, lighter perspective from which to view the earth.

From these observations, Whitman finishes this extraordinary passage with advice to the would-be poet:

> This is what you shall do: Love the earth and sun and the animals, despise riches, give alms to every one that asks, stand up for the stupid and crazy, devote your income and labor to others, hate tyrants, argue not concerning God, have patience and indulgence toward the people, take off your hat to nothing known or unknown or to any man or number of men, go freely with powerful uneducated persons and with the young and with the mothers of families, read these leaves in the open air every season of every year of your life, re examine all you have been told at school or church or in any book, dismiss whatever insults your own soul, and your very flesh shall be a great poem and have the richest fluency not only in its words but in the silent lines of its lips and face and between the lashes of your eyes and in every motion and joint of your body. . . . . The poet shall not spend his time in unneeded work. He shall know that the ground is always ready ploughed and manured . . . . others may not know it but he shall. He shall go directly to the creation. His trust shall master the trust of everything he touches . . . . and shall master all attachment.
>
> The known universe has one complete lover and that is the greatest poet. (LG 1855, v–vi)

The sentences that frame this passage — beginning with the claim that the poet shows the way between the "dumb" objects of nature and the soul, giving voice to an otherwise silent nature, and closing with the view of the "greatest poet" as the "one complete lover" of the "known universe" — suggest that the trend to aggrandize the poet's function was already stewing in 1855, but still we are a long way from the conception of the poet in "Passage to India" as the "true Son of God." In the 1855 passage, the poet needs merely to touch and to look to realize his vocation, to trust his body and the information that comes to him in strong resonances from the natural world. But as early as 1856, in the image of the hairy wild-bee, the soul grows hungry, the creative function becomes aligned with consumption — the bee gathering food becomes the metaphor for sex — the desire for connection with others and with the earth appears as "The greed that eats me day and night with hungry gnaw," and only through ejaculation ("I saturate what shall produce boys to fill my place when I am through"), releasing the stuff of desire upon the world, can the poet enjoy the "wholesome relief, repose, content" that his soul hungers for (Blue Book 1:307).

The struggle we see in these passages from the first three editions of *Leaves of Grass* — Whitman's struggle with how to find the language to reconcile the gnawing greed of humanity with the equally powerful drive to live at peace with the earth — provides a faithful image of the modern environmental dilemma. One key issue, which reaches deep in language and culture, concerns the conflict between the impulse to consume and the impulse to conserve. Tropes of identity may be pressed into service of both. In the old fable, the grasshopper is a joyous child of the earth that eats and dances its way into the winter of its own oblivion; its counterpart, the ant, is a stern-minded child of the earth whose way is to preserve and persevere. The roots of the conflict may well reach to the difference between the older hunter-gatherer lifestyle and the more recent agricultural lifestyle devoted to careful planning and organizing and to the cultivation and preservation of food, producing through technology the kinds of surpluses, specialized crafts, and community hierarchies associated with modernity.[12] The success of either lifestyle depends upon local environmental conditions, which may in turn point toward the limits of human imagination and creative potential.

CHAPTER FOUR

The Island Poet and the Sacred Shore

"This Compost" spans the rural landscape of pasture, field, and forest but returns for its climactic realization of nature's power to an image of the poet surrendering to the ocean's waves, the "transparent green-wash of the sea which is so amorous after me," the water rising "to lick my naked body all over with its tongues" (LG 1891–92, 286). In the "voluptuous earth" passage of the 1855 "Song of Myself" (Section 22), the shoreline appears as the point of most complete contact with the earth, the intensity of which the poet summons with the language of sexual orgasm: "You sea! I resign myself to you [. . .] Dash me with amorous wet" (LG 1855, 27). In "Spontaneous Me," the poet's erotic imagination drifts from the hillside whitened with the spring blossoms of mountain ash — an earthy analog for his own body littered with his "seed," the semen, "this bunch plucked at random from myself" — to the familiar ground of the ocean shore, with "The souse upon me of my lover the sea, as I lie willing and naked" (Blue Book 1:307). The scene, or some variation of it, appears in all of Whitman's major poems. "Out of the Cradle Endlessly Rocking" (1859, 1860) offers perhaps the most complete version, the narrative of the child-poet's first deep experience of the pains and joys of life, the realization of the power of love and death, represented in his encounter with the mockingbird mourning the loss of its mate at the edge of the sea and the ocean itself figured as the ancient mother lisping the "low and delicious" word "death." But we also have "The Sleepers" (1855), with its vignette of the "beautiful gigantic swimmer" dragged to his death on dangerous currents in sight of shore; "Crossing Brooklyn Ferry" (1856), with its images of the great city at the water's edge; "As I Ebb'd with the Ocean of Life" (1860), in which low water is associated with depressed spirits; and "When Lilacs Last in the Dooryard Bloom'd" (1865–66), in which the poet retreats to the swamp to mourn the death of the beloved president.

This chapter offers a reading of four shoreline poems considered as two overlapping pairs, each framing a life crisis. The first pair to be considered as the clearest models of what I call Whitman's island poetics — "Out of the Cradle Endlessly Rocking" and "When Lilacs Last in the Dooryard Bloom'd," the poet's greatest contributions to the genre of the elegiac lyric in English — were published in 1859–60 and 1865–66, respectively, one just before, the other just after the national crisis of the Civil War. The second pair, "Crossing Brooklyn Ferry" and "As I Ebb'd with the Ocean of Life," frame what was for Whitman an intense period of personal crisis in the late 1850s, during which he came to doubt his poetic vocation and the confident optimism and sympathy that informed the first two editions of *Leaves of Grass*. While it has become commonplace in Whitman criticism to treat the two 1860 poems "Out of the Cradle" and "As I Ebb'd" as a unit, a pair of darker poems indicating the new mood of the poet at the end of his personal crisis and on the eve of war, I find it illuminating to pair "As I Ebb'd" with "Crossing Brooklyn Ferry" because of their tidal tropes, the poem of the soul's ebb tide set against the earlier celebration of life's abundance as a "Flood tide below me." Geographical metaphors prevail in the other pair as well. "Out of the Cradle" establishes the shoreline as the site of the poet's original vocation, to which he returns in later life as a pilgrim in need of renewal after personal and vocational troubles, and "Lilacs" depends upon a return to and a poetic identification with the shoreline as a place especially suited for mourning and renewal.

At the seaside, marsh, swamp, or riverbank — the meeting place of land and water — the events narrated in these poems and others like them in *Leaves of Grass* occur with all the power of the primal scene as Freud envisioned it but stripped of the Victorian trappings of dimly remembered parlors, bedrooms, and nurseries. Traditional psychoanalytical criticism suggests that "nature" in these scenes is merely a displaced version of the inner rooms of the family home (which may in turn represent the organization of the poet's troubled mind). In *My Soul and I: The Inner Life of Walt Whitman*, for example, David Cavitch writes that in "Out of the Cradle" and "As I Ebb'd," Whitman "confronts an obsessive early memory of abasement and neglect" (139): "His recollection in old age includes innumerable but possibly misleading suggestions of a primal scene of sexual intercourse that a child, waking at night, might misinterpret as distress or even interrupt with mortifying consequences" (140; see also Miller). Instead of nature being substituted for history, as in the model posed by the ideological critic, nature is for the psychoanalytical critic an empty shell filled with the fantasy life of the poet. His desire for a forbidden form of love — incestuous or homosexual, for example — is displaced upon the body of the earth: the mockingbird singing for a dead mate (the denied Other) or the "savage" mother the sea "laving me softly all over."

Ecological criticism would be ill-advised to deny the validity of such interpretations, but neither can it fully accept the treatment of nature as a

100

🦥

*The
Island Poet
and the
Sacred
Shore*

"mere" anything. The place of writing must be defined far more broadly than the virtual reality of memory, imagination, and desire. It must take account of the material contexts of both historical and physical reality, including the bioregion — the land defined not so much by social and political boundaries, the imposition of human will upon the landscape, but by long-standing cultural ties and the natural markers of waterways and other elements of physical geography — to which the author is born or is attached by choice or happenstance. The concept of bioregionalism in ecocriticism, environmental philosophy, and ecoactivism suggests that a person is bound to the land of birth or settlement by strong forces of identity, often unconscious or underrated, "a connection — even a necessary unity — between the natural world and the human mind," a "spiritual" connection that is "archaic, primitive, and so obvious that it hasn't received much attention since the rise of Christian dominion and fossil-fuel industrialism" (Dodge 10). As Jim Dodge suggests, in acknowledging the way that place shapes character and consciousness through a sense of kinship and indwelling, bioregional thinking embraces renewal and resistance. It renews links to places of inhabitation (or more often these days, reinhabitation), taking on an ecopoetical purpose in the search for beauty and meaning in local conditions. Robert L. Thayer Jr. argues that "without a fundamental realization of the question 'Where are we?' human meaning is not stable, and the logic of our own being collapses" (1). Renewal through the questioning of our place on the earth involves resistance to the modern condition of homelessness. "Just past the turn of the millennium," writes Thayer, "we have all become, in certain fundamental ways, homeless," a state resulting from factors all too familiar to ecocritics: "the Cartesian assumption of separation of mind from body; the evolution from ecosystem-based to globally based economies; the drug trip of fossil fuel; the substitution of mechanism for organism; the dissolution of space and time by electronic communication; and the erasure of uniquely placed culture by all of the above" (1–2). In redirecting critical attention to the importance of place in literature and resisting the modernist division between a "merely regional" literature and a literature with "universal" appeal, ecopoetics participates in bioregional theory and practice.

In dealing with nineteenth-century writers like Whitman, we can see that the transportation and communication technologies were having their globalizing effects well before the age of oil and the advent of computers. Just as his assertion of artisanal republican values in political life represents something of a reversion to outmoded systems, as scholars such as Wynn Thomas and Bryan Garman have shown, Whitman's bioregional intensity oddly anticipates and resists the globalizing motives of his culture, motives that would from time to time influence his own writing. He found new value in his attachment to the New York islands after a journey beyond his own region in the late 1840s, when he sought career advancement through geo- 101

The
Island Poet
and the
Sacred
Shore graphic mobility by briefly taking a job as a journalist in New Orleans. Later he would feel the recurrent need for renewal and return to his island home after forays in the big city of Manhattan and the power center of Washington, D.C. His poems of the late 1850s and early 1860s arise from his need for relief from the pressures of social and geographical mobility, of city life and mass communication, of homelessness in the bioregionalist sense. He had by that time entered upon a career as a high-profile national poet with claims of universality. His attitude toward the forces of modernity, which he would do his best to celebrate in poems like "Passage to India" and "Song of the Redwood-Tree," was deeply conflicted in the late 1850s when he saw the nation headed for war and his own work threatened by ridicule and failure. At this point, he turned back to the land of his origins and again discovered his inspiration. In Whitman's poems of the shoreline, we have a bioregion- alist success story. On the theme of renewal, there can be no doubt; the theme of resistance, largely implicit in these poems, would rise to the surface in *Calamus* and *Specimen Days* (discussed in chapters 5 and 6, respectively).

Such an approach to the seaside poems takes seriously the idea that, for Whitman, the shoreline, and particularly the shoreline of his native Long Island, amounts to a sacred place, a scene to which he ritualistically returns to revive his sense of beauty and meaning, a site to which his identity as poet and person is anchored. Though Justin Kaplan rightly remembers Whitman as America's "first urban poet" (107), Jerome Loving makes an equally strong case that Whitman is "essentially an island poet" (*Walt Whitman* 26).[1] Within the historical and geographical contexts, both appel- lations make sense. Whitman grew up on Long Island and later associated himself with Manhattan, which, though highly urbanized even in the mid- nineteenth century, also demands to be remembered as one of many sea islands on the Atlantic Coast. The realization often overtook Whitman (as he suggests in "When Lilacs Last in the Dooryard Bloom'd") when he caught the scent of the sea breeze in the city, anticipating the sensation of John Crowley's protagonist in the wonderfully impressionistic novel *Little, Big*: "He could smell tide, and shore and sea detritus, sour and salt and bitter- sweet. And realized that the great City was after all a sea island, and a small one at that." "A sea island," he muses. "And you could forget so basic a fact for years at a time if you lived there. But there it was, amazing but true" (Crowley 12).

In an often-quoted passage from his late prose work *Specimen Days*, Whitman identifies

three leading sources and formative stamps to my own character, now solidified for good or bad, and its subsequent literary and other outgrowth — the maternal nativity-stock brought hither from faraway Netherlands, for one, (doubtless the best) — the subterranean tenacity and central bony structure (obstinacy, willfulness) which I get from my paternal English elements, for another — the combination of my Long Island birth-spot, sea-shores, childhood's scenes, absorptions, with teeming Brooklyn and New York — with, I suppose, my experiences afterward in the secession outbreak, for the third. (SD 705–706)

Of the three influences Whitman enumerates here — family, environment, and war — the biographers have made much of family and war and somewhat less of environment. But in fact geography plays a role in all three of the elements, each of which suggests a particular set of personal conflicts linked to the coordinates of land and sea. First, the inherited qualities of the mother are set at odds with those of the father, and each is associated with a place of origin, the Netherlands and England (the one country in need of constant redemption from the threatening sea, the other an island nation). Second, the open land and seashore of Long Island are contrasted with the densely populated human cities, "teeming Brooklyn and New York," and the isolation of the child in nature set against the immersion of the adult in society. Third, the war is described as a "secession outbreak," the South pulling away from the North.

In this drama of selfhood in situ, the island becomes a metaphorical crucible for identity, mixing the paternal and maternal, the introspective (or introverted) and the social (or extroverted), childhood and adulthood, the empty wilderness and the teeming city. "I roam'd, as boy and man, and have lived in nearly all parts" of Long Island, says the poet, "from Brooklyn to Montauk point" (SD 695). The island becomes a metaphor for the full range of individuality. Its special character comes through its isolation from the continent and its emergence out of the sea, but the processes that form it give insights into the great continental masses and the flow of the mighty oceans. In this sense, the island is at once a unique individual and a microcosm. Its relationship to the sea hints at the alternating cosmic processes of stability and flow, particle and wave, space and time, permanence and change.[2] The sea shapes the special character of the island but also threatens to dissolve it into the primordial element.

The history of the island metaphor is long and deep. In English poetics, it takes on a special meaning, for English is the language of an island people. The seventeenth-century master of the metaphysical conceit, John Donne, is rightly remembered for claiming this native space as a metaphor for individuality, albeit negatively. In his Meditation XVII, in one of the most frequently quoted passages from English literature, Donne writes:

103
The
Island Poet
and the
Sacred
Shore

> No man is an *Iland*, intire of it selfe; every man is a peece of the *Continent*, a part of the *maine*; if a *Clod* bee washed away by the *Sea*, *Europe* is the lesse, as well as if a *Promontorie* were, as well as if a *Mannor* of thy *friends* or of *thine owne* were; any mans *death* diminishes *me*, because I am involved in *Mankinde*; And therefore never send to know for whom the *bell* tolls; It tolls for *thee*. (339)

The key theme of the passage is how, upon reflection, the appearance of individuality, isolation, or alienation gives way to connectedness. Seemingly separate, every island is grounded in the bedrock of the continental mass. England has an essential connection to Europe, and the life, even the death, of every human being affects every other.

Bringing their language to the New World, descendants of Donne's island people would find that what seemed a solid continent by comparison to their homeland could in fact also be understood in terms of insularity (if nothing else, because of its isolation from the Old World) and that the island metaphor resonated with the Native American mythos. In his Pulitzer Prize–winning 1974 collection *Turtle Island*, the ecologically awakened poet Gary Snyder would explain his title in a snippet of prose (remarkably Whitmanian in style if not in its political thrust) at the beginning of the book:

> Turtle Island — the old/new name for the continent, based on many creation myths of the people who have been living here for millennia, and reapplied by some of them to "North America" in recent years. Also, an idea found world-wide, of the earth, or cosmos even, sustained by a great turtle or serpent-of-eternity.
>
> A name: that we may see ourselves more accurately on this continent of watersheds and life-communities — plant zones, physiographic provinces, culture areas; following natural boundaries. The "U.S.A." and its states and counties are arbitrary and inaccurate impositions on what is really here.
>
> The poems speak of place, and the energy-pathways that sustain life. Each living being is a swirl in the flow, a formal turbulence, a "song." The land, the planet itself, is also a living being — at another pace. Anglos,

Black people, Chicanos, and others beached up on these shores all share such views at the deepest levels of their old cultural traditions — African, Asian, or European. Hark again to those roots, to see our ancient solidarity, and then to the work of being together on Turtle Island. (n.p.)

104

🦌

*The
Island Poet
and the
Sacred
Shore*

As with Donne, we see in Snyder a desire both to assert and to overcome insularity. The naming, or renaming, of North America as Turtle Island is the means of at once setting it apart (as distinct from Europe and a tradition of naming that suggests colonization, empire, and exploitation of land and Native peoples) and reconnecting it to the subsurface strata of common myth and mother earth. Snyder's commitment to what he calls a "reinhabitory move," which involves reconnecting with or returning to the sacred, the original, the crusted over, despoiled, or forgotten root of being — a personal and political commitment for him but also an ecopoetic commitment that resonates with Whitman's treatment of the seashore as the place of origins and returns — finds reinforcement with the concern over names in Gerald Hausman's *Turtle Island Alphabet*:[3]

> Perhaps the most regrettable corruption is the name used for this country, America. Originally, this earth, the mother of Native American legend, The People called Turtle Island. And it was thought that the ancient and sacred creature carried the earth upon her back. Turtle was a deity, an ancestor creature, a symbol of long life.
>
> However, Turtle Island was taken from those who named her. And a thing was done that Native Americans have never fully understood: The sacred land was used, sold, bartered, bought and paid for with blood and money. In the end, The People had no part in it, and hardly any place in it. And Mother Earth, Turtle Island, was owned by people who did not seem to know who she was. (xviii)

As Snyder puts it, "speak of the United States and you are talking two centuries of basically English-speaking affairs; speak of 'America' and you invoke five centuries of Euro-American schemes in the Western Hemisphere; speak of 'Turtle Island' and a vast past, an open future, and all the life communities of plants, humans, and critters come into focus" (*Place in Space* 248).

Though Snyder's adoption of Turtle Island looks respectfully backward to the old traditions (or downward to the root of being), he creates a double appeal typical of the ecological imagination, embracing within a single worldview the discourses of tribal mythology and modern science.[4] The appeal to scientific ecology in Snyder's diction — "watersheds and life-communities — plant zones, physiographic provinces" — hints at another connection. In *The Song of the Dodo*, the science journalist David Quammen tells the story of how island tropology came to prominence in the field of biogeography. The story begins in Whitman's time with the work of Charles Darwin and Alfred Russel Wallace, cofounders of the theory of evolution, both of whom had their chief insights in the study of island species. The seminal text, according to Quammen, was Wallace's "On the Natural History of the Aru Islands," published in 1857 in the *Annals and Magazine of Natural History*. Wallace found "his own version, in Aru, of what Darwin saw belatedly in the Galápagos: synecdoche ... a set of small facts that hinted toward big truths" (Quammen 88). Islands offer the observer "a simplified ecosystem, almost a caricature of nature's full complexity" (19). Synecdoche and caricature allow bold patterns to stand forth clearly. The patterns that island biogeographers have observed since Wallace and Darwin "give clarity to evolution"; on islands there are "fewer species and therefore fewer relationships among species, as well as more cases of species extinction" (19). The fact of extinction is crucial, as we have come to realize in the century and a half since Darwin: "evolution is best understood with reference to extinction, and vice versa. In particular, the evolution of strange species on islands is a process that, once illuminated, casts light onto its dark double ... : the extinction of species in a world that has been hacked into pieces" (117). In the early twenty-first century, "we're headed toward understanding the whole planet as a world of islands, and evolution itself as a consequence of insularity" (130). In this sense, "island biogeography is no longer an offshore enterprise. It has come to the mainlands. It's everywhere. The problem of habitat fragmentation, and of the animal and plant populations left marooned within the various fragments under circumstances that are untenable for the long term, has been showing up all over the land surface of the planet."[5] In this world of islands, which "exists wherever Homo sapiens has colonized and partitioned a landscape, . . . critical thresholds are being reached and passed" (549). The story of island biogeography suggests that the question of origins that dominated all the talk about evolution in the era of Wallace, Darwin, and Whitman always contained questions about survival that predominate in our times.

Imagine, then, an island poetics. Synecdoche becomes a key trope. It is the trope of representation, the part standing for the whole. It inhabits or possesses a place, a site, a segment that, while distinctive or even unique, exposes a pattern that reappears in other places, sites, segments. While not reducible to one another, they are linked by shared attributes represented as common ground. When Gary Snyder discovers similar patterns in the

105

The
Island Poet
and the
Sacred
Shore

cultural traditions of the various ethnic groups washed up on the shore of North America, he is practicing island poetics.

What is synecdochic at the microlevel of the word or phrase may be mythic at the macrolevel of narrative. Like metaphor, metonymy, and synecdoche, which work at the level of the phrase or sentence, myth is a linguistic means of identity formation. Metaphor forces an identification between two seemingly unlike objects: the poet is a spider; the man (or no man) is an island. Myth offers a story that stands for seemingly disparate experiences. The boy watching the mockingbird sing on the beach at night stands for the poet's (or any adolescent's) coming into awareness, finding the voice, hearing the vocation. The extinction of the dodo stands for the possible extinction of every creature, including human beings.

In addition to elements of form (metaphor, synecdoche, myth), island poetics comprises issues of theme or content. It has to do with evolution and extinction, origins and survival. In this sense, it is intimately connected to the concept of sacred places, each of which is a fragment of the earth, an island as it were, isolated from a predominantly secular or desecrated mass (the mainland or "mainstream") because of its history (whether mythic or mundane), set aside as a place for pilgrimage, retreat, ceremony, prayer, sacrifice, or any act of reverence. The sacred place is bound up with stories of heroic acts, miracles, or divine revelations. It is full of power and possibility.[6]

The seashore of the poet's Long Island homeland becomes in *Leaves of Grass*, and especially in the cluster of poems that Whitman eventually named *Sea-Drift*, the equivalent of a sacred place. The family connection — which gives force to psychoanalytical readings of the poems and which Whitman himself celebrates in *Specimen Days* — provides the communal foundation for the shoreline's special status. It is a site of origins — the literal birthplace of the poet's body, the place of his family's settlement, and the scene of his passage into manhood, including sexual initiation: scenes with strong sexual overtones are associated with the landscape of the "headland" in key moments of at least two major poems — "The Sleepers" and "Song of Myself," Section 28 (see Bloom; see also Killingsworth, *Whitman's Poetry of the Body*). The island or seashore is most certainly the site of the soul's first onset and deepest revelations — and it is a site of survival, to which the poet returns again and again to reconnect with the earth and regenerate his energy.

The birth of the poet, in the sense of initiation into the mysteries of his vocation, finds its fullest and most successful treatment in "Out of the Cradle Endlessly Rocking," published first as "A Child's Reminiscence" in the 1859 *Saturday Press* and then as "A Word Out of the Sea" in the 1860 *Leaves*.[7] Of all the poems that would be grouped together in the 1881 edition and thereafter under the title *Sea-Drift*—a section dominated by compositions from the crisis years (personal and national) just before and after the Civil War — "Out of the Cradle" has rightly received the greatest critical attention. The style of the overflowing sentences of the poem, its structural mimicry of the operatic form, the many sources both poetic and scientific that engaged the poet, the powerful treatment of the themes of adolescent realization of individuality in terms of sex and death (or childhood awareness of sexuality displaced onto adolescence), the awakening of the poet's sense of the tragic, the connection of nature and the body, the confrontation of the ego and the unconscious mind, the transcendence of loss and death, the sublimation of sexual emotion in artistic production, the problem of representing natural objects and sense impressions in poetic language, and many more topics have occupied the best of Whitman's readers. The critical view that predominates sees "Out of the Cradle" as a spiritual autobiography in the Romantic tradition, the older poet's reflection on the time when he was first awakened to the need for transcending individual joy and pain through artistic "translation"—"uniting here and hereafter," as he says, recalling the requirement of the poet, as explained in the 1855 Preface, to show the path between reality and the soul. It is the story of a boy who goes to the beach each night to watch a pair of mockingbirds and one night, finding the male bird left alone and singing mournfully for his lost mate, discovers within himself the power to "sing" (that is, to write) in a different register, translating into human language the song of the bird as well as the word out of the sea (the savage old mother "hissing melodious"): "death." The bird, the "singer solitary," "projects" the poet, and the poet "perpetuates" the bird. What's missing, or understated, in this impressive biographical and critical literature are the profound sense of place that the poem communicates and the special quality of the tropes of identity that the poet employs. The critics who get closest to capturing Whitman's sense of sacred space are those who focus on the poem as a problem of *translation*. In confronting the limits of language, the poet engages the question of limits in a broader sense — the limits of land at the ocean's edge, the limits of life at the edge of death.[8]

The poem dramatizes the poet's struggle against such limits. From an ecocritical point of view, he indulges heavily in anthropomorphism, personification, and the pathetic fallacy, imposing upon a scene of nature (a mockingbird defending its territory at the seaside) aspects of a personal crisis that (the biographers tell us) he suffered in the late 1850s, probably a failed love affair with a man, or a psychological crisis (the psychoanalytical critics tell us) that had pursued him from childhood, probably the fear of losing the love and approval of his parents, as well as the worry over a

national crisis involving the increasing tensions between North and South (as the historical critics tell us).[9] But the poem's tropes reverse the pathways of imposition. The moon (like the poet) is "swollen as if with tears," the bird (not the poet) sings of lost love, and the sea (not the poet) lisps the word "death" and appears as a wise if somewhat witchy old crone. It is the poet (not the moon, bird, or ocean) who feels imposed upon, possessed by the wild night scene, the demon bird, and the sea witch. The great poet of selfhood becomes the poet of self-abnegation, opening to the influences of the earth spirits.[10] Dying to his old ways of innocence and self-centeredness — with death, the word out of the sea, serving as the metaphor for the end of the old ways — the boy-poet is overwhelmed by the experience of otherness and must overcome his fear and open himself completely before he can master the forces that threaten the integrity of his individuality.

The language of the poet as represented in the poem contrasts strongly with the "language" of the bird and ocean, figured here as demons or spirits. While the poet's language is rich with imagery — "the sterile sands and the fields beyond, where the child leaving his bed wander'd alone, bareheaded, barefoot," "the mystic play of shadows twining and twisting as if they were alive," "the patches of briers and blackberries" (LG 1891–92, 196–197) — the song of the bird is highly schematic with stark contrasts, musical in its rhythms but impoverished in its imagery. Just as the man's tears wet the beach but lightly compared to the soaking of the waves from the great ocean, the "hints" from the bird and ocean, on the basis of which he must become "uniter of here and hereafter" (showing the way between reality and the soul), do not amount to much. From one bird's song a flock of aroused words must take flight, and from the ocean's one word ("death" — "stronger and more delicious than any") must come many words. The poetic experience of the earth is thus synecdochic and elaborative.

The bird is an island unto itself. Trapped in the repetitive cycles of love and death, insulated first by the experience of mating and nesting, then by the grief that comes from losing its mate, the mockingbird trills a song that compulsively repeats the refrain of "two together," unable to imagine life outside the charmed circle of love.

Shine! shine! shine!
Pour down your warmth, great sun!
While we bask, we two together.

Two together!
Winds blow south, or winds blow north,
Day come white, or night come black,
Home, or rivers and mountains from home,
Singing all time, minding no time,
While we two keep together. (LG 1891–92, 197)

The bird's song comprehends the earth only in broad strokes and general outlines — the four directions of the compass, the white of day and black of night. Everything is either home or not ("Home, or rivers and mountains [away] from home"). And once love is lost, the bird sees all of nature refracted through the lens of sorrow, in a classic instance of the pathetic fallacy — actually a double instance of the fallacy: the poet imposes his emotions upon the bird, and the bird imposes upon the moon:

O brown halo in the sky near the moon, drooping upon the sea!
O troubled reflection in the sea!
O throat! O throbbing heart!
And I singing uselessly, uselessly all the night.

O past! O happy life! O songs of joy!
In the air, in the woods, over fields,
Loved! loved! loved! loved! loved!
But my mate no more, no more with me!
We two together no more. (LG 1891–92, 200)

The bird appears as a closed system of love and sorrow. By contrast, the boy-poet remains open. Just as he is open to the song of the bird, he is open to the influences of the earth, sensitive to finer perceptions of the landscape's details — the "moss-scallop'd stake," the "yellow half-moon [. . .] swollen as with tears" (the "as" indicating his awareness of a poetic intrusion missing in the more metaphorically engaged mockingbird's song), the "lilac-scent [. . .] in the air and Fifth-month grass . . . growing," the "four light-green eggs spotted with brown" — as well as to the more careful distinction of places, such as Paumanok and Alabama, and above all, to the multiple tropes applied to the ocean (the "hoarse surging of the sea," the "slapping waves," the "white arms out in the breakers tirelessly tossing") that gradually resolve into the vision of the "savage old mother incessantly crying, / [. . .] some drown'd secret hissing, / To the outsetting bard."

The ultimate image of the child-poet's openness is that of an island receiving the waves of the ocean as the tide comes in, threatening dissolution (death) but promising fusion, connection, fluidity, and release in the face of rigid compulsion. Turning from the demon bird, the poet invokes the greater power of the sea:

110

*The
Island Poet
and the
Sacred
Shore*

> O give me the clew! (it lurks in the night here somewhere,)
> O if I am to have so much, let me have more!
> A word then, (for I will conquer it,)
> The word final, superior to all,
> Subtle, sent up — what is it? — I listen;
> Are you whispering it, and have been all the time, you sea-waves?
> Is that it from your liquid rims and wet sands? (LG 1891–92, 201)

And the sea responds, bringing not only the word but, more important, perhaps, something close to a mother's affection, which arouses the body of the child-poet much as the soul is said to arouse the body in Section 5 of "Song of Myself." The sea whispers to the inspired child, "laves" him with soft waves, and sings sweetly. And as in the passage from "Song of Myself," the heart responds, the womb-heart that represents the creative faculties of the poet, the part of the individual that receives influences from outside the self and then pours forth the words that align the poet with the natural world and the cosmos:

> Whereto answering, the sea,
> Delaying not, hurrying not,
> Whisper'd me through the night, and very plainly before daybreak,
> Lisp'd to me the low and delicious word death,
> And again death, death, death, death,
> Hissing melodious, neither like the bird nor like my arous'd child's heart,
> But edging near as privately for me rustling at my feet,
> Creeping thence steadily up to my ears and laving me softly all over,
> Death, death, death, death, death. (LG 1891–92, 201)

The poem is about origins in the reminiscence of the time when the child's poet-heart was awakened, but it is also about survival and renewal in the grown poet's return. From the perspective of biography, the adult poet — "A man, yet by these tears a little boy again, / Throwing myself on the sand, confronting the waves" — comes seeking release from the compulsive cycle of the demon love represented by the mockingbird. We might say that Whitman, in bringing to the poem his grief for his lost love and his anxiety over the troubled nation, began in the position of the mockingbird — forlorn, depressed, alienated, and compulsive — and found transcendence and survival by prostrating himself before the earth spirits on the sacred site of his origins. In a pattern we will see again in *Calamus* (see chapter 5), the experience of romantic love involves an alienation from community and even from oneself. Survival outside the charmed circle depends upon a return to the elemental and a sacrificial gesture that opens outward. After retreating deep into the recesses of the island, the lover must risk the sea again, where the only word is death.

111
28
*The
Island Poet
and the
Sacred
Shore*

The word out of the sea has a deeply ecopoetical significance. The threat and the promise of the earth is death. The hysterical turning away from the earth — and from the body, that human island of clay, beset on every side by forces of dissolution — is a function of the human fear of death. Anticipating the womb-tomb imagery of Dylan Thomas, "Out of the Cradle" confronts the human dilemma that the forces driving life also take it away. The tide that brings nutrients to the shore returns to the sea with an equal measure reclaimed. Like "This Compost," "Out of the Cradle" hints strongly that the trouble with focusing ecological awareness and even sustaining ecopolitical activism is rooted in the human alienation from the earth as "the place of graves," as Whitman calls it in "Passage to India" (LG 1891–92, 318). Identity requires the kind of mystical self-abnegation that makes death sound "delicious" and that is beyond the power of ordinary consciousness, which recoils from the very thought of death. The effort of environmentalists to tie the survival of the human race to the survival of nature as the source of life always runs up against this formidable psychological limit. The human will to power understood as the struggle against death can only countenance a parallel struggle against the earth. The great Mother becomes the great Other, and reconciliation becomes the chief task of the poet as a sort of mystical ecologist.

In treating death alternately as a fearful end of living things and as a joyful reunion with the earth, a return to origins that can be simulated, understood, and rendered less frightening through meditative and poetic interactions with nature, Whitman was following, to some degree, the poetic conventions of his day, beginning perhaps with the nature mysticism of the English Romantics and their early followers in the United States, notably William Cullen Bryant, Whitman's fellow New Yorker.[11] Among the most widely read poems in American literature, Bryant's "Thanatopsis" attempts to domesticate death with its famous injunction to "approach thy grave, / Like one who wraps the drapery of his couch / About him, and lies down to pleasant dreams" (Bryant, in Ellmann 32), but not before looking stoically into the reality of the most complete and final identification with nature:

112

🐜

*The
Island Poet
and the
Sacred
Shore*

                    Earth, that nourished thee, shall claim
              Thy growth, to be resolved to earth again,
              And, lost each human trace, surrendering up
              Thine individual being, shalt thou go
              To mix for ever with the elements,
              To be a brother to the insensible rock
              And to the sluggish clod, which the rude swain
              Turns with his share, and treads upon.[...] (Bryant, in Ellmann 30–31)

Whitman surely had these lines in mind when he enjoined the reader of "Song of Myself" to "look for me under your boot-soles" (CRE 89).

The strategy of familiarization, moving from the fearful coldness of nature to the warmth of the domestic scene of death, undergoes an ironic reversal in another key text of nineteenth-century American ecopoetics, Emerson's "Hamatreya," which was almost certainly a source for Whitman's "operatic" poems. "Hamatreya" begins with a reflection on the ownership of land, ironically noting that the New England farmers who boast of their holdings — "'T is mine, my children's and my name's" — and even of their identity with the land — "I fancy these pure waters and the flags / Know me, as does my dog: we sympathize; / And, I affirm, my actions smack of the soil" — finally may be found "Asleep beneath their grounds: / And strangers, fond as they, their furrows plough" (Emerson, in Ellmann 51). As Whitman does with the mockingbird in "Out of the Cradle" and the thrush in "Lilacs," Emerson gives voice to the earth to provide a counterpoint to the boastful farmers. Schematic and even laconic, with lines shorter and more conventionally "musical" than the lines in which the poet speaks in more or less his own voice, Emerson's "Earth-Song" anticipates the song of Whitman's mockingbird:

> "Mine and yours;
> Mine, not yours.
> Earth endures;
> Stars abide —
> Shine down in the old sea;
> Old are the shores;
> But where are old men?
> I who have seen much,
> Such have I never seen.
>
> . . . .
>
> "Here is the land,
> Shaggy with wood,

With its old valley,
Mound and flood.
But the heritors? —
Fled like the flood's foam.
The lawyer, and the laws,
And the kingdom,
Clean swept herefrom.

"They called me theirs,
Who so controlled me;
Yet every one
Wished to stay, and is gone,
How am I theirs,
If they cannot hold me,
But I hold them?" (Emerson, in Ellmann 51–52)

113
⚡
*The
Island Poet
and the
Sacred
Shore*

The poet does not find consolation in the earth's song but rather humility and even fear. Upon hearing the song, he says, "I was no longer brave; / My avarice cooled / Like lust in the chill of the grave" (Emerson, in Ellmann 52).

Both "Thanatopsis" and "Hamatreya" represent the earth as humanity's ultimate home or resting place, the grave of humankind. Bryant treats this realization with stoic acceptance, Emerson with Romantic awe and irony. Both participate in the pastoral tradition, the literature of agricultural people who lay claim to the earth only to be claimed by it. Bryant reminds us that "the rude swain" (the very diction suggesting the English pastoral from Spenser on down) will roughly plow the ground that holds us; Emerson's earth "laughs in flowers" at the New England farmers' pretentious claims of ownership. The *ubi sunt* tradition of the pastoral lyric — represented here in the conventional query "where are old men?" — makes it particularly useful to the environmentalist imagination with its concern over loss and grief. No wonder, then, that Lawrence Buell argues in *The Environmental Imagination* that the pastoral tradition is a powerful influence. Whitman himself draws upon pastoralism in many poems, most clearly perhaps in "This Compost." And in "Out of the Cradle," he cleverly combines the stoic acceptance of Bryant with the sublime awe of Emerson in the image of the sea as an old crone, at once domestic and consoling but also threatening and not a little spooky.

But I would argue that with the island poetics of "Out of the Cradle," Whitman departs from, or at least extends, the pastoral tradition. If, as the cultural geographer Jonathan Smith suggests in his essay "The Place of Nature," nature seems big and imposing while people seem small and

114

⚶

*The
Island Poet
and the
Sacred
Shore*

ultimately threatened in nineteenth-century Romantic pastoralism, and if people seem imposingly big and nature small and threatened in the twentieth-century environmentalist imagination, a kind of inverted pastoralism — heroic nature giving way to abused nature — then Whitman is a bridging figure or something entirely different in "Out of the Cradle." The poet seems to expand beyond the limits of the natural beings and phenomena that inspire him. His song engulfs the lament of the bird and the whispered word of the sea and grows larger with these offerings. Adding his own sense impressions and layering his song with many returns to the sacred place, his words swamp the schematic utterances of bird and ocean. Even so, this poetic giant is "by these tears a little boy again." He depends upon the memory of the bird, the sacred place, and the roar of the ocean as a child depends upon the mother. Without renewed contact with the endless rocking of the cradle, he becomes diminished. Renewal depends upon the return to the sacred site and all that it signifies.

While in poems like "This Compost" and "Out of the Cradle" Whitman shares with his Romantic sources the tendency to approach nature as a spirit (in the manner of modern "deep ecologists" or nature mystics) rather than as an object (in the manner of modern science) or as a resource or commodity (in the manner of modern business and industry, or, for that matter, Bryant's swains and Emerson's farmers), the quality of spiritual interaction is distinctly different for him.[12] The nature of both Emerson and Bryant has a monotheistic or deistic flavor. Nature is a god term or an actual god before which the Romantic poets bow, either in submission or awe, but keeping their own relatively stable identities intact. The speakers in poems like "Thanatopsis" and "Hamatreya" modulate their voices only slightly, steadily maintaining the persona of something like Nature's priesthood. By contrast, Whitman's earth is not reduced to a single deity but is full of spirits competing for his attention; the poet's soul is one spirit among many.[13] Instead of bowing before them, he invokes them, invites them to fill him, transform him. If Bryant and Emerson come off as deistic or Unitarian, Whitman appears as charismatic or shamanistic.[14]

As with his treatment of the soul in "Song of Myself," it is hard to know how literally Whitman took himself when he called the bird a "demon" and referred to the child's aroused heart as "the sweet hell within." We cannot say exactly what the earth spirits mean to the poet, but we can say how they affect him. They change him, renew him, pull him out of the depression into which he has sunk, and restore his vital creativity. The suggestion is that the soul of the human being dwells in the earth and must be reintegrated with the living body and individual ego through ritual contact, preferably carried out in sacred sites. The ecopoetics suggested by this view subverts the Romantic categories of scale and hierarchy, the large and the small, the victim and the master, the god and the creature (or even the mediating high priest), hinting instead toward a model of interactive flow, of fluids and bodies interpenetrating, the opening and closing of inlets and pores, mouths and ears, with islands whose shorelines are formed by the sea, whose mineral substance and fresh waters feed the sea in turn, and the shape of whose very being stands as a monument to the power and wonder of the ocean.

115

The
Island Poet
and the
Sacred
Shore

"Out of the Cradle" offers consolation through an acceptance of death as a force that pervades nature and promises a dissolution into the mystic whole that will bring an end to compulsive and painful repetitions. The meditative posture of the poet prostrate upon the sacred shore indicates a release of the willful control by which the individual ego attempts to carve out an artificial island of protected life. The joyful, though admittedly frightening, abandon at the end of the poem results from the release that the poet feels.

By the time we come to the postwar poem "When Lilacs Last in the Dooryard Bloom'd," much has changed. Again we have the elegiac tone and structure, the singing bird that is a "brother" to the poet, a setting near the sacred shore, the poet going thence to mourn and seek redemption and atonement. But the attitude toward nature and toward death differs somewhat; the mood is more somber, the release less than joyful and not even complete. Whitman's experience of daily sickness and death in the war hospitals, the sacrifice of the many comrades and fellow citizens followed by the assassination of President Lincoln, has undermined his certainty that death "avails not." As Wynn Thomas puts it in *The Lunar Light of Whitman's Poetry*, "the path down to the swamp" that the poet follows in "Lilacs" "passed directly through the hospitals" (249).[15]

Like the ocean in "Out of the Cradle," the phenomena of nature represented in "Lilacs" speak of death to the poet, but this time they seem to reflect his own thoughts and knowledge and become tokens of his awareness — the great star "drooping" in the western sky, the dark cloud that threatens to hide the star, the lilac sending forth blossoms as if to resist the oppression of death and remind him of life but failing, only to become the token by which he vows to remember each springtime the president's death. The vow to remember accounts largely for the passion the poem communicates, as Thomas suggests in his reading; moreover, the memorial attitude is deeply tied to the poet's environmental sensibility. He sets up a virtual monument in the sacred places recast in the forge of memory and imagination.

And then there is the bird, the hermit thrush. Unlike the mockingbird, whose very life seems to depend upon his mate, the thrush is a "hermit withdrawn to himself, avoiding the settlements," hiding away in "the swamp in secluded recesses" (LG 1891–92, 256). The thrush is like the poet around the time of the national crisis, who by his own account hid away at the beginning of the war, going home to his mother's house in Brooklyn, and was there again when the announcement came of Lincoln's assassination (see Loving, *Walt Whitman* 2–17; see also French). "Lilacs" recounts a mythic journey during which the poet forms a more complete identification with the bird, making his way out of the settlements to the sacred site to find in solitary meditation his bearings in the face of the awful death. Whitman follows a path blazed by Henry David Thoreau in his essay "Walking," published in the year he died, 1862, as the war raged on and Whitman prolonged his retreat in Brooklyn. "Hope and the future for me," Thoreau writes in the prophetic mode that predominates in this essay, "are not in lawns and cultivated fields, not in towns and cities, but in the impervious and quaking swamps":

> When I wish to recreate myself, I seek the darkest wood, the thickest and most interminable and, to the citizen, most dismal swamp. I enter a swamp as a sacred place — a *sanctum sanctorum*. . . . A town is saved, not more by the righteous men in it than by the woods and swamps that surround it. A township where one primitive forest waves above while another primitive forest rots below, — such a town is fitted to raise not only corn and potatoes, but poets and philosophers for the coming ages. ("Walking" 646–647)[16]

Thoreau's swamp, in addition to drawing upon the contemporaneous ideas of George Perkins Marsh on how forests and wetlands regenerate soils, an early source of appeals for preserving wilderness (Nash 105), also recalls the "rot" of Whitman's compost as well as the concepts in island poetics of sacred places and the theme of survival. Though not a marsh (or estuary), which opens to the sea and thereby signifies the indefinite margin where solid earth (the father) gives way to open sea (the mother), the swamp (a forested wetland) represents a similar kind of nurturing margin. It feeds the forest and builds the general profile and strength of the soil — and thereby the people — and thus suggests regeneration and renewal. It is related to the shoreline in the sense that it is the place where civilization ends and the earth does its work without the interference of humanity. It is to the woodlands what the marsh is to the shoreline. In the midst of his encomium on swamps, Thoreau enjoys a moment of characteristic perversity that makes clear the relationship of the various wetlands (and drylands) by using the umbrella concept of wilderness: "My spirits infallibly rise in proportion to the outward dreariness. Give me the ocean, the desert, or the wilderness!" ("Walking" 647).

Whitman's "Lilacs," composed only a few years after Thoreau's essay, depends on many of the same themes. In tracing the path out of civilization and into the wilderness, the poem develops something like a narrative that, while not straightforward, is nevertheless fairly clear and recoverable from the hints of the poem's structure. As the story begins, the flowers are blooming in the dooryard of an old farmhouse. The place suggests a return (in memory or fantasy) to Whitman's childhood home, the "old homestead" on Long Island. From a bush of lilacs, the poet takes a sprig to toss upon the coffin of the dead president (never named in the poem but treated mythically as the representative comrade, "him I love") as the funeral train passes through the city on its circuitous route from Washington, D.C., to Springfield, Illinois. The movement suggested by the poem, from the farmyard to the city where the coffin passes (an event Whitman did not actually witness, according to the biographers), reconstructs the poet's own migration in his early manhood, which follows the pattern of Lincoln's life, too, as well as that of many thousands of young American men of the day who moved from the country to the city looking for opportunities (literally "openings"). The stately solemnity of the funeral procession recounted movingly in Section 6 — "the pomp of the inloop'd flags with the cities draped in black," the "mournful voices of the dirges pour'd around the coffin," the "dim-lit churches and the shuddering organs" — and even the placing of the lilac sprig on the coffin, an improvised ritual act fitted to the season and the American scene, fail to suffice, however. By Section 7, we find the poet sounding the depths of his mourning, which is not "for you, for one alone," he says, addressing the dead comrade, but for death itself, he imagines, "sane and sacred death," which he then addresses directly, telling of his desire to "cover you over with roses and early lilies" and copious sprigs of lilac — "For you and the coffins all of you O death." But the covering over fails to provide the release he needs. As the night advances, he tells us in Section 8, "my soul in its trouble dissatisfied sank," and in Section 9, the drooping star, which he now calls comrade and which some critics have identified with the fallen president translated in the classical manner into the heavens, "holds and detains" him (see CRE 329n). The feeling of being held, the inability to break free from the compulsive return of thoughts about the dead comrade, recalling the unbreakable cycles of the mockingbird's grief in "Out of the Cradle," drives the poet to other paths. In Section 10, he feels the sea winds and finds in them the breath that he says he will make into a chant with which to "perfume the grave of him I love," as if to augment the fragrance of the copious blossoms in his earlier offering, which failed to "cover over" death. The feeling imparted is that he is moving toward the sea. Along the way, he imagines a "burial-house of him I love" (Section 11) which he adorns with "Pictures of growing spring and farms and homes / [. . .] With floods of the yellow gold of the gorgeous, indolent, sinking sun, burning, expanding the air" and "With the fresh sweet herbage under foot, and the pale green leaves of the trees prolific" and "all the scenes of life and the workshops, and the workmen homeward returning." The adorned death-house bears a strong resemblance to his own book *Leaves of Grass*. Yet even the dedication of the poetry, the lovely pictures, will not suffice.[17] The clue to what will ultimately release him sounds repeatedly throughout the poem in the song of the hermit thrush (appearing in the interludes of Sections 9 and 13), which continues to draw him toward the swamp. But still "the star holds me" and "the lilac with mastering odor holds me," he says. Finally, in Section 14 he begins to find his way out of the deadening cycle. Cognizant now of the breadth and motions of the earth — the "arching heavens of the afternoon swift passing" and the "many-moving sea-tides" — and even the ordinary movements of the city's people — "the fields all busy with labor / And the infinite separate houses, how they all went on, each with its meals and minutia of daily usages" — he sees "enveloping them all" the cloud, "the long black trail," and with this vision, he says, "I knew death, its thought, and the sacred knowledge of death."[18] He communicates the closeness he feels with death through personification, the thought of death and the knowledge of death becoming as two comrades who take his hands and lead him to the thrush in the swamp:

> Then with the knowledge of death as walking one side of me,
> And the thought of death close-walking the other side of me,
> And I in the middle as with companions, and as holding the hands of
>   companions,
> I fled forth to the hiding receiving night that talks not,
> Down to the shores of the water, the path by the swamp in the dimness,
> To the solemn shadowy cedars and ghostly pines so still.
>
> And the singer so shy to the rest receiv'd me,
> The gray-brown bird I know receiv'd us comrades three,
> And he sang the carol of death, and a verse for him I love.

118

*The
Island Poet
and the
Sacred
Shore*

From deep secluded recesses,
From the fragrant cedars and the ghostly pines so still,
Came the carol of the bird.

And the charm of the carol rapt me,
As I held as if by their hands my comrades in the night,
And the voice of my spirit tallied the song of the bird.

(LG 1891–92, 259–260)

119

辤

*The
Island Poet
and the
Sacred
Shore*

The bird's song differs significantly from that of the mockingbird in "Out of the Cradle." Like the mockingbird's, the thrush's song has a regularity and a pattern of trilling repetition that distinguish it from the "voice" of the poet (helped along by the use of italic typeface). But the tone is soothing and calming, not only accepting of death but inviting or invoking death much as Whitman invites the soul in "Song of Myself": "*Come lovely and soothing death,*" sings the bird, "*Dark mother always gliding near with soft feet, / Have none chanted for thee a chant of fullest welcome?*" (LG 1891–92, 260). In one sense, the bird's acceptance of death represents the integration in natural cycles that all creatures except humans seem not to question. As Whitman says of animals in "Song of Myself," "they are so placid and self-contain'd":

They do not sweat and whine about their condition,
They do not lie awake in the dark and weep for their sins,
They do not make me sick discussing their duty to God,
Not one is dissatisfied, not one is demented with the mania of owning
    things,
Not one kneels to another, nor to his kind that lived thousands of
    years ago,
Not one is respectable or unhappy over the whole earth.

(LG 1891–92, 54)

But in another sense, the bird reminds the poet of his faculty of openness. In the notion of "tallying" — another term for what I called "resonance" in chapter 1, which entails the actions of opening and receiving, a pattern of response repeated in all the seashore and wetland poems — lies perhaps his greatest contribution to ecopoetics, the willingness and capacity of the sensitive person to be transformed in the face of undeniable otherness, both human and natural.

On this occasion, he must not only open himself to the word "death" but to the spirit itself, which replaces the ocean as "mother" in this poem, or rather reduces the figure of the ocean-speaking-the-word-death to the figure of death-as-ocean-and-mother. Death consumes all else before it. Moved by the song of the bird, the poet's spirit "tallies" with that of the singer, aligns with it, receives it, and is rewarded with a vision of death as "*deliveress*," a "*loving floating ocean*," a "*flood of [. . .] bliss*." The images that come to him in the vision remind him that the suffering of war, though terrible, is over for those soldiers who have died but not for the survivors, the sorrow of whom is drummed out with the relentless repetition of the word "suffer'd":

120
🐾
*The
Island Poet
and the
Sacred
Shore*

> And I saw askant the armies,
> I saw as in noiseless dreams hundreds of battle-flags,
> Borne through the smoke of the battles and pierc'd with missiles I saw
>   them,
> And carried hither and yon through the smoke, and torn and bloody,
> And at last but a few shreds left on the staffs, (and all in silence,)
> And the staffs all splinter'd and broken.
>
> I saw battle-corpses, myriads of them,
> And the white skeletons of young men, I saw them,
> I saw the debris and debris of all the slain soldiers of the war,
> But I saw they were not as was thought,
> They themselves were fully at rest, they suffer'd not,
> The living remain'd and suffer'd, the mother suffer'd,
> And the wife and the child and the musing comrade suffer'd,
> And the armies that remain'd suffer'd. (LG 1891–92, 261)

With the vision, the cycle of grief is redeemed if not broken. With "death's outlet song," the remembrance of the ones who are beyond suffering, the tide of grief is released to flow into the death-ocean, and the poet can try to let go and return to the flow of life — "Passing the visions, passing the night, / Passing, unloosing the hold of my comrades' hands," he says in the closing stanzas of Section 16. By "comrades" here, he means primarily the personified abstractions, "the thought of death" and "the knowledge of death," but he also implies the release of the dead comrades of his visions whom he tries to leave in peace, taking what comfort he can from the knowledge that in death their suffering has passed. The visions inspired by the bird's song are the gifts to show him that his obligation to the dead is fulfilled by his having opened himself to the spirit of death, by having sung in his own voice, and by his vow to remember. The "fragrant pines" and the "cedars dusk and dim" provide the necessary perfume, the celebratory incense.

    It is significant, however, that the poet never reaches the actual edge of the ocean, as he does in "Out of the Cradle." He never enters even the open marshland. He stops in the swamp with the thrush and seeks therein sufficient resolution to return to the city. He seems to be reaching for something — an artistic effect, a consolation, a fullness that he never quite attains: the ocean. This shortfall may help to explain why, though "Lilacs" has been generally regarded as one of the greatest poems in *Leaves of Grass*, Whitman himself was never completely satisfied with his performance. It is well known among Whitman scholars that the poet was upset over the popular reception of another of his Lincoln poems, "O Captain, My Captain," which he considered uncharacteristic of his work as a whole, but neither did he consider "Lilacs" one of his best poems (see Loving, *Walt Whitman* 288). Chances are that Whitman could never rest satisfied with any memorial to the death of Lincoln and the war itself. The effect upon him was simply too devastating.

121

The
Island Poet
and the
Sacred
Shore

So it is right that in the postwar imaginative landscape of "Lilacs," the swamp never yields a shoreline. Things just get murkier and messier. Though drawn forth by the scent and freshness of the sea winds, the poet fails to reach any place that resembles the Long Island coast that he knew so well, the kind of clear place where liquid meets solid. Perhaps he began the poem with his many restorative pilgrimages to that clear place in mind but found himself stuck instead in the kind of swamp that he always associated with the South, the kind that he first came to know during his time in New Orleans in the 1840s and celebrated in his 1860 poem "O Magnet-South" but which during the war in the environs of Washington, D.C., and northern Virginia took on a different meaning, more attuned with "This Compost," terrifying and awesome rather than picturesque. In "Lilacs," the swamp is the place of decomposition; its smells and its muck ooze decay. There's good reason — actual physical reason — that he can't get to the ocean (you can't walk a swamp to the open ocean). So the fact that he chooses a swamp as the place to walk into with the thought of death and the knowledge of death is no accident. In a way, he does not want to be released from this place: he wants to stand knee-deep in decay. The swamp presents a dangerous ecology, because in effect it is the place where the great continental island is half-dissolved in the sea beneath the ground, so the generating tension between self and other, between individual and collective, between life and death is erased (or held in suspension). It's the active place of compost, where we can feel and smell the decomposition taking place, where decomposition is in some ways all that there is.

And after the Civil War, there was a lot to decompose. In one section of *Specimen Days*— titled "The Million Dead, Too, Summ'd Up," in which the elided "summ'd" could mean either "summed" or "summoned" — he absorbs in one swampy sentence all "the dead, the dead, the dead" as "the corpses floated down the rivers," as they "lie at the bottom of the sea."[19] He seeks to compost "the infinite dead" back into a living present and future, but his efforts lead to horrifying results ("the land entire saturated, perfumed with their impalpable ashes' exhalation in Nature's chemistry distill'd, and shall be so forever, in every future grain of wheat and ear of corn, and every flower that grows, and every breath we draw") (SD 777). So in "Lilacs," as he opens his eyes on the dead and sees "the debris and the debris," the swamp is the only place to be, the only ecology capable of handling this much composting. To make the pattern explicit throughout his book, Whitman goes back to "This Compost" after the war and changes it just slightly by adding that one phrase to the catalog of things that grow out of death: "the lilacs bloom in the dooryard." In a way, it's easier for him to absorb the Civil War dead by gently altering his more innocent compost poem than to write a new swamp poem. "Lilacs" is the terrifying entry into an ecology that has no shoreline, and the "retrievements" he manages to make are "out of the night," destined to be "dusk and dim," oozy, neither solid nor liquid. When, at the end of "Lilacs," he says, "I leave thee lilac [...], I leave thee there in the door-yard, blooming, returning with spring," he is in effect transferring that image of spring and rebirth back to "This Compost," where it can still offer hope. The swamp is no place for lilacs.[20]

The retreat implied in the poem's ending sadly manifests not only in theme (the stopping short of the sacred shoreline) but also in form. Whitman falls back on poetic strategies that had worked for him before, the method of the reprise that summons again the key symbols and scenes at the end of the poem, a technique that he had used with outstanding results in "Out of the Cradle" but which seems ever so slightly shopworn in "Lilacs." More significantly yet, in this poem — as in later poems like "Song of the Redwood-Tree" — he falls back on the well-worn conventions of traditional poetry, in this case the conventions of the English elegy. The recourse to the personification of abstractions is especially telling, as is the metaphorical substitution of death for the ocean.[21] Instead of speaking the word "death" and thereby illuminating the poet, contributing to the fullness of his song, the ocean has become death itself and threatens to swamp the poet. He professes to have been changed by his experience of hearing the thrush's song, but that change is weakly dramatized compared to the way the boy-poet's initiation into mystery and the man-poet's revitalization are dramatized in "Out of the Cradle." Indeed, the voice of "Lilacs" is only slightly modulated throughout, the solemn tone of the elegy pervading all parts. The wild fluctuations and transformations of a character

122

🙚

*The
Island Poet
and the
Sacred
Shore*

fully open to the influences of the earth's spirits — a quality that had distinguished him from the other great poets of nature and death in his time, Bryant and Emerson and even Tennyson — appear much diminished in "Lilacs." From the character of "Out of the Cradle" we might have expected before the resolution the crazy keening of Irish mourners or the comparable self-wounding of American Indian grief (see Eastman 150–152).

123

The
Island Poet
and the
Sacred
Shore

Worn out from the war, Whitman was likely struggling to keep his inspiration alive. The struggle makes for moving poetry, no doubt, a poetry that has a special resonance to twenty-first-century readers in an America beset by the threat of violence from within and without. The recent surge of critical interest in Whitman's wartime writings — in the work of Davis, Loving, Morris, Maslan, and Coviello, for example — bespeaks the effect of what Kenneth Burke in *Counter-Statement* calls a "symbolic charge," a historical resonance that accounts for a work's continuing appeal, or renewed appeal, in later times. But what's troubling from an ecopoetical perspective is the tendency toward abstraction and alienation that begins to prevail at the end of "Lilacs." Part of the struggle in the poem involves the poet's failed effort to find consolation in his "pictures" of simple scenes of people and earthly phenomena. He no longer seems able to connect in the old way. Now he holds the personified hand of the thought of death and the knowledge of death rather than the fleshy hands of his loving friends in "I Sing the Body Electric" and *Calamus* or the wounded soldiers in "Drum-Taps." For all his claims to release, he seems unable to break the compulsive cycle. The poet and the bird from "Out of the Cradle" seem to have changed places in "Lilacs."

Throughout his career Whitman returned again and again, with new poems and annual lectures, to the death of Lincoln, unable to find the resolution he seeks throughout "Lilacs." He worried that his fellow Americans had forgotten the struggle and the sacrifice exacted by the war. The war consumed him and ate away at his inspiration, already damaged by the crisis of the late 1850s.

The failure of inspiration, represented as being held or restrained in "Lilacs," was a theme that had occupied Whitman in an earlier poem of the sacred shore, "As I Ebb'd with the Ocean of Life," which made its first appearance in *Leaves of Grass* in the 1860 edition. The opening lines, with their reference to the ocean as a "fierce old mother," indicate that the poem was intended as a companion to "Out of the Cradle." It is another poem about returning to the sacred site and being "seized" by earth spirits. It begins with these lines in its final version:

As I ebb'd with the ocean of life,
As I wended the shores I know,
As I walk'd where the ripples continually wash you Paumanok,
Where they rustle up hoarse and sibilant,
Where the fierce old mother endlessly cries for her castaways,
I musing late in the autumn day, gazing off southward,
Held by this electric self out of the pride of which I utter poems,
Was seiz'd by the spirit that trails in the lines underfoot,
The rim, the sediment that stands for all the water and all the land of
    the globe. (LG 1891–92, 202).

The drifted matter at the edge of the ocean closely noted and named —
"Chaff, straw, splinters of wood, weeds, and the sea-gluten, / Scum, scales
from shining rocks, leaves of sea-lettuce, left by the tide" — becomes the
"types" that he seeks in the poem, the symbols for the bard with depressed
spirits. Again, he feels "held" out of the flow. This time he says that he is
held "by this electric self out of the pride of which I utter poems." This line
was revised from the 1860 version, which read "Alone, held by the eternal
self of me that threatens to get the better of me, and stifle me" (Blue Book
1:195). The original line imparts the feeling of stifling and suggests a more
general depression, while the revision focuses particularly on the failure of
inspiration, the "pride [out] of which I utter poems," and substitutes the
curious word "electric" for the puzzling adjective "eternal." Both versions
suggest that some deep aspect of the self withdraws from the poet's will to
write, to mingle in the ocean of life. The word *electric* usually bears a positive connotation in *Leaves of Grass*, as in "I Sing the Body Electric," a poem
celebrating the magnetism of the sexualized and loving body. The word
electric did not appear in the 1860 version of that poem either but came
later, in 1867. In both poems, it seems to suggest an openness, like the valence
of a molecular bond, a willingness to engage. In "I Sing the Body Electric,"
which dates from 1855, the poet is "engirthed" by the bodies of the people
he loves; they "will not let me off, nor I them, till I go with them, respond
to them [...] and charge them [full] with the charge of the Soul" (Blue Book
1:291). The electric self, then, is the self possessed fully by the soul. But in
"As I Ebb'd," there is no means of release. The poet is alone, and like the
noiseless patient spider, he opens outward but is unable to find a place for
the creative filament to attach. Such are among the saddest moments in
Leaves of Grass, the soul engaged, charged up, but without a connection by
which to release the charge. In this case, the "electric self" cannot form a
circuit with the "pride" of his earlier poems. He feels alienated from the

ocean of delight that infuses poems like "Song of Myself" and "Crossing Brooklyn Ferry." The "types" he finds for himself, insofar as he identifies with his works, are the bits of sea-drift, rubbish left on the beach at low tide.

In Section 2, he gives full vent to his discontent. The "shores I know" become "the shores I know not," and indeed the very self, the "real Me," eludes him, and Nature rebukes him for daring to sing and mocks him with the sound of a dirge:

125

The
Island Poet
and the
Sacred
Shore

> As I wend to the shores I know not,
> As I list to the dirge, the voices of men and women wreck'd,
> As I inhale the impalpable breezes that set in upon me,
> As the ocean so mysterious rolls toward me closer and closer,
> I too but signify at the utmost a little wash'd-up drift. (LG 1891–92, 202)

Anticipating another crisis poem, "The Prayer of Columbus," the poet hears not the joyous voices of lovers and comrades but the "voices of men and women wreck'd," washed up on the shore. Now the electric self, sensitive to the suggestions of the "spirit" of the drift that confronts him, specifies the doubt that haunts him. The great barbaric yawp of "Song of Myself" has come to seem mere "blab" to him; he has internalized the dismissive attitude of the critics who pursued him after publication; he feels mocked by the "real Me," the electric self that will not be satisfied with his offerings:

> O baffled, balk'd, bent to the very earth,
> Oppress'd with myself that I have dared to open my mouth,
> Aware now that amid all that blab whose echoes recoil upon me I have
>   not once had the least idea who or what I am,
> But that before all my arrogant poems the real Me stands yet
>   untouch'd, untold, altogether unreach'd,
> Withdrawn far, mocking me with mock-congratulatory signs and
>   bows,
> With peals of distant ironical laughter at every word I have written,
> Pointing in silence to these songs, and then to the sand beneath.
>   (LG 1891–92, 202)

Much as the ecstasy that comes from merging with the soul that "arose and spread around" him in Section 5 of "Song of Myself," the penetrating doubt inspired by the spirit of the ebb tide now expands into a general skepticism that causes him to doubt his understanding of the earth. And the "real Me" has become, like the objects of the earth and the unknowable place of origins, a thing that resists poetic language, that remains "untouch'd, untold, altogether unreach'd." Nature joins the electric self in mocking the poet:

I perceive I have not really understood any thing, not a single object,
    and that no man ever can,
Nature here in sight of the sea taking advantage of me to dart upon
    me and sting me,
Because I have dared to open my mouth to sing at all.

(LG 1891–92, 203)

126

⚜

*The
Island Poet
and the
Sacred
Shore*

Reproached by the ocean-mother, hitting bottom as it were, he extends the familial mythos and appeals to his island home, addressing Paumanok as "father":

I too Paumanok,
I too have bubbled up, floated the measureless float, and been wash'd
    on your shores,
I too am but a trail of drift and debris,
I too leave little wrecks upon you, you fish-shaped island.

I throw myself upon your breast my father,
I cling to you so that you cannot unloose me,
I hold you so firm till you answer me something.

Kiss me my father,
Touch me with your lips as I touch those I love,
Breathe to me while I hold you close the secret of the murmuring I
    envy. (LG 1891–92, 203)

The identity with the island-father seems to give the poet the strength to face again the ocean's ebb-tide dirge so that he can, in the concluding Section 4, affirm the necessity of it and gather hope in the turning of the cycle: "Ebb, ocean of life, (the flow will return,) / […] Rustle not up so hoarse and angry against my feet as I touch you or gather from you" (LG 1891–92, 203). The image suggests the poet prostrate on the land beseeching the father just as the tide begins to turn, the water reaching up to his feet. The end of the poem offers only the slightest lift of spirits, the poet saved like a drowning man who has thrown himself in desperation on the shore, but barely alive.

Typical of the religious trend of the 1860 poems and consonant with Romantic ecopoetics, "As I Ebb'd" tends to deify as well as personify Nature, the poem ending with the apostrophe, "Whoever you are, we too lie in drifts at your feet" (LG 1891–92, 204). But the poem also suggests a contrary movement, resisting an explanatory or priestly function as well as a confident monotheistic logic in its acceptance of uncertainty about earthly objects and the deified Nature ("Whoever you are"). Like the objects of nature, the poet's very self is a thing that cannot be fully comprehended; it is a presence known only by traces, "drifts" upon the shore. The spiritual lift at the end of the poem comes from the acceptance of uncertainty and the possibility of insignificance — the vision of "loose windrows, little corpses," ephemeral "Froth, snowy white, and bubbles," analogous to "my dead lips the ooze exuding at last" (LG 1891–92, 203). As the poet's acceptance of the thingish otherness of the earth in "This Compost" allows him to turn from fear to awe, so in this poem the acceptance of possible insignificance ironically allows him to pursue the attempt at signification.

127

The
Island Poet
and the
Sacred
Shore

The familial mythos that runs through all the seashore poems — completed in "As I Ebb'd" with the vision of the island-father to fill out the group that includes the ocean-mother and the bird-brother — deserves attention for its ecopoetical suggestiveness. To some extent, the familial group represents an alternative to the idea of the land as lover (or victim of acquisitive passion), and it resonates with the Native American mythology of mother earth, father sky, and filial animals — brother fox and brother bear — as well as Brer Rabbit and his fellow creatures in the stories of Joel Chandler Harris, who drew upon the Gullah traditions of storytelling from the southeastern sea islands. It's interesting that mother earth (and her quasi-scientific incarnation as "Gaia" in recent years) is the one survivor in modern times of this rich mythology. The reduction follows the trend toward monotheism and abstraction in the representation of human relations to nature. The introduction of the father in "As I Ebb'd" allows the poet a greater symbolic range in confronting the earth. In Whitman's case, the designation is particularly poignant. His own father, five years dead by the time the poem was published in 1860, had been by many measures a good example of human insignificance against the background of grand schemes — a carpenter and house builder who lived from hand to mouth much of the time, leaving little behind as evidence of his work ("straw, sand, fragments," as the poem says). Whitman's desperate identification with the father and his own frailties open him to new ways of encountering himself and the earth. He dismisses the "pride" of his early poems, rejecting the kind of hubris that many ecocritics see at the root of modern environmental troubles. This rejection creates a powerful balance in the whole of his book, with its alternating patterns of assertion and withdrawal, imposition and receptiveness. He emerges from the poem chastened but realigned, the electric self reconnected in the charged space between the island-father and the ocean-mother.

The idea of having been "wreck'd" on the shore in "As I Ebb'd," dragged down close to death by the grip of the electric self, corresponds to the images of sinking and even drowning that come to pervade "When Lilacs Last in the Dooryard Bloom'd." In the later poem, the sun sinks with its golden light, the star droops in the west threatened by the dark cloud, and the poet himself, when his practices of grieving at first fail to suffice, confesses that "my soul in its trouble dissatisfied sank." The feeling of being held out of the flow, suspended, trapped in his grief, gives way only when he releases the "hold of my comrades' hands," as if the dead ones and his own thoughts of death are pulling him down. He must fill himself again with the breath of the living earth and return to the flow. The saving "lift" at the end of "As I Ebb'd" is expressed as buoyancy. "Buoy'd hither from many moods, one contradicting another" (LG 1891–92, 204), the drift appears on the edge of the ocean, waiting to be carried hither into the flow.

The tidal trope as well as the notion of the buoyant soul had been established powerfully in "Crossing Brooklyn Ferry," which dates from 1856, a time when Whitman was riding the high tide of excitement over the fullness of his inspiration and Emerson's praise for the first (1855) edition of his book. As in Section 5 of "Song of Myself," the poem suggests the ecstatic response to the earth and its creatures that characterized the poet fully possessed of his soul, his creative imagination gathering up sense impressions arriving at every pore and his mind striving against the limits of time and mortality. This time, the poem begins in the voice of the inspired poet and maintains the ecstatic voice throughout. The great river running to the sea buoys him up, carrying him from one sea island to another, all connected by the powerful flood tide of the ocean-mother. With the long lines of the verses suggesting a chest-expanding confidence full of spirit-breath, he looks directly into the challenge of the ancient sign of mortality, the setting sun. He feels a filial interest in the men and women near him and no less interest in the people of the future who fill his meditations:

> FLOOD-TIDE below me! I see you face to face!
> Clouds of the west-sun there half an hour high — I see you also face
>   to face.
>
> Crowds of men and women attired in the usual costumes, how curi-
>   ous you are to me!
> On the ferry-boats the hundreds and hundreds that cross, returning
>   home, are more curious to me than you suppose,
> And you that shall cross from shore to shore years hence are more to
>   me, and more in my meditations, than you might suppose.
>
> (LG 1891–92, 129)

128

The
Island Poet
and the
Sacred
Shore

Here we have the voice of the poet fully integrated with nature, having broken free of the islands and his fear of the sea, going fully with the flow. Using the favorite figure of the mystical poet, paradox, Whitman hints that the integration he feels requires disintegration, the openness to all things, the possibility that they will feed him and support him:

129

The
Island Poet
and the
Sacred
Shore

> The impalpable sustenance of me from all things at all hours of the day,
> The simple, compact, well-join'd scheme, myself disintegrated, every
>   one disintegrated yet part of the scheme,
> The similitudes of the past and those of the future,
> The glories strung like beads on my smallest sights and hearings, on
>   the walk in the street and the passage over the river,
> The current rushing so swiftly and swimming with me far away,
> The others that are to follow me, the ties between me and them,
> The certainty of others, the life, love, sight, hearing of others.
>
> (LG 1891–92, 129)

The linking of "the walk in the street and the passage over the river" suggests a seamless flow on the flood tide, the islands of individuality smoothly connected in a "well-join'd scheme," for which the current becomes a metaphor, engulfing time itself.

With the claims to have transcended time, the troubles with the poem begin, at least if it is read within the historical-ecological context, with special reference to urbanization and the imperialistic or manic trend of the poet's persona. Such will be the approach of my next chapter. But before closing this chapter, I want to consider the seeming transcendence of time in its relation to the sanctification of place implied in what I have been calling island poetics.

Rather than saying that the poem implies a transcendence of time, it might be better to call it a rejection of temporal limits or a denial of history. In this sense, the poem allows for the kind of spatially situated view of experience that modern environmentalists and nature mystics long for in their concepts of conservation and protection, a view of place elevated above the imposition of a transcendent concept of human progress that values development and human evolution over the sanctity of the land. The view is implied in the "Earth-Song" of Emerson's "Hamatreya," with its view of the old earth that laughs at the quickly passing life span of her "boastful boys." The view gathers political momentum in the writings of Vine Deloria Jr., who argues, "Ecology, the new left politics, self-determination of goals by local communities, and citizenship participation all seem to be efforts

130

🌺

The
Island Poet
and the
Sacred
Shore

to recapture a sense of place and a rejection of the traditional American dependence on progress — a temporal concept — as the measure of American identity" (74). Temporal concepts of religious experience, he suggests, lead inexorably to the secularization of religion and the dominance of doctrines such as manifest destiny and other concepts of a divine plan for the human race, a grand narrative whereby local deities expand and devour all the competition. Finally, Deloria argues that "whereas religions that are spatially determined can create a sense of sacred time that originates in a specific location, it is exceedingly difficult for a religion, once bound to history, to incorporate sacred places into its doctrine. Space generates time, but time has little relationship to space" (71).

One possible example of "a sense of sacred time that originates in a specific location" is Whitman's treatment of the tides in his island poetry. The tides become associated with the availability of certain spiritual forces and states of mind. The change of the tides provides a needed analog to the ebb and flow of the human soul and its susceptibility to different influences. And the tidal cycles, along with the rising and setting of the sun, generate the poet's faith that future generations will participate in the "vast similitude" that "interlocks all," as he says in another island poem dating from 1856, "On the Beach at Night Alone" (CRE 261).

Though the poet claims in Section 3 of "Crossing Brooklyn Ferry" that neither time nor place "avails," it is the distance of time that he especially denies. He specifies the particulars of the place he loves so thoroughly as to undermine any claim that differences of place are insignificant. But beyond the cycles of sunup and sundown, earthbound definitions of time, he clearly rejects the power of historical time to alter the human soul. As he writes in Section 5, in what seems to be one of many examples of his directly addressing future readers:

> What is it then between us?
> What is the count of the scores or hundreds of years between us?
>
> Whatever it is, it avails not — distance avails not, and place avails not,
> I too lived, Brooklyn of ample hills was mine,
> I too walk'd the streets of Manhattan island, and bathed in the waters
>   around it,
> I too felt the curious abrupt questionings stir within me,
> In the day among crowds of people sometimes they came upon me,
> In my walks home late at night or as I lay in my bed they came upon me,
> I too had been struck from the float forever held in solution,
> I too had receiv'd identity by my body,

That I was I knew was of my body, and what I should be I knew I
   should be of my body. (LG 1891–92, 131)

The "I" in this passage, and throughout the poem, is the soul talking, "struck
from the float forever held in solution," inhabiting the body and animating the islands, making holy whatever it touches, as the poet says in "Song
of Myself." Time never touches it.

The concepts of sacred space and sacred time celebrated in the poem
hold powerful appeals for the environmentalist imagination. But the poem
falters, from an ecocritical viewpoint, when the celebration of the human
perceptive and creative faculty — the soul — extends to include the secular products of human creativity, the vast spread of houses and buildings
and businesses, ships and docks and landings that fringe the shores of
Manhattan and southeastern Long Island. For all their glory in the eyes of
the admiring poet, these phenomena are historically bound and subject to
the whims of time. To that less than holy realm, the following chapter
returns.

131

🐾

*The
Island Poet
and the
Sacred
Shore*

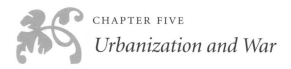

CHAPTER FIVE

Urbanization and War

With the onset of the Civil War, Whitman was, according to his own accounts, drawn out of nature and into history. His attention to the sacred time of tides and seasons and the sacred places of ancestors and origins yielded to a worldview in which time is measured by the events of social and political life and the sense of place is colored by the geographic mobility and dislocation associated with modernity. Not that he was ever actually absent from history or that his concept of nature was not historically conditioned, but his sense of historical mission gave way at times to a mythically oriented immersion in ceremonial time and sacred place. With the intrusion of the tides of war, the island poet was again suffused with historical consciousness.

We have seen how in poems like "This Compost" and "Passage to India" Whitman employs a rhetoric of turning away from the earth, questioning the intent of nature toward human life, only to turn back again, affirming finally a deep connection to the earthy root of all being, usually in an effort to reconcile human concerns with natural forces. And we have seen how in "Song of the Rolling Earth," while questioning our ability to communicate directly with the great mother and even our own bodies, which form "substantial words" outside the limits of language, the poet left open the possibility of knowing the body and the earth from the resonances that sound within the human soul. The "silence" of the earth and its indifference to the words and actions of its wayward human children were themes that continued to haunt Whitman in his writings from the war years, nowhere more clearly than in the remarkable *Drum-Taps* poem "Give Me the Splendid Silent Sun," which is perhaps his most powerful dramatization of the inner conflict over the enticements of a quiet life that resonates with calm creativity and a tumultuous existence amid the dense humanity of urban life, as well as his most direct treatment of the intertwined forces of urbanization and war.

The poem begins with a rejection of urban life and an affirmation of the pastoral pleasures he associates with living close to nature. "Give me the splendid silent sun with all his beams full-dazzling," the poet says, then reels off a catalog of pleasurable images — "the unmow'd grass," "the trellis'd grape," "fresh corn and wheat," "serene-moving animals teaching content," landscapes wild as well as enclosed and cultivated ("high plateaus west of the Mississippi," "a garden of beautiful flowers where I can walk undis-turb'd"), a simple domestic life with wife and family ("a sweet-breath'd woman of whom I should never tire," "a perfect child") — all the senses engaged and the general impression of the calm and quiet necessary for close communion with the earth, the desire for which gains emphasis with each repetition of the anaphoric "Give me," as if forming a prayer to Nature with a capital N: "Give me solitude, . . . give me again O Nature your pri-mal sanities!" (LG 1891–92, 244). But at the midpoint of the poem, the poet turns back, and the rejection of Nature that follows is never reversed as it was in earlier poems. This time it is not the earth that conceals its meaning from the curious poet or seems cold, indifferent, and thingish so much as it is the poet who, after looking first for comfort in nature — "tired with ceaseless excitement" in the city and "rack'd by the war-strife" (LG 1891–92, 244) — rejects the prospects of the silent earth and allows himself to be consumed by the clamor of the big city and the big war.

He adheres to the city, which holds him "enchain'd" till the soul itself, "glutted" by stimulation, yields to the attraction and tramples on his desire to escape (LG 1891–92, 245). On the one hand, the pejorative connotations of "enchain'd," "glutted," and "trampling" hint at the poet's resistance, but on the other hand, the diction suggests a version of rough erotic appeal, which, as critics such as Byrne Fone and Mark Maslan have suggested, was deeply attractive to Whitman in certain moods. Now the intensity of the city completely possesses the poet, obliterating his taste for simple pastoral comforts. "Keep your splendid silent sun," he says at the turning point of the poem: "Keep your woods O Nature, and the quiet places by the woods . . . your fields of clover and timothy, and your corn-fields and orchards." The promise of high stimulation overwhelms his resistance: "Give me faces and streets — give me these phantoms incessant and endless along the trot-toirs! / Give me interminable eyes — give me women — give me comrades and lovers by the thousand!" (LG 1891–92, 245). Instead of the country wife faithful and steady, he seeks promiscuous phantoms, the objects of his fan-tasy, their contact brief and ephemeral, reduced here to the exchange of looks and signs of consent — again the synecdoche of "eyes" recalling the war notebook with the manuscript version of "A Noiseless Patient Spider," the stranger communicating by "certain signs / O eyes wishfully turning!" (UPP 2:93). The poem ends by connecting the city's crowded eroticism with images of a Manhattan alive with preparations for war:

Give me Broadway, with the soldiers marching — give me the sound
    of the trumpets and drums!
(The soldiers in companies or regiments — some starting away,
    flush'd and reckless,
Some, their time up, returning with thinn'd ranks, young, yet very
    old, worn, marching, noticing nothing;)

. . . .

The dense brigade bound for the war, with high piled military
    wagons following;
People, endless, streaming, with strong voices, passions, pageants,
Manhattan streets with their powerful throbs, with beating drums as
    now,
The endless and noisy chorus, the rustle and clank of muskets, (even
    the sight of the wounded,)
Manhattan crowds, with their turbulent musical chorus!
Manhattan faces and eyes forever for me. (LG 1891–92, 245)

"Give Me the Splendid Silent Sun" is not usually listed among the "recruit-
ing poems" like "Beat! Beat! Drums" that Whitman wrote during the early
part of the war and later included in *Drum-Taps* (see Loving, *Walt Whitman*
9), but in many ways it fits the genre. If we think of the central voice of the
poem not first as the lyric embodiment of the poet turning from nature to
society but as the persona of a young rustic leaving the farm and the coun-
tryside to answer the call to war, which for the adventurous (and naive) soul
could only intensify the city's already seductive lure of economic opportunity and erotic enticement, then we might read the poem as an attempt to
put thoughts into the heads of young men of the type whom Whitman would
come to see as the heroes of the war, who left comfortable homes in the farm-
ing villages of America and joined the "dense brigade bound for the war." But
such a reading addresses only one of the poem's aspects — "aspect" in the
original sense of "face." Like many of the tropes in Whitman's best poetry, the
persona effect in this poem operates on an alternating gestalt, showing several faces (or facets) and sounding many voices at once. In harmony with the
voice of the prospective soldier is the voice of the older poet recalling that he
followed a similar path in earlier times, moving from the Long Island homestead of his ancestors to the small town of Brooklyn as a young boy, then on
to the great city of Manhattan as a youth in search of his fortune.[1]

Yet another voice in the harmonic texture sounds the theme of the reju-
venated poet, coming back to the city after the crisis period in the late 1850s

when doubts about his poetic achievement coincided with uncertainty over the particular version of urbanity he celebrated in such poems as "Song of Myself" and "Crossing Brooklyn Ferry," a view of the city founded on the excitement of exchanges with strangers and the electricity of America "en masse." By the time he published the first *Sea-Drift* and *Calamus* poems in 1860, the note of doubt had sent him searching for his lost inspiration on "paths untrodden" and the lonely shores of the old home place. "Give Me the Splendid Silent Sun" dramatizes the opposite movement, during which the poet "patched up his quarrel and resumed city life," as Wynn Thomas suggests, rejecting "as misanthropic and shallow his previously recorded wish to 'live absolutely alone' and 'to hear nothing but silent Nature in woods, mountains, far recesses'" (*Lunar Light* 167). In a provocative passage in *Whitman and the Romance of Medicine*, Robert Leigh Davis argues that the poem "suggests not only the urban basis of Whitman's vision but a change in his self-conception. The whole will not come back again, the poet knows; 'archaic' satisfactions no longer obtain" (114). Davis understands the new self-concept as one in which the old totalities of nature and soul give way to a "mature" understanding of the poet's vision as partial and fragmentary.[2] I would substitute the word "modern" for Davis's term "mature." With *Drum-Taps*, Whitman drifts toward a modernist understanding of nature and the city, revising what had been his Romantic or transcendental poetics, which Davis calls "epic" and "archaic." The terminology is interesting because it reveals a modernist bias against notions like the soul and the sacred (wholeness and holiness), which from the perspective of deep ecology and ecopoetics, as well as the "Native" or ethnographic views offered by such writers as Deloria, Hyde, and Hutchinson, may yet to have outlived their value. Davis's reading (and, to some degree, Whitman's own self-concept) follows a Whiggish or progressive trend that imposes a model of human growth upon cultural history, so that modern means grown up and archaic means childlike.

In my view, Whitman's work of the 1850s was fully "mature," moving to a level well beyond the work of his literary apprenticeship in the 1840s. What changes over the course of the 1860s is that his adherence to the theory of progress intensifies along with his renewed commitment to urbanization and his experience of total war. Whitman becomes a modernist, albeit reluctantly. "Give Me the Splendid Silent Sun" forms a record of his recruitment to the new ideology (or the ideology of newness). The war revitalized his lagging enthusiasm for his nation, his community, and his city and reenergized his mission as a citizen-poet — citizen in the sense of city-dweller as well as engaged democrat. But the war also substantially altered his understanding of his relationship with the earth, so that the attractions of solitary communion with nature began to fade and the resonances of a largely forsaken earth could only nag at him from the edges of consciousness. The shift is suggested in "Give Me the Splendid Silent Sun" and in a looser fashion appears as a feature in the very structure of the *Drum-Taps* collection, in which we find poems related directly to the battlefield, home front, and hospital juxtaposed with "nature poems" like "When I Heard the Learn'd Astronomer" and westward-expansion poems like "Pioneers! O Pioneers!" Jerome Loving has noted how Whitman used poems on topics other than the war to fill out the empty spaces in the short collection of *Drum-Taps* (*Walt Whitman* 286–287), so that to read them as "fillers" largely irrelevant to the theme of war makes some sense. A similar pattern recurs in the reflective prose work of Whitman's later years, *Specimen Days*, in which we find a long section of war remembrances ending abruptly, followed by an odd mix of prose snippets that Whitman claims were developed spontaneously during visits to the country for purposes of restoring his health through direct contact with the earth. What the nature writing has to do with the war memoranda is not totally clear.[3]

This chapter follows the development of an ambivalence in the poems written in the late 1850s that hardens into an opposition of nature and society in the writings associated with the war. One theme I wish to suggest is that the tension between war and nature explicit in "Give Me the Splendid Silent Sun" and implicit in the structure of *Drum-Taps* and *Specimen Days* — a tension already present in the poems of 1860 but intensified and clarified by the war — bespeaks not only the general trends of modernization but also the inner turmoil of a man wrestling with two modes of human existence that are extremely difficult to reconcile: on the one hand, the active principle of emotional intensity, human control over natural processes, and even aggression that characterizes the experience of total war and the building of big cities (as well as the pioneering mentality and the drive to empire), and, on the other hand, the more passive and contemplative openness that characterizes a meditative approach to life on earth. The turmoil leads to a sense of division between one's work (the province of human creation) and one's experience of the natural world (the province of divine creation and human recreation). In this turmoil and the resulting division of life experience, though without a fully realized political consciousness, Whitman anticipates the conditions that ultimately give rise to the environmentalism of the late twentieth century.

In the modern world, as viewed from the perspective of the environmentalist, the sense of connection with the sacred places of one's origin and the feeling of integration with earthly life grow distant. Life moves indoors; outdoor life becomes an occasion for recreation or something to be "weathered" and endured. Instead of the very medium of existence, the earth becomes first Nature — the mysterious and unpredictable godlike force, at times benign, at times hostile — and then the "environment," the indifferent setting of life, the place of resources and nonhuman objects. For the environmentalist, the mobility and prosperity of a modern, urban, technologically enhanced way of life come to seem, if not an outright curse, certainly a program of mixed blessings. The environmentalist outlook foreshadowed by Whitman's later poetry and prose is imbued with a sense of loss that may ultimately hinge on the loss of one's place in the world. It represents the dark side of the progressive ideology of the Enlightenment. It is the quiet voice that sounds in the background amid the loud celebration of human progress. It wants to know "What are we forgetting?" In the early editions of *Leaves of Grass*, Whitman represented himself as the poet of the New World garden, the poet of presence and the present, striding forth like "Adam early in the morning," full of health and hope. In the years following the assassination of Abraham Lincoln, however, Whitman became something like a refugee from the war, the poet of survival in a devastated land, the old ways haunting him from the past and his hope displaced onto an uncertain future.

Whitman's modernization begins with his shifting attitude toward the city in the prewar years — his own urbanization, as it were. Scholars have embraced the concept of Whitman as America's "first urban poet" (Kaplan 107), and rightly so.[4] Though he shares with such contemporaries as Emerson, Bryant, and the "schoolroom poets" a predilection for nature poetry, Whitman is distinguished among the best-known poets of his own time by his celebration of the streets and ports, the transformed environments and amassed peoples, the energetic movements, extensive technology, and myriad occupations of the great metropolis. As an urban writer — or at the very least, an urbanizing writer — he stands at the beginning of a new tradition in American poetry, which would ultimately include the quintessential modernists T. S. Eliot, Marianne Moore, and Ezra Pound as well as more identifiable followers such as Hart Crane, Langston Hughes, Carl Sandberg, Allen Ginsberg, Jack Kerouac, and Lawrence Ferlinghetti.

Whitman's urbanizing motifs resonate with the island poetics discussed in chapter 4 not only because he made an island city the focal point of many of his finest poems — including "Song of Myself," in which the poet appears as "Walt Whitman, a kosmos, of Manhattan the son" (CRE 52) — but also because the metaphor of the modern city as one island among many attains a special significance within the figurative systems of recent biogeography and environmental history. In one sense, every identifiable fragment of landscape has the character of an island; the condition of such a "world in pieces" — "the problem of habitat fragmentation," the insularity that "exists wherever Homo Sapiens has colonized and partitioned a landscape" — is largely an outcome of widespread urbanization (Quammen 549). And yet while fragmentation and partition are certainly facts of modern life, the pace of which increased dramatically in Whitman's time, we need to recognize the essential relationship among the parts. We need, for one thing, a better understanding of the flow between city and country, wilderness and civilization. As the environmental historian William Cronon argues, "The journey that carried so many people into the city carried them out again, and in that exchange of things urban for things rural lies a deeper truth about the country and the city" — a truth that contradicts "our nostalgia for the more 'natural' world of an earlier time," the "pastoral or wilderness landscapes . . . unscarred by human action" — the truth that city and country "can exist only in each other's presence," that "the world of civilized humanity is . . . created in the continuing movement of their encounter": "They *need* each other, just as they need the larger natural world which sustains them both" (18). If the city is an island, according to this view, it is not "entire of itself" but ultimately "a piece of the continent, a part of the main."

The critic who best captures Whitman's movement between city and country, or rather his sense of existing between the two poles of a burgeoning and shifting discourse in his day, is Christopher Beach in his chapter on Whitman and the city in *The Politics of Distinction*, which anticipates many of my readings though with a different slant. Beach argues that while Whitman is the only major poet of the nineteenth century commonly associated with urban life, it is not as a city poet that he achieves his primary distinction but as the celebrant of that "curiously liminal space," the "open road": "Rather than a regressive turn to the traditional dichotomies — city and country, urban and pastoral, prosaic and poetic, public and personal, sociolectic and idiolectic — the open road represents a new opposition in poetic discourse, one not merely between two types of environments and the linguistic structures needed to represent them, but between two opposing modes of sociopolitical experience" (107). Ultimately, he aims toward the obliteration of the boundaries between public and private existence, the unleashing of a powerful "sympathy" upon the world of social distinctions. Beach follows the evolution of this drive and its metonymic association with the representation of place over several editions of *Leaves of Grass*. He traces Whitman's development of a kind of documentary poetics, an "aesthetic of indifference" that illuminates but does not judge or form ideological associations with urban realities, a perspective both encouraging in a general portrait of humankind and discouraging in opening the theater of human suffering to public scrutiny. Finally, Beach shows the difficulty Whitman encountered in sustaining over the years his claim to have obliterated personal distinction as a paradoxical means of achieving poetic distinction. In his later poems that deal with urbanization, Whitman drifts toward the "extremes of rejection or idealization" in portraying the city and its inhabitants, appearing at times unable to absorb, to stand "indifferently" within the whirl of an urban space that over the course of his lifetime had grown violent beyond the poet's resources of identification and sympathy (148). In short, he had to face his own "inability to deal with the new urban environment" that evolved in the postwar years (149). Rapid urbanization appears to have become entangled in Whitman's mind with the failure of *Leaves of Grass* to attract an appreciative audience. He found himself appealing to the future and to the forms of traditional "authorship" and social legitimacy.

In the early poems, I would argue, it was neither the city proper nor the open road but the alternating insularity and openness of urban environments that attracted Whitman, a movement suggested even in the poet's self-concept with its wide swings from global (kosmos) to local (Manhattan's son). In joyful moments, he directs the attention of his city-dwelling ideal readers to the open road and exults over the flood tide that carries the ferry back and forth across the waterways between the big city and the surrounding small towns and farms. The city retains a strong appeal so long as it is separated from the country only by permeable boundaries, in the manner suggested by Cronon. Like many men and women of his generation, Whitman moved from country to city and back again many times. The urban experience of the poet's middle life, the experience that prompted many of his best poems, was inflected by his experience of the Long Island towns and villages, seashores and pastures. His poems bear the signs of a mind undergoing constant readjustments to new perceptions of geographical identity and community.

Whitman's love of the city was never uncritical, as he often shows even in his early journalism. "How it deadens one's sympathies, this living in a city," he wrote in the *Brooklyn Daily Eagle* in the late 1840s (qtd. in Burrows and Wallace 707).[5] But the first poems published in *Leaves of Grass* embrace a universalizing rhetoric that cuts through the problem of urban alienation by energetically denying it. In the opening poem of the 1855 edition, the earliest version of "Song of Myself," Whitman proclaims, "I CELEBRATE myself," to which he adds an imposition on the reader — "And what I assume you shall assume" — then completes the flourish with a negation of the difference between "me" and "you": "For every atom belonging to me as good belongs to you" (LG 1855, 13). The poet's unabashed use of the first person and even his own nickname — "Walt Whitman, an American, one of the roughs, a kosmos" (LG 1855, 29) — struck readers as an outrageous display of ego in his own day, but from a modernist perspective, his self-absorption is less outrageous than his assumption of what he called "sympathy," the ability through which he claimed to know the minds and hearts of others: "whatever is done or said returns at last to me" (LG 1855, 29). For the inspired poet, the sympathetic imagination knows no bounds, neither gender ("My voice is the wife's voice, the screech by the rail of the stairs" [38]), nor race ("I am the hounded slave . . . . I wince at the bite of the dogs" [39]), nor the extreme ranges of experience, such as crime ("Not a youngster is taken for larceny, but I go up too and am tried and sentenced" [43]), great adventure, and even death ("I am the mashed fireman with breastbone broken" [39]). The distance that the poet claims to overcome through sympathy is comparable to the distance that strangers feel from one another in the great city and also the distance between the poet and the mass audience in the age of print — another gap across which the poet reaches, addressing his readers as lovers in the second untitled poem of 1855 (later "A Song of Occupations"):

> COME closer to me,
> Push close my lovers and take the best I possess,
> Yield closer and closer and give me the best you possess.
>
> This is unfinished business with me . . . . how is it with you?
> I was chilled with the cold types and cylinder and wet paper between us.
>   (LG 1855, 57)

The untamed flow of sympathy, which Whitman may have seen as a corrective to the actual experience of city life and its tendency to deaden sympathies, culminates in "Crossing Brooklyn Ferry," which dates from 1856. In this, his finest celebration of urban life, the poet muses upon the pressing crowds and the traffic on the great fast-flowing river that separates Manhattan from Brooklyn. "Thrive, cities," he sings out in his closing section, "bring your freight, bring your shows, ample and sufficient rivers" (LG 1891–92, 134). The city and its natural environment flow together in

Whitman's imagination, as we see in a metaphor he applied to Broadway in a feature article from the same period: "that ever-flowing land-river, pouring down through the center of Manhattan Island" (qtd. in Loving, *Walt Whitman* 6). In an even more extravagant trope from his earlier journalism, he pictured Grace Church as "a ghostly light-house looming up over the porpoise-backs of the omnibuses, as they lift and toss in that unquiet sea" (qtd. in Burrows and Wallace 709). On the ferry, one of the city's earliest forms of mass transportation — "a striking instance of how, in a democracy, what used to be a privilege of the few was now being made available to all" (Thomas, *Lunar Light* 108) — the poet enjoys a magnetic connection with the throngs of people he meets: "What gods can exceed these that clasp me by the hand, and with voices I love call me promptly and loudly by my nighest name as I approach?" (LG 1891–92, 133). And now the human kinship the poet feels among his fellow citizens extends to the future, the distance of both the print medium and time itself yielding before the sympathetic imagination:

> It avails not, time nor place — distance avails not,
> I am with you, you men and women of a generation, or ever so many
> generations hence,
> Just as you feel when you look on the river and sky, so I felt,
> Just as any of you is one of a living crowd, I was one of a crowd,
> Just as you are refresh'd by the gladness of the river and the bright
> flow, I was refresh'd,
> Just as you stand and lean on the rail, yet hurry with the swift
> current, I stood yet was hurried,
> Just as you look on the numberless masts of ships and the thick-
> stemm'd pipes of steamboats, I look'd. (LG 1891–92, 130)

Whatever readers in his own time may have thought about the poet's faith in his oneness with others, readers in the twenty-first century are likely to look with cynical irony or with a deep sense of loss upon the poet's faith that his experiences would align with those of future readers. Whitman could not have imagined the isolation that comes with automobile travel — each individual enclosed within his or her own bubble of glass and steel, protected from contact with other people and from the choking atmosphere of exhaust, careening across the river on asphalt high above the water. It would take an act of denial on the Whitmanian scale for the modern reader not to feel the tug of resistance when the poet asserts, after a long catalog of waterfront images — the high-masted ships with white sails, sailors scrambling in the riggings, even the ferry itself, which came to be replaced by the Brooklyn Bridge — "These and all else were to me the same as they are to you" (LG 1891–92, 131).

Whitman's insistent universalizing has roots in Romanticism and may owe a particular debt to Emerson, whose concept of "self-reliance" included the dictum: "To believe your own thoughts, to believe that what is true for you in your private heart is true for all men, — that is genius. Speak your latent conviction, and it shall be universal sense" (259). But Whitman added a communal element that bespoke his experiences among classes of people and kinds of places that would have been utterly foreign to a person like Emerson. Historical scholarship has identified Whitman's outlook in the early *Leaves* with the artisanal republican culture of his father's time, a culture of artisans rooted in local life and marked by an almost fanatical devotion to comrades and an equally fervent suspicion of the centralizing forces of government and corporate industry. Wynn Thomas argues that the poems of the 1850s struggle to preserve the face-to-face democracy of artisanal culture against the insurgence of large-scale industrialism and what Alan Trachtenberg calls "the incorporation of America." According to Thomas, Whitman's vision was out of touch with the times even in his own day. The "old artisanal dream of a free, egalitarian commonwealth," which Whitman celebrated in the "aggressive new form" invented by the likes of Thomas Paine and Frances Wright, "was already antiquated by the 1820s and totally out of step with the giant strides of capitalist development" (*Lunar Light* 29). The 1855 *Leaves*, in Thomas's view, was "the direct result of a plunging economic crisis that severely hit the bastard artisan class to which Whitman then loosely belonged" (*Lunar Light* 33). Finding himself, like many Americans, unable to get work as a house carpenter, a job he had undertaken with his father in the early 1850s after stints at schoolteaching and writing for newspapers, Whitman began to write exuberantly hopeful poems whose energy partly conceals social and political fears just beneath the surface, which Thomas sees as a source of aesthetically powerful tension. Granting the aesthetic appeal of the poems, Bryan Garman has recently asserted that Whitman's artisanal republicanism was not only belated but in fact reactionary and that the attractiveness of Whitman's stance to later social thinkers, poets, and songsters — from Horace Traubel and Eugene Debs down to Woody Guthrie, Bob Dylan, and Bruce Springsteen — led to the development of an image of the working class that preserves sexist and racist elements at the core of American liberal thinking. According to Garman, the democratic character of the village artisans and farmers that Whitman admired tended to exclude people of other races and ethnic origins from the tightly knit workingmen's camaraderie and to closely circumscribe the position of women as well. Along these lines, Whitman's grandiose denial of the distance between himself and others (on the street, in the print medium, and across historical and cultural distances) may seem uncomfortably close to the rhetorical strategies that critics these days associate with imperial, colonial, racist, and masculinist discourses (see Anderson, Erkkila, Grünzweig, Pollak, Simpson, and Sorisio).

The historical critics focus primarily on social and political aspects of Whitman's artisanal republicanism, but we might also add a geographical dimension. The old artisans were the product of village or small town life. Their ways of life as well as their mode of production could not withstand urbanization and incorporation. Whitman's poems represent an effort to transplant the old ways or translate village life for use in the city. From this perspective, *Leaves of Grass* gives us a protagonist typical of urbanizing fictions, from Hawthorne's "My Kinsman, Major Molineaux" down to contemporary popular films like *Crocodile Dundee*. The Whitmanian "myself" appears in this light not as the arrogant misogynist, stealthy racist, or imperial self but as the overly familiar bumpkin, treating city strangers like old family friends, confronting urban aliens with the kind of insistent recognition formed in towns where everyone knows you, as Whitman would say, by your "nighest name."

Significantly, whenever Whitman reaches for a strong example of the kind of public intimacy he longs for in the 1855 and 1856 *Leaves*, his mind drifts back to the rural setting he knew as a village boy on Long Island. The model characters he presents to the reader come from his parents' generation, such as the old farmer in "I Sing the Body Electric," a poem that dates from 1855:

> I knew a man. . . . he was a common farmer . . . . he was the father of
>   five sons . . . and in them were the fathers of sons . . . and in them
>   were the fathers of sons.
>
> This man was of wonderful vigor and calmness and beauty of
>   person;
> The shape of his head, the richness and breadth of his manners, the
>   pale yellow and white of his hair and beard, the immeasurable
>   meaning of his black eyes,
> These I used to go and visit him to see . . . . He was wise also,
> He was six feet tall. . . . he was over eighty years old. . . . his sons were
>   massive clean bearded tanfaced and handsome,
> They and his daughters loved him . . . all who saw him loved him . . .
>   they did not love him by allowance . . . they loved him with
>   personal love;

He drank water only. . . . the blood showed like scarlet through the
    clear brown skin of his face;
He was a frequent gunner and fisher . . . he sailed his boat himself . . .
    he had a fine one presented to him by a shipjoiner . . . . he had
    fowling-pieces, presented to him by men that loved him;
When he went with his five sons and many grandsons to hunt or fish
    you would pick him out as the most beautiful and vigorous of the
    gang,
You would wish long and long to be with him . . . . you would wish to
    sit by him in the boat that you and he might touch each other.

(LG 1855, 78–79)

The portrait gives us the image of the village patriarch whose age and fertility, as well as his skill as a farmer, hunter, and sailor, account partly for his status, which is acknowledged by gifts given by local admirers and craftsmen — the fowling piece and the boat, and finally the poem itself, given by the artisan poet, whose admiration for the old man is rooted in the physical magnetism of his presence. The memory of how the patriarch commands the love of others inspires the general principle that follows in the next lines of the poem, which express the universalizing trend of Whitman's vision for the new urban life. "I have perceived that to be with those I like is enough," he says, "To be surrounded by beautiful curious breathing laughing flesh is enough, / To pass among them . . . to touch any one. . . . to rest my arm ever so lightly round his or her neck for a moment" (LG 1855, 79). But we should note how in these lines the kinds of specific details that grace the passage about the beautiful old man are now absent, leaving a generalized picture of an abstract community (that involves "any one" and "his or her neck"), a model for current life waiting to be filled in (or not).

When Whitman tries to imagine himself as the center of admiration in an urbanized culture of artisans, the result is similarly vague. In another 1855 poem, the fantastical dream vision entitled "The Sleepers" in later editions, appear these lines, for example:

Well do they do their jobs, those journeymen divine,
Only from me can they hide nothing and would not if they could;
I reckon I am their boss, and they make me a pet besides,
And surround me, and lead me and run ahead when I walk,
And lift their cunning covers and signify me with stretched arms, and
    resume the way;
Onward we move, a gay gang of blackguards with mirthshouting
    music and wildflapping pennants of joy. (LG 1855, 71)

The use of the term "journeymen" is significant in hearkening back to a group of skilled artisans who remained free to work from job to job and were thus not fully subject to corporate control — the very group that was disappearing into the new system. The movement in the streets and the unruly camaraderie suggest the conditions that erupted into workers' riots frequently during the economic troubles of midcentury New York, with its growing pains associated both with urbanization and with market fluctuations arising from foreign trade, the emerging globalization on which the great port of New York depended for its ascendancy (see Spann; see also Burrows and Wallace). But again the detail is missing. These "journeymen divine" have no faces and are ironically reduced to their function, serving the boss who is also their pet. So schematic is the representation of this "gay gang of blackguards" that we are tempted to see them as symbolic, perhaps a trope for some characteristics of the speaker himself, or again as a hopeful model yet to be filled in or fleshed out, Whitman's artisanal ideal applied but vaguely to the realities of urban life.

When the "Sleepers" does give us a more vivid picture of human sympathy, it comes in the form of another vignette from village life taken from the previous generation. The story seems intended to provide a model for affection arising from chance encounters, a situation that becomes for Whitman (as it did for Baudelaire and other urbanizing poets) a poignant phenomenon of city life:

Now I tell what my mother told me today as we sat at dinner
  together,
Of when she was a nearly grown girl living home with her parents on
  the old homestead.

A red squaw came one breakfastime to the old homestead,
On her back she carried a bundle of rushes for rushbottoming chairs;
Her hair straight shiny coarse black and profuse halfenveloped her face,
Her step was free and elastic . . . . her voice sounded exquisitely as she
  spoke.

My mother looked in delight and amazement at the stranger,
She looked at the beauty of her tallborne face and full and pliant limbs,
The more she looked upon her the more she loved her,
Never before had she seen such wonderful beauty and purity;
She made her sit on a bench by the jamb of the fireplace . . . . she
  cooked food for her,
She had no work to give her but she gave her remembrance and
  fondness.

> The red squaw staid all the forenoon, and toward the middle of the
> afternoon she went away;
> O my mother was loth to have her go away,
> All the week she thought of her .... she watched for her many a month,
> She remembered her many a winter and many a summer,
> But the red squaw never came nor was heard of there again.
>
> (LG 1855, 74)

The passage holds out the possibility of love among strangers, momentary
but deep. But the setting of the "old homestead" seems to matter in a special way. The possibility of chance intimacy increases with the old habit of
entertaining strangers who come calling unexpectedly. The theme was still
viable in the rural setting of country blues music in the early twentieth century, as we see, for example, in Mississippi John Hurt's song "Make Me a
Pallet on Your Floor," with the lines, "Never turn a stranger from your door,
/ Might be your best friend come calling and you would never know."

The idea of admitting unknown visitors at the door can only seem dangerous to people weaned on urban experience in modern times, and yet
again and again Whitman celebrates the possibility of not only hospitality
but love among strangers in city life. The poem "Once I Pass'd through a
Populous City" offers a good example:

> ONCE I pass'd through a populous city imprinting my brain for
> future use with its shows, architecture, customs, traditions,
> Yet now of all that city I remember only a woman I casually met
> there who detain'd me for love of me,
> Day by day and night by night we were together — all else has been
> long forgotten by me,
> I remember I say only that woman who passionately clung to me,
> Again we wander, we love, we separate again,
> Again she holds me by the hand, I must not go,
> I see her close beside me with silent lips sad and tremulous.
>
> (LG 1891–92, 94)

The "sad and tremulous" lips — comparable to the synecdochic eyes of the
urban "phantoms" in "Give Me the Splendid Silent Sun" — offer the single
detail of an otherwise schematic portrait, which, compared to the loving
image conjured by the mother's memory of the American Indian woman,
seems sketchy to the point of being unconvincing.

Yet more remarkable is the fact that the manuscript for the poem reveals
that it was originally about a man, not a woman. Whitman changed the

gender for the first published version in the 1860 *Leaves of Grass* (Loving, *Walt Whitman* 249–250). Whatever his motive — whether to conceal the homosexual emotion or to balance the number of poems in the book devoted to same-sex and heterosexual love — we need also to recognize that the quality of interchangeability is made possible by the abstracting imagination associated with the urbanizing experience. The trend toward this particular version of abstraction points toward imagism and Ezra Pound's famous two-line poem of urban vision, "In a Station at the Metro" — "The apparition of these faces in the crowd; / Petals on a wet, black bough" (Pound, in Ellmann 502) — in which the people are reduced to the generality of faces, their lack of substance suggested in the word "apparition," anticipated by Whitman's "phantoms"; nature becomes a mere reference, the people substituting for the schematic tree of Pound's imagination (petals on a bough). In "Once I Pass'd through a Populous City," the faceless one who "detains" the poet is hardly a person at all but rather a fantasy figure, an image perhaps of unfulfilled longing reduced to the virtual synecdoche of "lips sad and tremulous," the gender a matter of seeming indifference.

But of course gender and sexuality can never be matters of indifference to close readers of *Leaves of Grass*, especially the 1860 edition, the first to include the notorious *Calamus* poems, which have come to be identified as Whitman's most transparent representation of homoerotic emotion and which, as it turns out, also exhibit a deep concern with the interplay of urban and rural life. Here, against a background of advancing ambivalence about the city and its attractions, we see Whitman beginning to struggle with his earlier faith in the sympathetic imagination as a foundation for the love of comrades. The *Calamus* poems alternate between a celebration of erotic opportunity in the city and a profound sense of tragic alienation from humanity en masse. The enthusiasm of the celebratory poems — such as Calamus 18 (later titled "City of Orgies"), a poem that treats the Manhattan themes repeated a few years later in "Give Me the Splendid Silent Sun" — may well arise from an increased opportunity for love among men in the urban setting, the kind of situation that, by the end of the nineteenth century, drew gay men out of the provinces and into the city. This movement, which may well have begun in Whitman's day, is powerfully documented in the work of the historian and ethnographer George Chauncey, beginning with *Gay New York*. The historical situation before 1860 is blurrier, though at least one scholar — Michael Milner in his essay "The Fear Passing the Love of Women: Sodomy and Male Sentimental

Citizenship in the Antebellum City" — has argued that "a constellation of feelings, many revolving around the sexual . . . , came to undergird an ideology of male sentimental citizenship . . . in the years of rapid urban growth and social transformation (economic and racial) before the Civil War as it became more difficult for (and thus more imperative that) white, middle-class men properly police their homosocial entitlement" (45–46).

Calamus seems less interested in policing than in expanding opportunities. In a typical moment, Calamus 18 acknowledges the "frequent and swift flash of eyes offering me love," the "continual lovers" encountered in the streets of Manhattan (Blue Book 1:363). The act of "cruising" suggested in these lines becomes in *Calamus* the very model for the relationship between the poet and his ideal readers, as recent critics have suggested (see Helms, "Hints"; see also Coviello). And yet the enthusiasm for urban promiscuity and the chance encounter in the "carousing" persona — which to readers in our own time can only appear as a gay version of the earlier figure from "Song of Myself," the "free and flowing savage" — contrasts with a variant of the *Calamus* persona: the "tenderest lover" who withdraws from the stimulating and high-profile life of the city to take a single lover and go out on "paths untrodden / In the growth by margins of pond waters," as he says in Calamus 1, "away from the clank of the world," "Escaped from the life that exhibits itself, / From all the standards hitherto published" — the word "published" suggesting the world of public information always associated in Whitman's discourse with the big city — preferring instead the distant pond side with its aromatic calamus grasses and the quiet whispers of the natural world. The phrase "paths untrodden" is of course paradoxical if not an outright oxymoron. A path is by definition a trodden patch of ground, a place where people or animals tread. The phrase could be an intensification of what he calls in another *Calamus* poem an "unfrequented spot" (Blue Book 1:355), or it could be an appeal to nature, a rhetorical strategy defending the naturalness of the homoerotic emotion. Such an emotion is figured as a path that in the "world as we know it" — the socially sanctioned, heterosexual world — is unacknowledged and thus grown over and all but lost.

The finest example of a poem in this mood is Calamus 11, later titled "When I Heard at the Close of the Day," which changed very little in later editions of *Leaves*:

WHEN I heard at the close of the day how my name had been
    receiv'd with plaudits in the capitol, still it was not a happy night
    for me that follow'd,

And else when I carous'd, or when my plans were accomplish'd, still I
    was not happy,
But the day when I rose at dawn from the bed of perfect health,
    refresh'd, singing, inhaling the ripe breath of autumn,
When I saw the full moon in the west grow pale and disappear in the
    morning light,
When I wander'd alone over the beach, and undressing bathed,
    laughing with the cool waters, and saw the sun rise,
And when I thought how my dear friend my lover was on his way
    coming, O then I was happy,
O then each breath tasted sweeter, and all that day my food nourish'd
    me more, and the beautiful day pass'd well,
And the next came with equal joy, and with the next at evening came
    my friend,
And that night while all was still I heard the waters roll slowly
    continually up the shores,
I heard the hissing rustle of the liquid and sands as directed to me
    whispering to congratulate me,
For the one I love most lay sleeping by me under the same cover in
    the cool night,
In the stillness in the autumn moonbeams his face was inclined
    toward me,
And his arm lay lightly around my breast — and that night I was happy.

                                (LG 1891–92, 102–103)

The poet retreats entirely from the uproar of the city and finds his way back
to the wild island seashore. The whispering waters recall the ocean-mother
of "Out of the Cradle Endlessly Rocking," and the poet's deafness to "plaudits in the capital" suggests the rejection of former poetic achievements,
such as we find in "As I Ebb'd with the Ocean of Life" (see chapter 4). Plaudits
in the capital and accomplished plans, the controlling concerns of a career
as a public and national poet, fall away before the happiness of quiet communion with the earth — "inhaling the ripe breath of autumn," "undressing [and] laughing with the cool waters" — actions in which the love of
nature anticipates the love of the "dear friend" and that are finally realized
with the lover himself: "sleeping [. . .] under the same cover in the cool
night," the waters and sand "whispering to congratulate me." In this vision
of loving communion, modeled on the quietness and subtlety of communion with the earth, nature stands in contrast with the city and becomes
the place of retreat away from the "blab of the pavements" and other young

men cruising and carousing. Ironically, Whitman gives us an image of gay love that requires fleeing the very city that creates the conditions for gay community in the first place, drawing young men out of the country and into the "midnight orgies" of the urban centers. Again, the movement between city and country tends to heighten the contrast in the manner critiqued by Cronon. The rural place where the lovers meet in this poem offers a setting "wholly other" from that of the urban environment. The Romantic division between the "world" of humankind and the nature of pagans and gods that we find in Wordworth's "The World Is Too Much With Us" now makes its appearance in *Leaves of Grass*.

What we begin to feel in *Calamus* is that the identifications celebrated in "Song of Myself" and "Crossing Brooklyn Ferry"—the one and the many, the urban and the rural, the universal and the particular — are beginning to divide. Even Whitman's insistent identification of his love for nature and the love he feels for his "dear friend" in "When I Heard at the Close of the Day" has a distinctive rhetorical quality, the hint of an argument. As Kenneth Burke remarks in *A Rhetoric of Motives*, identification generally proceeds from an original condition of division — the politician from the distant capital reminds an audience of farmers about his experience of growing up on the farm, for example. The 1860 *Leaves of Grass* displays an increasing awareness of divisions that beg to be bridged — country and city, nature and humanity, the love of man and the love of woman. The sense of difference between "the love of comrades" (primarily, for Whitman, male-male attraction) and the passionate sexual desire of man for woman — or to use the terms that Whitman borrowed from phrenology, adhesiveness and amativeness — is reinforced in the segregation of poems about the different kinds of male love in the two 1860 clusters *Calamus* and *Enfans d'Adam*.

Another instance of the old identities yielding to an analytical division and categorization is the replacement of a unified sense of time (the idea that time "avails not," as he claims in "Crossing Brooklyn Ferry," that past and future are "contained" in the present) with a more poignant recognition of the difference between past, present, and future. The theme of grief pervades the poems, centering on the experience of love lost into an irrecoverable past. The theme harks back to the origin of *Calamus* in a manuscript sequence of love poems that Whitman called "Live Oak, with Moss." The sequence seems to have chronicled the story of a failed love affair with a particular man, a story obscured in the more general celebration of "manly love" in the published version of *Calamus* (see Bowers; Helms, "'Live Oak'"; and Parker). In Calamus 9, a poem that appeared in the original manuscript and the 1860 cluster but was removed from *Leaves of Grass* in 1867 (after the war, when Whitman had to some degree recovered his sense of citizenship), the poet offers a lament in the darker mood. The past obsesses the poet and makes the present a living hell, the sense of place dissolving in grief:

> Hours continuing long, sore and heavy-hearted,
> Hours of the dusk, when I withdraw to a lonesome and unfrequented
>   spot, seating myself, leaning my face in my hands;
> Hours sleepless, deep in the night, when I go forth, speeding swiftly
>   the country roads, or through the city streets, or pacing miles and
>   miles, stifling plaintive cries;
> Hours discouraged, distracted — for the one I cannot content myself
>   without, soon I saw him content himself without me;
> Hours when I am forgotten, (O weeks and months are passing, but I
>   believe I am never to forget!)
> Sullen and suffering hours! (I am ashamed — but it is useless — I
>   am what I am;)
> Hours of my torment — I wonder if other men ever have the like,
>   out of the like feelings?
> Is there even one other like me — distracted — his friend, his lover,
>   lost to him?
> Is he too as I am now? Does he still rise in the morning, dejected,
>   thinking who is lost to him? and at night, awaking, think who is
>   lost?
> Does he too harbor his friendship silent and endless? harbor his
>   anguish and passion?
> Does some stray reminder, or the casual mention of a name, bring
>   the fit back upon him, taciturn and deprest?
> Does he see himself reflected in me? In these hours, does he see the
>   face of his hours reflected? (Blue Book 1:355–356)

The pain of separation leads him to a "lonesome and unfrequented spot," more an image of his mental desolation than a depiction of a place. He is in fact indifferent to place at this point; "speeding swiftly the country roads, or through the city streets, or pacing miles and miles," it's all the same to him. The anguish over the loss of the lover expands into a general sense of alienation: "I wonder if other men ever have the like, out of the like feelings? / Is there even one other like me — distracted — his friend, his lover, lost to him?"[6] It may well have been the pain of past and present that led the poet of the 1860 *Leaves* to a form of idealism that would color his works ever after — a displacement of his hopes for the realization of democracy onto the future, an indication of his dissatisfaction with the present. Dominant in works of the 1870s, such as "Passage to India" and *Democratic Vistas*, the theme appears in 1860 in Calamus 34 (later entitled "I Dream'd in a Dream"):

> I DREAMED in a dream, I saw a city invincible to the attacks of the
>   whole of the rest of the earth,
> I dreamed that was the new City of Friends,
> Nothing was greater there than the quality of robust love — it led the
>   rest,
> It was seen every hour in the actions of the men of that city,
> And in all their looks and words. (Blue Book 1:373)

Calamus thus gives us a view of the world divided — historical time stretched out into its component parts, the past and the future tugging anxiously at the experience of the present; the "clank" and "blab" of the urban world at odds with the whispers of nature; lovers on untrodden paths hiding away from the crowds of strangers on city streets; the poet alienated from his former work, his hope fixed on the future. Modernization has begun its work, and with the intervention of the war, the process is at once intensified and modified.

   Whitman's most direct poetic treatment of the war comes in the book *Drum-Taps*, which he published along with a sequel that included "When Lilacs Last in the Dooryard Bloom'd," among other poems, in 1865–66. The book was incorporated into *Leaves of Grass* in 1867. In the edition of that year and in all successive editions, the war poems (in various arrangements) appeared together in the *Drum-Taps* cluster. Whitman's reentry into the social life and historical work of his generation is signaled in the original book by his clear invocation of poetic genres — his heritage in literary history, an acknowledgment of belonging to a poetic community over time. His use of the elegy, for example, in poems like "Lilacs" conforms to the very conventions that earlier poems such as "Out of the Cradle" and *Calamus* seemed to challenge or extend. Instead of using the theme of death in lamentations for a lost lover or as a means of communicating a general sense of tragic loss and depression, as he did in the 1860 poems, Whitman turns to the contemplation of death's reality in *Drum-Taps*, mourning the fallen soldier and the murdered president.

   Another type of conventional poetry that makes its appearance in *Drum-Taps* is the reflective nature lyric — the genre we have seen represented by "A Noiseless Patient Spider," a poem also composed during this time and published just after the war. A notable example from *Drum-Taps* is "When I Heard the Learn'd Astronomer," which appears as one of the odd "filler" poems in the 1865 book and which was moved when the *Drum-Taps* cluster was developed for the 1867 *Leaves*. Like the spider poem, the astronomer poem has become one of the most widely anthologized of Whitman's works largely because of its brevity and its stand-alone quality, its independence of the clustered structure within *Leaves of Grass*. Its popularity may also arise from the poem's seeming conformity to the generic type and its adherence to Romantic ideology, easily recognized features that are especially clear in the portrayal of the poet as a member of nature's priesthood. His special claim on spiritual communion with nature appears to put him at odds with science, at least the kind of positivistic science that was emerging as the professional norm in the second half of the nineteenth century, when careful measurements in the field and close experimentation in the laboratory came to replace the almost mystical model of close observation in nature practiced by Whitman's friend John Burroughs and by such luminaries as Thoreau and Muir (see Sloan 9). During Whitman's later life, professional science, like many other forms of human existence, was moving indoors, as natural history came to be regarded as more of an amateur pursuit, or was mediated by powerful technology, as science in the field was undertaken with the help of an expanding array of complex instrumentation (see Killingsworth and Palmer, *Ecospeak*, chapter 3; see also Battalio). Whitman's concern over the possible contribution of modern science to our understanding of nature, represented in the poem by the persona's presence in the astronomer's lecture, hints at ecopoetical issues related at least indirectly to the emphasis in wartime on command, control, and centralization.

In the terms of analysis developed in chapter 2, "When I Heard the Learn'd Astronomer" favors the view of nature-as-spirit over the scientific perspective of nature-as-object-of-study and even suggests that the two attitudes are mutually exclusive:

> WHEN I heard the learn'd astronomer,
> When the proofs, the figures, were ranged in columns before me,
> When I was shown the charts and diagrams, to add, divide, and
>   measure them,
> When I sitting heard the astronomer where he lectured with much
>   applause in the lecture-room,
> How soon unaccountable I became tired and sick,

Till rising and gliding out I wander'd off by myself,
In the mystical moist night-air, and from time to time,
Look'd up in perfect silence at the stars. (LG 1891–92, 214)

In one sense, the poem bucks against the trend toward modernization, rejecting the mastery of nature implied in the analytical devices of science. The poet himself, like nature, is "unaccountable," resisting analysis and categorization; he greets the stars in a spirit of kinship, with "perfect silence" rather than with the objectifying measures of the astronomer. The stars thus retain their mystery, their thingishness, and the poem recalls "This Compost," with the poet standing in awe before the unspeakable wonder of the earth and sky in the "mystical moist night-air." But in another sense, the poem departs from "This Compost." It represents an abandonment of the scientist within the poet, the lecturer-persona who could show us the compost as a worthy demonstration of the earth's power, who could say, "Behold this compost" and exclaim, "What chemistry!" By stepping away from the lecture hall and relinquishing the demonstrative mode of discourse, by treating mystical awe as an alternative response to the earth, sufficient in itself, the poet ironically follows the trend of increasing specialization and professionalization that characterizes modernity. The poet separates from the scientist, enacting the division of science and the arts in modernity — the condition of the "two cultures" lamented memorably by C. P. Snow. By the end of the twentieth century, the division would be so complete that the very idea of ecopoetics, which hints at a combination of ecology and poetry, could only appear suspicious to some members of the scientific community. In the essay "The Place of Nature," for example, the geographer Jonathan Smith, because he equates the entire field of ecopoetics with the Romanticized version of late-twentieth-century environmentalism or deep ecology, calls for a more realistic assessment of humanity's ecological dilemmas, one based on factual understanding and scientifically generated knowledge.

Certainly Whitman's poem resonates with the Romantic critique of science as an overly intellectual, hubristic complication of life, a form of understanding based on reduction and control. By the mid-nineteenth century, the sentiment of the astronomer poem and even its plot — the movement from indoor science to outdoor communion — had thoroughly crystallized into a genre of the Romantic lyric. The most famous predecessor was perhaps Wordsworth's "The Tables Turned," in which the poet chides a friend for preferring the indoor ways of the serious scholar: "Books! 'tis a dull and endless strife." In contrast, the lessons of nature come to one as sweetly as the song of the woodland linnet — "There's more of wisdom in it" — and the blithe singing of the throstle — "He, too, is no mean preacher." "Come forth into the light of things," urges the poet, "Let Nature be your Teacher":

Sweet is the lore which Nature brings;
Our meddling intellect
Mis-shapes the beauteous forms of things: —
We murder to dissect.

Enough of Science and of Art;
Close up those barren leaves;
Come forth, and bring with you a heart
That watches and receives. (Wordsworth 107)

In coaxing his interlocutor out of the study and into nature and in valuing a "heart / That watches and receives" over the dissecting and reductive intellect of the scholar, Wordsworth's poet foreshadows Whitman. But for the father of English Romanticism, Nature (with a capital N) offers its own lessons freely, providing a powerful substitute for book learning and indoor life. For Whitman, a generation later, the mystical moist night air and the stars command attention and silence, but the poet is far less ready to claim them as teachers. Rather, they offer relief, providing an alternative but not necessarily a straightforward substitute for "Science and Art." In Whitman's poem, nature is not a transfigured lecture hall but rather a place of retreat, qualitatively different from the indoor space, a place of healing for the "tired and sick" soul.

Closer to home (in time and place, if not in theme and attitude) is another predecessor in the genre, an early poem of Edgar Allan Poe, "Sonnet — To Science":

Science! true daughter of Old Time thou art!
    Who alterest all things with thy peering eyes.
Who preyest thus upon the poet's heart,
    Vulture, whose wings are dull realities?
How should he love thee? or how deem thee wise
    Who wouldst not leave him in his wandering
To seek for pleasures in the jewelled skies,
    Albeit he soared with an undaunted wing?
Hast thou not dragged Diana from her car?
    And driven the Hamadryad from the wood
To seek a shelter in some happier star?
    Hast thou not torn the Naiad from her flood,

The Elfin from the green grass, and from me
The summer dream beneath the tamarind tree? (Poe 38)

For Poe, the chief objections to science are its tendency to objectify (with its "peering eyes" focused on "dull realities"), to deny the emotional response to nature (preying upon the poet's heart), and to demystify, demythologize, and disenchant the world. Science has "dragged Diana from her car" and, like the woodsmen of Whitman's "Song of the Redwood-Tree" (which echoes Poe's poem), has "driven the Hamadryad from the wood."[7] In this mood, Poe recalls Wordsworth's "The World Is Too Much with Us," which prefers a pagan view of nature over the dully materialistic and disenchanted perspective of modern industrial society. While Whitman shares with Poe a distaste for the objectifying trend of scientific learning, he stops short (like Oliver Wendell Holmes) of romanticizing the old pagan view. Like the scientist, Whitman wants to see nature on its own terms (at least in the poems written before "Redwood-Tree").

Recent Whitman scholarship offers many attempts to account for Whitman's attitude toward science in this and other poems. Overall, scholars are reluctant to see the poet at odds with the science of his day. Robert Scholnick's essay "'The Password Primeval': Whitman's Use of Science in 'Song of Myself'" makes a strong case that, in the 1855 poem at least, Whitman is able to reconcile science and natural mysticism. In *Romantic Turbulence: Chaos, Ecology, and American Space*, Eric Wilson argues that Whitman's enthusiasm for science remains active even in the astronomer poem, rejecting Joseph Beaver's claim that the poem shows an "impatience with science" (Beaver 90–91). According to Wilson, Whitman grows impatient not with science in general but only with this particular astronomer's version of science. The poet favors a competing version, a "gnostic" method inspired by Lucretius that involves a "playful wandering" and an "openness to what the landscape might yield" (Wilson 133). In his entry on "When I Heard the Learn'd Astronomer" in the Whitman encyclopedia, Ed Folsom takes a similar position but adds a valuable historical layer to his reading. The poem, Folsom argues, is clearly a product of the war years and fits thematically in *Drum-Taps*: "While the poem's subject is obviously not the Civil War, the tenor of the war times is nonetheless reflected in the speaker's desire to escape a place of fragmentation (where the unified cosmos is broken down and divided into 'columns') and to regain a sense of wholeness. Union and oneness, pulling together that which has been separated—these are the subjects of many of Whitman's Civil War poems, and they are also the focus of this poem" ("'When I Heard'" 769). Folsom goes on to suggest that even so, the poet absorbs science's lessons and employs them in poetic ways. In the earliest version of "Song of Myself," the poet proclaimed, "Hurrah for positive science!" and addressed scientists directly, saying, "Gentlemen I receive you, and attach and clasp hands with you, / The facts are useful and real . . . . they are not my dwelling . . . . I enter by them to an area of the dwelling" (LG 1855, 28).

It seems to me an important difference, however, that Whitman could say "Hurrah" over factual science in 1855 but by 1865 could only grow "tired and sick" when he faced the astronomer's charts and figures. We might in fact surmise that Whitman sees in the models and diagrams of science a diversion from nature not unlike the old mythologies, which humanize the earth and therefore make it manageable. For him, the correct response is not to extract lessons from nature (in the manner of Wordsworth) or to create a human version of the natural world (in Poe's recourse to pagan mythology or the astronomer's calculations) but rather to respond soul fully in "perfect silence." Though in light of the history of science I would take issue with Wilson's intimation that Whitman's gnostic "science" was still a viable alternative in the nineteenth century, his reading of Whitman's gnosticism as a competing epistemological or phenomenological paradigm — an ecopoetics of chaos that resists objectification and reductivity — rings true. The detail of "much applause in the lecture-room" hints that a kind of professional jealousy seems to have gnawed at Whitman. Like the artisanal republicanism that he championed belatedly in the 1850s, the gnostic "science" that he gleaned from his readings in classical philosophy and in the eclectic natural philosophy of his day (in such books as *The Vestiges of Creation* and the medical texts that Harold Aspiz discusses as sources for *Leaves of Grass*) was out of step with the mainstream science of his times. What's modern about the poem has less to do with Whitman's acceptance or rejection of modern science and more to do with the tendency to feel alienated and to go to nature as a retreat from the pressures and competition of indoor life. The very sense of feeling "out of touch" and the need to recover something lost appear in Whitman as a kind of protoenvironmentalism, as does the need for release from the kind of concentration and control demanded by modern versions of scientific investigation.

Whitman's discomfort in the world that history offered to him is reflected in the direction that his experimentation with poetic genres was taking at the time. He sought the stability of writing within a well-known form while at the same time pushing against the constraints imposed by the form, sometimes opening the way into an emerging genre. One trend enacted in "When I Heard the Learn'd Astronomer," for example, is to refrain from offering the kind of explicit sermonizing moral or metaphysical lesson typical of nineteenth-century American nature lyrics such as Bryant's "To a Waterfowl" or Holmes's "The Chambered Nautilus." What Whitman was moving toward, along with a few other contemporaries (Herman Melville, for example, in such poems as "The Maldive Shark"), was the kind of observational lyric associated in the twentieth century with the imagist movement led by Ezra Pound or the open-eyed approach to things-in-themselves pursued by William Carlos Williams.

One of the best examples of the imagist trend in *Drum-Taps* is "Cavalry Crossing a Ford":

> A LINE in long array, where they wind betwixt green islands;
> They take a serpentine course — their arms flash in the sun — Hark
>   to the musical clank;
> Behold the silvery river — in it the splashing horses, loitering, stop to
>   drink;
> Behold the brown-faced men — each group, each person, a picture
>   — the negligent rest on the saddles;
> Some emerge on the opposite bank — others are just entering the
>   ford;
> The guidon flags flutter gaily in the wind. (D-T 8)

Much like Pound's "In a Station at the Metro," Whitman's poem resists the urge to moralize or sermonize but nevertheless uses the devices of poetic association (metaphor and metonymy in this case) to hint at tension between the human and natural worlds. The cavalry in crossing the river resembles a river itself. It takes a "serpentine course," and like the "silvery river," the soldiers' armaments "flash in the sun." But then there is the "clank," which may sound "musical" to the poet's ear in this context but which is always the sound of industrial civilization in Whitman's verse. Even though the poet refrains from questioning the naturalness of a long line of men on horseback, fully armed and organized into flagged units (called "columns" in military argot, not totally unlike the rationalized constructs of the astronomer, as Folsom suggests), the contrast to the river through which it splashes and clanks is strongly implied.

The reportorial restraint of the poem is not surprising considering its source: a news dispatch that described the movements of Union troops, from which Whitman liberally borrowed, as Betty Barrett shows in her essay "'Cavalry Crossing a Ford': Walt Whitman's Alabama Connection." Barrett hints strongly that what she understands as an improvement in Whitman's overall style — the spare imagism of the poem contrasting boldly with the untrimmed organicism of his earlier work — owes as much to the source as it does to Whitman's own artistry. But she fails to note how Whitman heightened the tension already present in the language of the news report, in phrases such as "serpentine course," by the imaginative addition of sounds to the visual imagery, including the "clank," a characteristic touch. Moreover, by placing the report in the context of poetry, Whitman brings the public discourse of newswriting into the realm of the poetic in a manner unheard of before his time, collapsing the distinction between the penny press and the epic account of a people at war. The photographic qualities of the poem (noted by Doug Martin in an *Explicator* article on the poem's artistry) and the reportorial approach — which may owe something to the Quaker concept of "bearing witness" in addition to the practices of journalism — appear in other poems as well, such as "Bivouac on a Mountain Side." Here the "shadowy" and "flickering" forms of men and horses and the "scatter'd" campfires of the army's bivouac stand in contrast both to the solid barns and orchards of the valley below and the greatness of the sky "out of reach" and "studded with the eternal stars." The implication of human transience and nature's permanence (with the pastoral life of the farm providing a middle ground, a deep connection to the earth that lasts for generations) is strong enough to make a direct statement seem superfluous:

> I SEE before me now, a traveling army halting;
> Below, a fertile valley spread, with barns, and the orchards of
>   summer;
> Behind, the terraced sides of a mountain, abrupt in places, rising
>   high;
> Broken, with rocks, with clinging cedars, with tall shapes, dingily
>   seen;
> The numerous camp-fires scatter'd near and far, some away up on
>   the mountain;
> The shadowy forms of men and horses, looming, large-sized,
>   flickering;
> And over all, the sky — the sky! far, far out of reach, studded with the
>   eternal stars. (D-T 70)

Whitman would continue to pursue the imagist approach in later poems, one of the most famous of which is "The Dalliance of the Eagles," first published in 1880. For years, Whitman scholars have followed Clara Barrus in believing that, like "Cavalry Crossing a Ford," the eagle poem was based on a secondhand account that Whitman got from John Burroughs, who had written about eagles mating on the wing in the early 1860s before he met Whitman

(CRE 273n). But Jerome Loving challenges this view, suggesting that Whitman may have actually witnessed the phenomenon on his visit to Richard Maurice Bucke in Canada in 1880 (*Walt Whitman* 400). In the poem, at any rate, Whitman remembers (or imagines) viewing the scene himself:

SKIRTING the river road, (my forenoon walk, my rest,)
Skyward in air a sudden muffled sound, the dalliance of the eagles,
The rushing amorous contact high in space together,
The clinching interlocking claws, a living, fierce, gyrating wheel,
Four beating wings, two beaks, a swirling mass tight grappling,
In tumbling turning clustering loops, straight downward falling,
Till o'er the river pois'd, the twain yet one, a moment's lull,
A motionless still balance in the air, then parting, talons loosing,
Upward again on slow-firm pinions slanting, their separate diverse
    flight,
She hers, he his, pursuing. (LG 1891–92, 216)

The subtlety of the imagist poems in *Drum-Taps* carries over into this performance. The tension resulting from the contrast between the instinctual behavior of the animal and the mannered behavior of human society is borne almost entirely by the word "dalliance" in the title, with its connotations of coy flirtation. The diction reverses the tendency of early poems like "Song of Myself" and "A Woman Waits for Me," which apply terms normally reserved for animal sex, such as "copulation" and "breeding," to human actions. The rushing clash of the eagles is anything but coy and flirtatious so that the poem's title is perhaps the closest Whitman ever comes to modernist irony in the page of *Leaves of Grass.* The unspoken lesson underscores the call of the earlier poems for a soaring and eaglelike energy in human love, a forthrightly sexual union verging on the violent. The difference in the late poem is the degree to which Whitman relies on his famous indirection. Where we find forthright treatments of human sexuality in the poems of 1855 and 1856, we have images from nature and ironic implications to carry the message in the new genre.

In addition to working within the genre of the Romantic reflective lyric and experimenting with a lyrical form that anticipated imagism, Whitman also laid the foundations in *Drum-Taps* for what would become for him something of a personal genre — the rhetorically rich but ecopoetically bankrupt ode to manifest destiny, which would appear fully realized in "Passage to India" and "Song of the Redwood-Tree," both produced in the decade following the Civil War. The prototype appears in "Pioneers! O Pioneers!" which, like "When I Heard the Learn'd Astronomer," seems to fit awkwardly into the collection of war poetry and would be moved to other sections when Whitman revised the *Drum-Taps* cluster for inclusion in *Leaves of Grass.*[8]

Reading the poem in its original context, however, shows how thoroughly the war came to pervade Whitman's thinking about human life on earth. War metaphors dominate Whitman's celebration of the pioneering spirit in this poem. The tools of the pioneer are called "weapons" in the first stanza:

> Come, my tan-faced children,
> Follow well in order, get your weapons ready;
> Have you your pistols? have you your sharp edged axes? (D-T 25)

As early as 1856, in the poem later titled "Song of the Broad-Axe," Whitman referred to the ax as a weapon, as he does here, and even associated it with firearms ("The slow progress, the scant fare, the axe, rifle, saddle-bags" [CRE 185]). But in the earlier poem, the weapon reference was moderated by the ax's connection with the central theme of creativity — with birth ("Weapon shapely, naked, wan, / Head from the mother's bowels drawn" [CRE 184]), with building and growth ("The shapes arise!" [CRE 193]), and with a new history liberated from the old regime of the "European heads-man" (CRE 191): "I see the blood wash'd entirely away from the axe [. . .] I see the scaffold untrodden and mouldy" (CRE 192). In "O Pioneers," the poet's categorization of the ax as a weapon fits snugly into a metaphorical complex centered on the notion of war with nature. Accordingly, westward movements are figured in the terms of military deployment:

> We detachments steady throwing,
> Down the edges, through the passes, up the mountains steep,
> Conquering, holding, daring, venturing, as we go[. . .] (D-T 26)

The language of rape — "We the rivers stemming, vexing we, and piercing deep the mines within; / We the broad surface surveying, and the virgin soil up-heaving" (D-T 26) — alternates with the language of battle:

> On and on, the compact ranks,
> With accessions ever waiting, with the places of the dead quickly fill'd,
> Through the battle, through defeat, moving yet and never stopping,
> Pioneers! O pioneers! (D-T 27)

From the perspective of ecocriticism, especially in the ecofeminist mode of writers like Annette Kolodny, nothing could be more disturbing than this development — the substitution of the earth for the enemy in the metaphor of war with nature and the recourse to rape as the privilege of the conqueror. From a viewpoint conditioned by the history of feminism and environmentalism, such language is no doubt reprehensible. But to judge Whitman too harshly would be unfairly anachronistic. He did not live to see the full effects of clear-cutting and strip-mining and the chemical pollution of the land that accompanied large-scale industry and technology in the twentieth century. He got only the slightest introduction to the effects of high technology in war with the repeating rifle and the machine gun, devastating though they were; he never saw the mass death of World War I or the firebombing of Tokyo and Dresden or the nuclear destruction of Hiroshima and Nagasaki. He got an elementary lesson on the concept of total war in the campaigns of Grant and Sherman, but he never saw the regular targeting of civilian populations that became common practice in World War II or the terrorism that followed in our time as an extension of that practice. The martial spirit he saw in the young soldiers he admired, their willingness to sacrifice and to die for their country, impressed him as the kind of commitment that America needed on the frontier. In this outlook, he anticipated the 1910 essay of William James, "The Moral Equivalent of War." Arguing against the necessity and inevitability of war, James affirms the "war-party's" admiration for certain "martial virtues": "intrepidity, contempt of softness, surrender of private interest, obedience to command" (668). James ventures the question, how can we preserve the virtues but avoid the fact of war? Here is his answer:

> If now ... there were, instead of military conscription a conscription of the whole youthful population to form for a certain number of years a part of the army enlisted against *Nature*, the injustice [of some people having to bear a greater load of nature's hardships than others] would tend to be evened out, and numerous other goods to the commonwealth would follow. The military ideals of hardihood and discipline would be wrought into the growing fibre of the people; no one would remain blind as the luxurious classes now are blind, to man's relations to the globe he lives on, and to the permanently sour and hard foundations of his higher life. To coal and iron mines, to freight trains, to fishing fleets in December, to dish-washing, clothes-washing, and window-washing, to road-building and tunnel-making, to foundries and stoke-holes, and to the frames of sky-scrapers, would our gilded youths be drafted off, according to their choice, to get the childishness knocked out of them, and to come back into society with healthier sympathies and soberer ideas. They would have paid their blood-tax, done their own part in the immemorial human warfare against nature; they would tread the earth more proudly, the women would value them more highly, they would be better fathers and teachers of the following generation. (669)

From our side of the environmentalist movement, James's almost glib use of the warfare-with-nature metaphor can only read like a dictation from the grim reaper. But again, our reading is conditioned by nearly a century of history. The metaphor itself not only endured but flourished well beyond James's time; it informed the concept of several conservation and peace-making organizations much admired by environmentalists, notably the Civilian Conservation Corps and the Peace Corps, programs that would no doubt have pleased William James. Not until the cold war years of the 1960s did writers like Rachel Carson and Paul Ehrlich begin to invert the war-against-nature metaphor with their notions of biocides and the population explosion. The peace movement tied directly into the environmentalist movement after Vietnam, and two decades later the ecologist Barry Commoner strove to extend the war-against-nature metaphor beyond its old limits. In his book *Making Peace with the Planet*, published in 1990 in conjunction with the twentieth anniversary of Earth Day, he writes:

> Clearly, we need to understand the interaction between our two worlds: the natural ecosphere, the thin global skin of air, water, and soil and the plants and animals that live in it, and the man-made technosphere—powerful enough to deserve so grandiose a term. The technosphere has become sufficiently large and intense to alter the natural processes that govern the ecosphere. And in turn, the altered ecosphere threatens to flood our great cities, dry up our bountiful farms, contaminate our food and water, and poison our bodies — catastrophically diminishing our ability to provide for basic human needs. The human attack on the ecosphere has instigated an ecological counterattack. The two worlds are at war. (7)

As with Whitman's, James's outlook on the world, and that of his whole generation, was totally reconditioned by the experience of the Civil War.[9] Neither Whitman nor James fought in the war, but both were absorbed by its spirit, the total mobilization of consciousness that seems characteristic of modern war. They stand at the beginning of an era in which the nation is perpetually mobilized, on the verge of war, informed by martial values, defined by war. They were early witnesses to the transformation of a nation of farmers and shopkeepers into a nation of warriors. Thinking outside the terms of war had become all but impossible. And the way people understood their place on earth, filtered through this martial consciousness, was transformed with devastating results.

CHAPTER SIX

Life Review

In the troubled years of the 1870s, confronting the depression brought on by ill health, which he always associated with his service in the Civil war, Whitman devoted a good deal of prose and poetry to explaining his poetic aims and justifying his work in terms of national need and public trends. These were the years he published "Passage to India," *Democratic Vistas, Memoranda During the War*, "Song of the Redwood-Tree," and "Prayer of Columbus." A poem from this period entitled "When the Full-grown Poet Came" addresses the division of humanity from nature and the position of the poet between the two. It was first published in the 1876 *Leaves of Grass* as part of a little annex attached to the second issue of the "Centennial Edition" — the last poem in a group significantly named "Bathed in War's Perfume" (CRE 550n). Dropped from *Leaves of Grass* in 1881, it was resurrected for the final annex ("Good-Bye My Fancy") of the 1891–92 "death-bed edition," presumably as an enduring statement of Whitman's ecopoetical aims:

> WHEN the full-grown poet came,
> Out spake pleased Nature (the round impassive globe, with all its shows
>   of day and night,) saying, *He is mine*;
> But out spake too the Soul of man, proud, jealous and unreconciled, *Nay
>   he is mine alone*;
> — Then the full-grown poet stood between the two, and took each by
>   the hand;
> And to-day and ever so stands, as blender, uniter, tightly holding hands,
> Which he will never release until he reconciles the two,
> And wholly and joyously blends them. (LG 1891–92, 416)

The trope of the poet holding the hands of allegorical figures revives an approach he had employed ten years earlier in "When Lilacs Last in the Dooryard Bloom'd." Instead of the personified abstractions "the thought of death" and "the knowledge of death," which appeared in "Lilacs," here the poet takes the hands of other equally abstract figures, "Nature" and "the Soul of man," the one "impassive" and distant (as mother earth is also portrayed in "Passage to India"), the other "proud, jealous, and unreconciled."

The need for reconciliation (and the persistent lack thereof) connects the later poem thematically to "Lilacs." The great elegy had been devoted to healing the rifts left after the war — the tragic distance between the war's dead and its survivors as much as the rift between North and South that kept the Union divided in spirit if not in law. "When the Full-grown Poet Came," likewise a survivor's poem, focuses on the rift between nature and humanity. By the mid-1870s, Whitman was giving renewed energy to the problem of bridging that gap, which appeared to grow wider with the technological advancement and urbanization stimulated by the war. The fact that he would revive this poem and place it in the final cluster of the last edition of his book suggests that he considered the reconciliation perpetually incomplete and the work unfinished.

For the last decade and a half of his life, Whitman kept going back to questions about how people relate to the earth and the role of the poet in mediating that relationship. In the late prose work *Specimen Days*, published in 1882, we find him reversing the movement of *Drum-Taps*, in which the poet of war is drawn out of nature and into the city. Broken in body and injured in spirit, he returns to nature in *Specimen Days*, but with a vision colored by his experiences in war and an urban life increasingly confined indoors. He modifies the protomodernism he had cultivated in the 1860s with a renewed Romanticism; indeed, in his late-life writings Whitman is more conventionally Romantic than he has ever been, and as such he foreshadows the discourse of modern environmentalism with its debt to the Romantic perspective of an alienated humankind divided from nature. And yet he remains the man in the middle, holding hands, desperately at times, carelessly at others. He pursues the idea of nature as a retreat from the effects of war and urban existence, even as he delights in the organization of city and country into parks and farms. He urges readers to follow his example as he strives to recover his own spiritual connection to the earth, resisting the crass materialism of his age, even as he struggles to maintain his image as the national poet in sympathy with westward expansion and the technological sublime. He becomes the poet of survival and recovery in a war-torn land, concerned over the fate of American democracy, but he also experiments with the perspective of the comfortable tourist, the travel writer taking prose snapshots of landscapes, urban and rural, collecting experiences in the compressed time of the railroad stop or from the moving car itself.

In this final chapter, I trace these movements in *Specimen Days*, looking back with Whitman at his earlier accomplishments and forward to the future of the American people and their relationship with the land. The story that emerges is a sad one, an image of the old poet struggling to get back to what matters most and only occasionally succeeding even to his own satisfaction. From there, we go briefly to the old-age annexes of *Leaves*

of Grass, poems that Whitman scholars have many times hurried over, giving the impression that the prose works dominate the later years.[1] From the perspective of ecopoetics, however, the late poems perform at least two functions of great value. First, they reprise important ecopoetical themes and genres developed over the different editions of *Leaves of Grass*, offering a kind of life review that through poetic practice rivals the prose version of *Specimen Days*. Second, they extend the idea that the body forms an ecological analog to the earth and suggest that it continues to commune with the old spirits, even to the point of death. In these inspired and inspiring little lyrics, Whitman takes us to the compost one more time. But we are not "going back to nature" so much as giving in. Now the compost becomes the aging body of the poet with death at the door.[2]

Specimen Days resembles the kind of life review familiar in studies of the aging process, as George Hutchinson has suggested in the Whitman encyclopedia. Embodying the literal and figurative ramblings of an old man, the book is loosely organized at best — Whitman himself called it a series of "garrulous notes" (SD 924). The sections roughly resolve into a five-part structure, as Linck Johnson has noted in "The Design of Walt Whitman's *Specimen Days.*" In an initial attempt to recover the mythic or ceremonial attitude toward place and time, the poet begins with the reflections on his ancestry and geographical origins that provide us with the image of the island poet (discussed in chapter 4). Next, as if to show how he came undone from these moorings, Whitman offers reminiscences and reflections on the war years, a slight reworking of his earlier book *Memoranda During the War* (1875–76), which he claimed to have composed as the war unfolded, often working in camps and army hospitals, and then published during his recovery from the paralytic stroke of 1873, when he was worried that America was forgetting the sacrificial war in its rush toward materialistic development. Apparently, he wrote the next section of *Specimen Days* during those same troubled years, a series of reflections composed outdoors on visits to Timber Creek and other rural sites away from the city of Camden, New Jersey, where he lived his largely indoor life. The last two sections are travel writings based on trips to the prairie states as far west as the Rockies, to Canada, and to northeastern sites closer to home, and finally a series of commentaries on other writers, including Poe,

Emerson, and Carlyle, in which Whitman situates his own work in literary history, a kind of intellectual geography.

The nature notes, which stand at the center of the book and which tend to puzzle readers interested primarily in the war writings, have won the admiration of recent ecocritics. Daniel J. Philippon, for example, argues that, like the best nature writers in our own times, Whitman's aim is not merely to describe the objects of nature in the spectatorial fashion of a travel writer or scientific essayist but rather to "encourage engagement with the non-human world" and that "the writing of *Specimen Days* was itself a functional tool for Whitman, a form of therapy to help him recover from the devastating series of physical and emotional difficulties he faced in the decade following the Civil War" (179–180). In using this approach, Whitman introduced methods and values that would inform the "back to nature movement" of the late nineteenth century. But he had to overcome the philosophical and formal problems of writing about an object (nature) that he considered largely beyond the limits of language, a problem he tried to solve with a special rhetoric appealing to spontaneity, intimacy, and immediacy and by structuring the text as "a series of discontinuous fragments" that "emphasize the ongoing, organic process of sensory perception" (Philippon 185).[3]

The strategy does not succeed entirely in overcoming the objective stance of the scientist or the abstraction of the philosophical observer. Witness the poet's impulse toward giving the specific names of trees, birds, and weeds, making lists and counting species, a practice likely influenced by his naturalist friend John Burroughs, who is mentioned several times in *Specimen Days*. The lists and names have the additional effect, however, of locating the notes in a particular geographical region and establishing the local quality of the observations. His lists lack the cold rigor of scientific analysis and accounting; they hardly even suggest the urgency of master birders with their "life lists" or amateur botanists and rockhounds with their near-obsession over collecting samples. Whitman makes lists casually, "negligently," in the same spirit in which he lovingly listed the names and descriptions of young working men he met in the cities. He was often moved by the merest acquaintance. The poet extends this practice to his nature writing, I suspect, to offset the tendency in these reflections to fall into philosophical abstraction in his praise of nature, treated here in the spirit of the Romantic capital N, complete with references to the identity theories of Schelling and Fichte. He virtually fights to maintain closeness to the earth — a struggle comically rendered in the memorable image of the old poet tugging and wrestling with hickory saplings and oak branches to "get into my old sinews some of [their] elastic fibre and clear sap" (SD 808). The passage recalls the theme of returning to nature in *Calamus*, especially when we consider what is obscured in *Specimen Days*, the fact that the elderly Whitman went to Timber Creek not only to be alone with nature but to visit his young friend Harry Stafford, whose family owned the land Whitman describes in these passages.[4] Instead of setting himself up as the bold exemplar striking out on paths untrodden, however, now Whitman confesses that, like other city-dwellers, he must fight to feel the "*emotional* aspects and influences of Nature," to counter the influences of "modern tendencies (from all the prevailing intellections, literature and poems)" (SD 813–814).

He very nearly succeeds. The section entitled "A Sun-Bath — Nakedness" comes close to recovering the spirit of 1855 as invoked in the earliest version of "Song of Myself," in which the poet vows, "I will go to the bank by the wood and become undisguised and naked, / I am mad for it to be in contact with me" (LG 1855, 13). Some of the madness may have departed, but *Specimen Days* offers an attractively mellow, old-age version of what he always called "the merge." "It seems indeed as if peace and nutriment from heaven subtly filter into me as I slowly hobble down these country lanes and across fields, in the good air," he writes, "as I sit here in solitude with Nature — open, voiceless, mystic, far removed, yet palpable, eloquent Nature. I merge myself in the scene, in the perfect day" (SD 806). The paradoxically "voiceless" yet "eloquent" earth affirms identity not by way of language and the mind but through the senses and the body of the old poet: "Somehow I seem'd to get identity with each and every thing around me, in its condition. Nature was naked, and I was also. It was too lazy, soothing, and joyous-equable to speculate about" (SD 807). Ultimately, however, he cannot resist the tug of philosophy and the need to divide and categorize: "Yet I might have thought somehow in this vein," he continues, giving in to the habit of interpreting and making intellectual sense:

> Perhaps the inner never lost rapport we hold with earth, light, air, trees, &c., is not to be realized through eyes and mind only, but through the whole corporeal body, which I will not have blinded or bandaged any more than the eyes. Sweet, sane, still Nakedness in Nature! — ah if poor, sick, prurient humanity in cities might really know you once more! Is not nakedness then indecent? No, not inherently. It is your thought, your sophistication, your fear, your respectability, that is indecent. (SD 807–808)

It may well be this irresistible recourse to the contrast between life by the bank of the creek and life in the city that appeals to ecocritics in our own time, who can identify with Whitman in his primary condition as an urban, indoor being. Despite the identification made possible by exposing the naked body to the naked earth, nature in *Specimen Days* is largely represented from the perspective of urban life. It is something to come back to — to re-turn to, re-treat to, re-create, re-cover, to get "back to nature." In this sense, nature is always a re-source rather than the source and ground of life itself. "After you have exhausted what there is in business, politics, conviviality, love, and so on — have found that none of these finally satisfy, or permanently wear — what remains?" the poet asks. "Nature remains; to bring out from their torpid recesses, the affinities of a man or woman with the open air, the trees, fields, the changes of the seasons — the sun by day and the stars of heaven by night" (SD 780–781).

Whitman returns to his old habit of direct address and urges the reader to join him as he moves out of his confinement into "soothing, healthy, restoration-hours — after three confining years of paralysis — after the long strain of the war, and its wounds and death" (SD 781). It is a commonplace in Whitman biography that the poet associated his own illness with the condition of war veterans and the recovering nation as a whole, but ecopoetics suggests that he also associated his confinement in paralysis and infirmity with the general condition of urban life:

> Away then to loosen, to unstring the divine bow, so tense, so long. Away, from curtain, carpet, sofa, book — from "society" — from city house, street, and modern improvements and luxuries — away to the primitive winding [. . .] wooded creek, with its untrimm'd bushes and turfy banks — away from the ligatures, tight boots, buttons, and the whole cast-iron civilizee life — from entourage of artificial store, machine, studio, office, parlor — from tailordom and fashion's clothes — from any clothes, perhaps, for the nonce, the summer heats advancing, there in those watery, shaded solitudes. Away, thou soul, (let me pick thee out singly, reader dear, and talk in perfect freedom, negligently, confidentially,) for one day and night at least, returning to the naked source-life of us all — to the breast of the great silent savage all-acceptive Mother. Alas! how many of us are so sodden — how many have wander'd so far away, that return is almost impossible. (SD 782)[5]

How far, he laments, has modern humanity departed from the likes of "a fine yellow poplar, quite straight, perhaps 90 feet high, and four thick at the butt. How strong, vital, enduring! how dumbly eloquent! What suggestions of imperturbability and *being*, as against the human trait of mere *seeming*" (SD 789).

Turning to the theme of language, and (I suspect) still bristling over a newspaper reviewer's dismissal of "Song of the Redwood-Tree," the poet falls into the mood of his astronomer poem in a brief critique of the kind of knowledge that does not go far enough to engage the soul:

> Science (or rather half-way science) scoffs at the reminiscence of dryad and hamadryad, and of trees speaking. But, if they don't, they do as well as most speaking, writing, poetry, sermons — or rather they do a great deal better. I should say indeed that those old dryad-reminiscences are quite as true as any, and profounder than most reminiscences we get [. . . .] Go and sit in a grove or woods, with one or more of those voiceless companions, and read the foregoing, and think. (SD 790)

The same scoffing attitude toward the most highly regarded products of human language — an attitude recalling the famous lines from "Song of Myself," "Logic and sermons never convince, / The damp of the night drives deeper into my soul" (LG 1891–92, 53) — is repeated in a section headed "Hours for the Soul." Here the poet extols the pure experience of night as a "placid and untellable lesson, beyond — O, so infinitely beyond! — anything from art, books, sermons, or from science, old or new" (SD 825).

The poetic merges with the rhetorical in such passages, for Whitman is giving us not the earth itself, his ostensible subject — no one could give that, as he well knew — but rather art, book, and sermon on the text of nature. In his attempts to merge again with the spirits of the earth, to get "back to nature," what the poet generally succeeds in recovering is not his own most original achievement — a poetic drama that aims to create a resonance in the reader analogous to the vibrations of the soul in direct communion with the earth. Instead, what we get is something closer to a recapping of the Romantic party line, enlivened somewhat by Whitmanian direct address: "Go and sit in a grove [. . .] and think." The appeal over time proves effective in ecocritical readings of *Specimen Days* largely because the same Romanticism informs modern environmentalist ideology, a perspective that has in recent years been seriously questioned as overly simplistic by works on urban history, environmental rhetoric, ecological justice, and sustainable development, though it continues to thrive in some circles of ecoactivism and ecocriticism. The general trend of the nature writings in *Specimen Days* points back to a few short poems of Wordsworth, notably "The Tables Turned" and "The World Is Too Much with Us," and points forward to such works as Rachel Carson's *Silent Spring*, Barry Commoner's *Making Peace with the Planet*, and Bill McKibben's *The End of Nature*. The key theme is alienation, the division of ecosphere and technosphere, or what Wordsworth called Nature and "the world."[6] Romanticism claims that the technosphere (the human "world") dangerously threatens the ecosphere (all of "Nature," including human life somehow) by failing to follow natural models, by playing god with the materials of the earth, by giving way to human hubris and greed regardless of long-term consequences. Though there is much to recommend in the more humble attitude toward the earth advocated in eco-Romanticism, the problem from the perspective of ecopoetics is that the language of one sphere tends to invade the other and create a dissonance that remains largely unchallenged. When the poet of "The Tables Turned" calls his interlocutor forth out of the study and into nature, he wittily lures him by claiming the superiority of nature's lessons, sermons, and moral truths. Nature speaks, we are told. But what does it say? It tells of truth and beauty most often; it tells us of the need to retreat and read poetry. Its power lies in its critique of industry, technology, science, and modernity; but the power is limited by its dependence upon its opposite. It tells us what we have lost but not how to get it back and certainly not how to go beyond where we are now. A cynic might say with some justice that the whole Romantic critique of modernity has to do with who is in charge of the Republic; it's the poet's bid for attention, if not control. If such is the case, it is no wonder that Whitman should adopt this perspective in his late writings when he was feeling neglected if not abandoned by postwar America.

The rhetoric of recovery — and along with it, the theme of survival in a devastated land and an equally devastated body — haunts every section of *Specimen Days*. Whitman offers specimens of his late-life experience to gauge the health of his country and himself, much as a patient gives tissue or fluid samples to the doctor. He explicitly uses the metaphor of the physician diagnosing disease in his critique of American political and spiritual life in *Democratic Vistas*, while in *Specimen Days* he adds an ecological examination and offers his own body as a synecdoche for the ills besieging the postwar nation.

In the section just before "Hours for the Soul," with its wonderful meditation on the night sky and its indictment of human products, appears a celebration of city life entitled "Human and Heroic New York." The dissonance between the two contiguous and seemingly contradictory specimens is resolved somewhat if we notice that the city is praised not for its wealth and civilization so much as for its mass of people, the aggregate of ordinary bodies, and the raw human energy that speaks to the old poet's soul, the kind of thing he still finds within his own experience at Timber

Creek undisguised and naked. He reactivates the themes of the island poet as he mingles in the "great seething oceanic populations," reviving the original spirit of "Crossing Brooklyn Ferry" and the early journalism (SD 823). The island city with its flood tide of people metaphorically unites with the ocean itself, "bubbling and whirling and moving like its own environment of waters"; the "mighty channels of men" become "current humanity" — in both senses of current, the flow as of water and the directly present now, the historical moment through which democracy seeks its outlet (SD 824). The island city, dissolved poetically into its oceanic medium, offers a tonic for the poet's soul:

> In old age, lame and sick, pondering for years on many a doubt and danger for this republic of ours — fully aware of all that can be said on the other side — I find in this visit to New York, and the daily contact and rapport with its myriad people, on the scale of the oceans and tides, the best, most effective medicine my soul has yet partaken — the grandest physical habitat and surroundings of land and water the globe affords — namely, Manhattan island and Brooklyn, which the future shall join in one city — city of superb democracy, amid superb surroundings. (SD 824)

The implicit appeal to nature in this representation of city life strives to overcome the division of wild nature and urban humanity at the heart of *Specimen Days*. So long as the island partakes of its environment, so long as the people of the crowds dissolve, blend, and merge, they speak to the soul, revive the creative spirit, form an analog with the earth.

Yet there remains one current of humanity, even in the island city, that is decidedly unnatural in the poet's view — "the full oceanic tide of New York's wealth and 'gentility,'" on which he comments in a section entitled "A Fine Afternoon, 4 to 6":

> Ten thousand vehicles careering through the Park this perfect afternoon. Such a show! and I have seen all — watch'd it narrowly, and at my leisure. Private barouches, cabs and coupés, some fine horseflesh — lapdogs, footmen, fashions, foreigners, cockades on hats, crests on panels — the full oceanic tide of New York's wealth and "gentility." It was an impressive, rich, interminable circus on a grand scale, full of action and color in the beauty of the day, under the clear sun and moderate breeze. (SD 845)

The poet is prepared to be impressed by the show, open to it, ready with his island metaphors, but the impression fails when he encounters the actual bodies, the flesh of the rich:

Family groups, couples, single drivers — of course dresses generally elegant — much "style," (yet perhaps little or nothing, even in that direction, that fully justified itself.) Through the windows of two or three of the richest carriages I saw faces almost corpse-like, so ashy and listless. Indeed the whole affair exhibited less of sterling America, either in spirit or countenance, than I had counted on from such a select mass-spectacle. I suppose, as a proof of limitless wealth, leisure, and the aforesaid "gentility," it was tremendous. Yet what I saw those hours (I took two other occasions, two other afternoons to watch the same scene,) confirms a thought that haunts me every additional glimpse I get of our top-loftical general or rather exceptional phases of wealth and fashion in this country — namely, that they are ill at ease, much too conscious, cased in too many cerements, and far from happy — that there is nothing in them which we who are poor and plain need at all envy, and that instead of the perennial smell of the grass and woods and shores, their typical redolence is of soaps and essences, very rare may be, but suggesting the barber shop — something that turns stale and musty in a few hours anyhow. (SD 845–846)

Whitman is obviously fascinated with the wealthy class that rises like a great tide above the ordinary flow of "we who are poor and plain" — just as he is fascinated with the beauty of Central Park and sympathetic with the employees who have more trouble, he insists, from "malarial fever, chills, and the like" than "from tramps, roughs, or in keeping people 'off the grass'" (SD 845). The very idea of keeping people off the grass draws no comment from the formerly self-proclaimed "rough" and loafer on the grass, but he seems at pains to stretch his metaphor of oceanic humanity to include the wealthy class, the steep ascent of which had been phenomenal in the years after 1860 when Whitman left New York, never to return as a citizen (see Beckert; see also Beach). The strain on democracy created by class distinction on this order was clear to the poet, and the distance from nature, from outdoor life, served him as a figure for representing the difference between common humanity and the moneyed classes. The trope is so important that he repeats it in the final section of *Specimen Days*:

Democracy most of all affiliates with the open air, is sunny and hardy and sane only with Nature — just as much as Art is. Something is required to temper both — to check them, restrain them from excess, morbidity. . . . American Democracy, in its myriad personalities, in factories, work-shops, stores, offices — through the dense streets and houses of cities, and all their manifold sophisticated life — must either be fibred, vitalized, by regular contact with out-door light and air and growths, farm-scenes, animals, fields, trees, birds, sun-warmth and free skies, or it will certainly dwindle and pale. We cannot have grand races of mechanics, work people, and commonalty, (the only specific purpose of America,) on any less terms. I conceive of no flourishing and heroic elements of Democracy in the United States, or of Democracy maintaining itself at all, without the Nature-element forming a main part — to be its health-element and beauty-element — to really underlie the whole politics, sanity, religion and art of the New World. (SD 925–926)

The appeal to nature applies to the book *Specimen Days* itself, which Whitman refers to in his last pages as "these garrulous notes"; the seeming aimlessness in fact conforms to a poetic principle, he says: "a humiliating lesson one learns, in serene hours, of a fine day or night. Nature seems to look on all fixed-up poetry and art as something almost impertinent" (SD 924).

The linking of nature and democracy, along with Whitman's appeal to nature as the foundation for an organic theory of art, must be seen as a rhetorical appeal, a plea for reconsideration of values. In *Experience and Nature*, John Dewey suggests that what we call real is what we value most highly. The same is true of what we call natural within the human realm of art and politics. Reality and Nature are what Kenneth Burke and others have called "god terms," an appeal to which represents the straining after authority in desperate times. Whitman's recourse to such rhetoric is a sign of his desperation, a part of his survivor's discourse. The mention of the wealthy classes in New York gives the game away. Democracy is threatened, but to let it go is to lose our connection with Nature itself, with God in effect. No wonder, then, that Whitman's mystical hours alone with the night sky become for him a vision of deification:

> As if for the first time, indeed, creation noiselessly sank into and through me its placid and untellable lesson, beyond — O, so infinitely beyond! — anything from art, books, sermons, or from science, old or new. The spirit's hour — religion's hour — the visible suggestion of God in space and time — now once definitely indicated, if never again. The untold pointed at — the heavens all paved with it. The Milky Way, as if some superhuman symphony, some ode of universal vagueness, disdaining syllable and sound — a flashing glance of Deity, address'd to the soul. All silently — the indescribable night and stars — far off and silently. (SD 825–826)

Nature is, in short, the god of a democratic people who forthrightly acknowledge the material base of their culture — silent perhaps, but quietly at work within the successes, and withdrawing from the failures, of the earth's wayward children in the New World.[7]

In contrast to the passages in which Whitman rhetorically reads God into Nature and Nature into Democracy, the travel-writing section of *Specimen Days* offers a prose variation on the protomodernist genre of imagist lyrics, such as the reportorial poems of *Drum-Taps* and late-life poems like "The Dalliance of the Eagles," in which a scene is represented with a minimum of commentary and the primary appeal is to the sense of sight. A good example appears in a single long paragraph entitled "Seeing Niagara to Advantage," worth quoting in full as an indication of the attitudes informing and effects arising from Whitman's touristic discourse:

June 4, '80. — For really seizing a great picture or book, or piece of music, or architecture, or grand scenery — or perhaps for the first time even the common sunshine, or landscape, or may be even the mystery of identity, most curious mystery of all — there comes some lucky five minutes of a man's life, set amid a fortuitous concurrence of circumstances, and bringing in a brief flash the culmination of years of reading and travel and thought. The present case about two o'clock this afternoon, gave me Niagara, its superb severity of action and color and majestic grouping, in one short, indescribable show. We were very slowly crossing the Suspension bridge — not a full stop anywhere, but next to it — the day clear, sunny, still — and I out on the platform. The falls were in plain view about a mile off, but very distinct, and no roar — hardly a murmur. The river tumbling green and white, far below me; the dark high banks, the plentiful umbrage, many bronze cedars, in shadow; and tempering and arching all the immense materiality, a clear sky overhead, with a few white clouds, limpid, spiritual, silent. Brief, and as quiet as brief, that picture — a remembrance always afterwards. Such are the things, indeed, I lay away with my life's rare and blessed bits of hours, reminiscent, past — the wild sea-storm I once saw one winter day, off Fire island — the elder Booth in Richard, that famous night forty years ago in the old Bowery — or Alboni in the children's scene in Norma — or night-views, I remember, on the field, after battles in Virginia — or the peculiar sentiment of moonlight and stars over the great Plains, western Kansas — or scooting up New York bay, with a stiff breeze and a good yacht, off Navesink. With these, I say, I henceforth place that view, that afternoon, that combination complete, that five minutes' perfect absorption of Niagara — not the great majestic gem alone by itself, but set complete in all its varied, full, indispensable surroundings. (SD 877)

Significantly, the famous falls, known for their roaring splendor, are silent in this poem, seen at a distance, framed by the experience of train travel. Likewise, the kind of tactile impressions that mean so much in the early poems, along with the tastes and smells both pleasant and offensive from the nature poetry and war writings, are never invoked. He seems to forget his own insistent advice that "rapport" with nature depends upon the "whole corporeal body" (SD 807). In his moments of greatest ecopoetical awareness, Whitman would have agreed with the powerful outdoor novelist Jim Harrison, who has a sententious narrator say in a moment of insight, "Books and television can't really extrapolate a world you must learn on foot as our ancestors learned it. True comprehension requires all the senses" (91). Likewise, in the odd little novel *The Day I Met Walt Whitman*, by Gregory Leifel, the narrator encounters the spirit of the old poet in a nature preserve only after donning a blindfold and allowing his sense experience of the earth to expand.

But here the sense of sight predominates, combined with the work of light and air. The scenic, photographic quality, a sort of poetic collecting of snapshots, becomes the norm in Whitman's travel notes, looking forward to Ezra Pound's imagism with its "intense, fragmentary, momentary seeing," as Ed Folsom puts it in his chapter on photography in *Whitman's Native Representations*: "Pound's definition of the image ('that which presents an intellectual and emotional complex in an instant of time') tied the movement to photography, and he even defined poetry in chemical terms. Out of imagism emerges Williams with his photopoetics, no ideas but in things, brief present-tense-captured glimpses on which so much depends" (111). The linking of photographic technology and tourism bears out the argument of Jonathan Bate in *The Song of the Earth* that "it is not a coincidence that picturesque tourism emerged . . . at exactly the same time as modern technology. Modern technology turns all things into what Heidegger calls 'standing-reserve' (*Bestand*). When a mountain is set upon, whether it is made into a mine or a nature reserve, it is converted into a standing-reserve. It is then revealed not as a mountain but as a resource for human consumption — which may be tourism's hungry consumption with the eye as much as industry's relentless consumption of matter" (254).

As if to make the analogy of his prose images with photography complete, Whitman places the "gem" of his Niagara impression into a kind of photo album or gallery of favorite images at the end of the section, momentary instances of rapturous or sublime experience — in the theater, at the opera, on the battlefield, or sailing off Navesink. What's missing in the gallery, I can't help but notice, is any mention of the sacred shoreline of Long Island, the sensual and intellectual center of Whitmanian consciousness in the most memorable poems from *Leaves of Grass*. The sacred site would not fit into this album of touristic images because its associative power is personal, private, and poetic, whereas the images of Niagara, the opera, the Great Plains (viewed mainly from the train, as it turns out), yachting in New York Bay, and the battlefield (prepared for viewing by the news reporter's sketch or the camera's eye) represent publicly sanctioned "sights," to which one travels for the purpose of "sightseeing" and the gathering of souvenir postcards. *Sights* such as Niagara are consumed in a few minutes and collected in the gallery of memory; *sites* such as the sacred shoreline of the island poet are absorbed over a lifetime and incorporated into one's very identity.

The brevity, the dating, and the specific mention of a short duration of time in the "Niagara" specimen conform to a general concern with temporality throughout the travel notes of *Specimen Days*. In the Niagara passage, Whitman describes his "lucky five minutes" and repeats himself at the end, as if the account of time deserves special emphasis: "that five minutes' perfect absorption of Niagara." The specimen on New York's "wealth and gentility," to take another example, is titled "A Fine Afternoon, 4 to 6." Even an episode entitled "Loafing in the Woods" shows a concern with time: "A snowstorm in the morning, and continuing most of the day. But I took a walk over two hours" (SD 876). This time-consciousness arises in part from the dependence of the partially paralyzed Whitman on train schedules and appointments with friends who can help him get around. Thus he begins the notes on his "jaunt" to Canada to visit Dr. Bucke by writing, "I left Philadelphia, 9th and Green streets, at 8 o'clock P. M., June 3, on a first-class sleeper, by the Lehigh Valley (North Pennsylvania) route, through Bethlehem" and so on, giving every major stop and the time consumed in travel, completing the journey to London, Ontario, he tells us, in "less than twenty-two hours altogether" (SD 877–878).

The concern over time has symbolic dimensions that go along with the practical considerations. His gradual loss of mobility and control suggests a corresponding depletion of his humanity. With both pathos and humor, Whitman would compare himself to a lower order of being in the introductory note to the last annex for *Leaves of Grass*, "Good-Bye, My Fancy," published a decade after *Specimen Days*:

In fact, here I am these current years 1890 and '91, (each successive fortnight getting stiffer and stuck deeper) much like some hard-cased dilapidated grim ancient shell-fish or time-bang'd conch (no legs, utterly non-locomotive) cast up high and dry on the shore-sands, helpless to move anywhere — nothing left but behave myself quiet, and while away the days yet assign'd, and discover if there is anything for the said grim and time-bang'd conch to be got at last out of inherited good spirits and primal buoyant centre-pulses down there deep somewhere within his gray-blurr'd oldshell . . . . (Reader, you must allow a little fun here — for one reason there are too many of the following poemets about death, &c., and for another the passing hours (July 5, 1890) are so sunny-fine. And old as I am feel to-day almost a part of some frolicsome wave, or for sporting yet like a kid or kitten — probably a streak of physical adjustment and perfection here and now. I believe I have it in me perennially anyhow.) (LG 1891–92, 407–408)

This "late-years palsied old shorn and shell-fish condition of me," set in contrast with the kittenlike spunk of his mood in this passage, Whitman goes on to say is the "indubitable outcome" of his years of service in the Civil War (LG 1891–92, 408).

The tragicomic loss of time and motion becomes a key theme in Whitman's old-age writings. He collects sights when he can no longer make an effort to comprehend places and thus captures the touristic mentality of modern life. To his credit, however, Whitman treasures more than any other the sights that cannot be reduced to a single, time-limited stop or captured in a photographic moment. He loves the Great Plains so well that the island poet in him yields for the moment to the prairie poet, a transition he very nearly completed in his late prose and poetry.[8] In a specimen he calls "America's Characteristic Landscape," he ranks the Plains higher than other vaunted sights in the tourist's repertoire. "I know the standard claim is that Yosemite, Niagara falls, the upper Yellowstone and the like, afford the greatest natural shows," he says, but he prefers the "Prairies and Plains," which "while less stunning at first sight, last longer, fill the esthetic sense fuller, precede all the rest, and make North America's characteristic landscape" (SD 864). Far from empty, the Plains offer human and natural details that entrance the camera-like eye of the traveling poet:

My days and nights, as I travel here — what an exhilaration! — not the air alone, and the sense of vastness, but every local sight and feature. Everywhere something characteristic — the cactuses, pinks, buffalo grass, wild sage — the receding perspective, and the far circle-line of the horizon all times of day, especially forenoon — the clear, pure, cool, rarefied nutriment for the lungs, previously quite unknown — the black patches and streaks left by surface-conflagrations — the deep-plough'd furrow of the "fire-guard" — the slanting snow-racks built all along to shield the railroad from winter drifts — the prairie-dogs and the herds of antelope — the curious "dry rivers" — occasionally a "dug-out" or corral — Fort Riley and Fort Wallace — those towns of the northern plains, (like ships on the sea,) Eagle-Tail, Coyotè, Cheyenne, Agate, Monotony, Kit Carson — with ever the ant-hill and the buffalo-wallow — ever the herds of cattle and the cow-boys ("cow-punchers") to me a strangely interesting class, bright-eyed as hawks, with their swarthy complexions and their broad-brimm'd hats — apparently always on horseback, with loose arms slightly raised and swinging as they ride. (SD 863)

Ultimately, however, he must condense and move on. He is not a settler but a tourist; he adds a snapshot of the Plains to his own album of sublime sights — "the peculiar sentiment of moonlight and stars over the great Plains, western Kansas" mentioned in the Niagara specimen — and writes an imagistic poem, "A Prairie Sunset," focusing on a time-limited moment, a scene yearningly remembered from the vantage of his final years spent as an invalid in urban New Jersey. But the task of comprehending the vastness of the prairies he leaves to poets of the future.

Whitman was destined to remain the island poet to the end, as we see in the remarkable first annex to *Leaves of Grass*, "Sands at Seventy," a life review somewhat different from that of *Specimen Days*, with an emphasis not on the sights of public life collected in the temporal increments of a railroad schedule but rather facing the elemental forces of sacred sites and the wide swings of seasonal change and whole human lives. Like the prose work, the annex begins by rooting the poet firmly in his place of origin with three short poems. The first, "Mannahatta," picks up the old theme of "aboriginal" naming that carries the past into the present, offers a personal definition, and treats the American Indian name as something worth recovering, "resuming":

MY city's fit and noble name resumed,
Choice aboriginal name, with marvellous beauty, meaning,
A rocky founded island-shores where ever gayly dash the coming, going,
    hurrying sea waves. (LG 1891–92, 385)

The second poem also "resumes" (or reassumes) an American Indian name, Paumanok, for Long Island and communicates the poet's identity with the place by picking up the theme of "When the Full-grown Poet Came," in which the poet mediates between Nature and the Spirit of Man, "tightly holding hands" with each for the purpose of reconciliation. In this work, he replicates the position of the island between the wild ocean and the lanes of commerce:

> SEA-BEAUTY! stretch'd and basking!
> One side thy inland ocean laving, broad, with copious commerce,
>   steamers, sails,
> And one the Atlantic's wind caressing, fierce or gentle — mighty
>   hulls dark-gliding in the distance.
> Isle of sweet brooks of drinking-water — healthy air and soil!
> Isle of the salty shore and breeze and brine! (LG 1891–92, 385)

In the third poem, for which again he chooses a place name of American Indian origin, "From Montauk Point," the dominant image gives us the poet standing at the farthest edge of the sea island, with all view of land and people obscured, "nothing but sea and sky":

> I STAND as on some mighty eagle's beak,
> Eastward the sea absorbing, viewing, (nothing but sea and sky,)
> The tossing waves, the foam, the ships in the distance,
> The wild unrest, the snowy, curling caps — that inbound urge and
>   urge of waves,
> Seeking the shores forever. (LG 1891–92, 385)

Though they were each published individually (within a single week in February and March 1888, in the *New York Herald* [CRE 507]), taken together as they appear in "Sands at Seventy," the three poems indicate a progressive movement outward, from the city (reduced to its island foundations) to the sea island with its strategic location and ample resources for human life ("sweet brooks of drinking-water — healthy air and soil"), to the point, where the poet faces the power of wild nature itself. Writing in the imagistic mode without commentary and moral, Whitman leaves the reader to work out the hints and indirections of "that inbound urge and urge of waves, / Seeking the shores forever." The suggestion is that the ocean brings in "the ships in the distance" but also comes to claim its own, and there the aged poet stands, on the sacred shore where he first heard the old mother hiss the low and delicious word "death." The sea is now stripped of human figuration, reduced to a "wild unrest" with "snowy, curling caps," an "urge" lacking the comfort of a human face and promising nothing but to continue, "Seeking the shores forever." The image is bleak but powerful, the poet uplifted "as on some mighty eagle's beak" — a Native image, with the poet's transcendence coming not in orthodox religious or transcendental terms but with the help of an earthly being, one suggesting the end of life as well as the ends of the earth, the limits of being. Though he gives the sense that he is somehow standing on the beak of the eagle (literally the island's point), the suggestion of his nearness to death also hints that he has become the prey of the great bird, carried away from the land that has been his home in life toward the wild ocean of uncertainty.

In the poems of "Sands," Whitman continues to seek metaphors that blend and reconcile people with the earth. He still personifies with some gusto. In "Broadway," his favorite city image of "human tides" appears again (LG 1891–92, 394). The movement of democracy in "Election Day, November, 1884" is portrayed as "stormy gusts and winds" that "waft precious ships" (LG 1891–92, 391). The sea sometimes resumes its human face, as in "With Husky-Haughty Lips, O Sea!" with its "tale of cosmic elemental passion" that "Thou tellest to a kindred soul" (LG 1891–92, 392), and in "The Voice of the Rain" the poet finds another analogous self — the rain that composes "the Poem of Earth" (LG 1891–92, 399). Following his lifelong habit of turning journalism (his own and that of others) into art and allegorizing in the genre of the reflective nature lyric, "Of That Blithe Throat of Thine" adopts yet another kindred figure from an account of arctic exploration: a "solitary bird" that continues to sing even in "the profoundest chill," and which reflects the chilled conditions of the poet's own old-age "singing" and "gay heart" (LG 1891–92, 394). In "You Tides with Ceaseless Swell," Whitman muses in the mystical style of William Cullen Bryant with an apostrophe to the ocean: "What central heart — and you the pulse — vivifies all?" (LG 1891–92, 389). And he pursues his organic theory of art in "Had I the Choice" with its appeals to nature, claiming that he would forego the offer of Homer's and Shakespeare's powers if he could choose instead the power of earthly forces:

> These, these, O sea, all these I'd gladly barter,
> Would you the undulation of one wave, its trick to me transfer,
> Or breathe one breath of yours upon my verse,
> And leave its odor there. (LG 1891–92, 389)

Here the poet's continuing experiment with meter — the irregular second line representing the undulation of the sea in contrast with the relatively regular iambs of the other lines — creates a sonic effect that, along with the mention of "odor" in line four, suggests communion with the earth that engages all the senses.[9]

But the most striking features of these poems, some of the best in American literature on the theme of old age, have to do with the stirring of life and hope within the reduced circumstances of a human being confronting his own demise. Again, the themes of the island poet come to the fore—survival and extinction. A striking example appears in "Continuities," which closes with these lines:

> The body, sluggish, aged, cold — the embers left from earlier fires,
> The light in the eye grown dim, shall duly flame again;
> The sun now low in the west rises for mornings and for noons
>   continual;
> To frozen clods ever the spring's invisible law returns,
> With grass and flowers and summer fruits and corn.

(LG 1891–92, 396)

The idea comes straight from "This Compost," with this difference: the composting matter, offensive and scary, is no longer out there, in the pasture or the woods, but in here, the body, which must pass from its current life if the frozen clods are to be transformed into the summer fruits and corn that follow "the spring's invisible law."

The thingishness of the body in old age, hinted at in Whitman's fanciful comment about his "old shorn and shell-fish condition" (LG 1891–92, 408), figures again in one of the last poems he ever wrote, "To the Sun-Set Breeze," included in the second annex to *Leaves of Grass*, "Good-bye My Fancy." The body is immobile and confined inside in the summer heat, a suffering lump of flesh, "sick, weak-down, melted-worn with sweat," until it is graced by a refreshing wind that enters the windows and doors of the dying poet's dwelling. When the heat breaks, the breeze comes like a muse, a spirit that takes him and revives for a moment the soul's creative power, awakening all the senses and inspiring the poetic vision of distant places full of beauty and meaning. The result is perhaps Whitman's finest old-age poem:

> AH, whispering, something again, unseen,
> Where late this heated day thou enterest at my window, door,
> Thou, laving, tempering all, cool-freshing, gently vitalizing
> Me, old, alone, sick, weak-down, melted-worn with sweat;
> Thou, nestling, folding close and firm yet soft, companion better than
>   talk, book, art,

(Thou hast, O Nature! elements! utterance to my heart beyond the rest
   — and this is of them,)
So sweet thy primitive taste to breathe within — thy soothing fingers
   my face and hands,
Thou, messenger-magical strange bringer to body and spirit of me,
(Distances balk'd — occult medicines penetrating me from head to
   foot,)
I feel the sky, the prairies vast — I feel the mighty northern lakes,
I feel the ocean and the forest — somehow I feel the globe itself
   swift-swimming in space;
Thou blown from lips so loved, now gone — haply from endless
   store, God-sent,
(For thou art spiritual, Godly, most of all known to my sense,)
Minister to speak to me, here and now, what word has never told,
   and cannot tell,
Art thou not universal concrete's distillation? Law's, all Astronomy's
   last refinement?
Hast thou no soul? Can I not know, identify thee?

(LG 1891–92, 414)

The spirit of life in the wind (the etymological root of "spirit," after all)
brings life back to the poet's tired and lumpish flesh. He is "laved" by the
breeze, the earth-lover to the end. He inflates with the vast prairies, northern lakes, ocean, and forest; the wind has touched them all, brings them to
him — places he can no longer go and could never completely comprehend. The spirit that comes over him now appears first as "something," a
suggestion of the "universal concrete's distillation" and "Astronomy's last
refinement" but resisting the poet's names, abstractions, and questions.
What it is remains unclear; what it does is to restore the sense of life and
the creative spirit of the questioner (and quester) in the poet.[10]

In the mode of ecopoetical awareness dramatized in this poem and in
such earlier works as "This Compost," the poet knows that the earth is what
resists the questionings and impositions of the human mind and what
remains when the human body dissolves into the medium of its own existence. The limits of human life become tolerable for the poet when he knows
that others will feel the breeze that refreshed him and walk on the sands
and see the night sky.

In the middle of writing this book, I felt a kind of Whitmanian thrill
myself, walking on a sea island beach at night and seeing the same formation of midsummer stars that I had read about that very morning in

Specimen Days: "In the northwest turned the Great Dipper with its pointers round the Cynosure. A little south of east the constellation of the Scorpion was fully up, with red Antares glowing in its neck; while dominating, majestic Jupiter swam, an hour and a half risen, in the east" (SD 825). Remembering the episode, it occurs to me that Whitman was right to say to the sunset breeze that "thou art spiritual, Godly, most of all known to my sense." The elements of the earth and the sky with their long lives and power of survival — the things of nature, including "the globe itself swift-swimming in space" — though they are never immune from extinction, are, by comparison to the brief life of human beings, eternal, the closest we may ever come to eternity at any rate. Sympathy with the earth, love for it, is a tonic we can count on as Whitman did, if not a cure, still the only balance for overweening human pride, imperial intelligence, and fleshly ambition.

Notes

1. In American literature, ecocriticism that canonizes prose nature writing as the central expression of the "environmental imagination" includes Scott Slovic's *Seeking Awareness in American Nature Writing: Henry Thoreau, Annie Dillard, Edward Abbey, Wendell Berry, Barry Lopez*; John P. O'Grady's *Pilgrims of the Wild: Everett Ruess, Henry David Thoreau, John Muir, Clarence King, Mary Austin*; Lawrence Buell's *The Environmental Imagination: Thoreau, Nature Writing, and the Formation of American Culture*; and Randall Roorda's *Dramas of Solitude: Narratives of Retreat in American Nature Writing*. Of these, only Buell's magisterial work mentions Whitman. The trend in American studies to focus on prose works as the key texts for advancing thinking about environmental politics is reinforced in the field of environmental rhetoric, which emerged alongside ecocriticism in the 1990s. See, for example, M. Jimmie Killingsworth and Jacqueline S. Palmer, *Ecospeak: Rhetoric and Enviornmental Politics in America*; James G. Cantrill and Christine Oravec, eds., *The Symbolic Earth: Discourse and Our Creation of the Environment*; Carl Herndl and Stuart Brown, eds., *Green Culture: Environmental Rhetoric in Contemporary America*; and Craig Waddell, ed., *"And No Birds Sing": The Rhetoric of Rachel Carson*. Another recent trend is to develop a canon of American poets who self-consciously develop environmentalist themes, such as Gary Snyder, Robert Bly, and Wendell Berry. In this vein, see Bernard W. Quetchenbach's *Back from the Far Field: American Nature Poetry in the Late Twentieth Century*, which begins with the prose canon before switching to the late modern practice of nature poetry in defining the limits of his study. Similar thematic limits but a somewhat broader scope characterize the 1985 book *Imagining the Earth: Poetry and the Vision of Nature* by the pioneering ecocritic and nature writer John Elder. An exception to the trend of first-wave American ecocritics to neglect poetry, Elder steers mostly clear of nineteenth-century poets who wrote before the conservation movement at the end of the century, but he does try to recover the late Romantic Robinson Jeffers as a key figure in modernity who represents nature as a model community, an alternative to the decadence of culture that appears in T. S. Eliot's work. Interestingly, the old division of poetics and rhetoric holds up all too well in the greening of the humanities. With the exception of Buell, who reads more widely than anybody, and such recent proponents of "ecocomposition" as Sidney Dobrin and Christian R. Weisser, literary ecocritics and scholars in environmental rhetoric rarely cite and respond to one another's work. In *Greening the Lyre: Environmental Poetics and Ethics*, David W. Gilbert takes a bold step across the divide between rhetoric and poetics and draws heavily upon rhetorical theorists from Aristotle to Kenneth Burke but still cites no recent work in environmental rhetoric and ethics. Angus Fletcher's *A New Theory for American Poetry: Democracy, the Environment, and*

the Future of the Imagination, which appeared after I finished writing this book, departs radically from previous work in its focus on poetry that has, in Fletcher's view, a more tenuous thematic connection to ecology. He treats Whitman in a historical tradition of descriptive poets rooted in the eighteenth century and including John Clare on one side and John Ashbery on the other in a two hundred–year continuum. As a genre, the "environment-poem," according to Fletcher, originates with Whitman. The poems in *Leaves of Grass* "are not *about* the environment, whether natural or social," Fletcher argues, "they *are* environments" (103). Fletcher arrives at what seems to me a special version of formalism that insists on a radical separation of these poetic environments from the natural and social world, which entails a further separation of rhetoric from poetics and a separate treatment of place and space. While American democracy, according to this theory, may have created the conditions for a shift in focus from place to space, the environment-poem does not seem to sustain a dialogic relationship with the social context that made it possible. Though he does not make the connection himself, Fletcher's treatment of the environment-poem in Clare, Whitman, and Ashbery seems to foretell not the ecological crises of modern times — the historical trajectory that I am eager to trace in my project — so much as the concern with virtual reality and cyberspace in artificial intelligence, computer engineering, and science fiction.

2. In the introduction to *The Ecocriticism Reader*, Cheryll Glotfelty follows Wallace Stegner in arguing for a definition that is "large and loose and suggestive and open" (xxii), but in comparing ecocriticism to Marxist and feminist models, she makes clear the importance of the political edge, as do the majority of the writers included in this influential collection.

3. See, for example, Jonathan Bate's *Romantic Ecology: Wordsworth and the Environmental Tradition* and Karl Kroeber's *Ecological Literary Criticism: Romantic Imagining and the Biology of Mind*.

4. In addition to Bate, see the outstanding sourcebook *The Green Studies Reader: From Romanticism to Ecocriticism*, edited by Laurence Coupe, in which Whitman appears briefly but significantly. We have also seen good article-length treatments of Whitman, including a protoecocritical essay by Gay Wilson Allen from 1980: "How Emerson, Thoreau, and Whitman Viewed the Frontier." Another well-known Whitman scholar, James Perrin Warren, has studied the relationship of the poet and his famous friend the naturalist John Burroughs. Lawrence Buell takes an ecocritical perspective on Whitman's urban journalism and poetry in *Writing for an Endangered World: Literature, Culture, and Environment in the U.S. and Beyond*. In *Romantic Turbulence: Chaos, Ecology, and American Space*, a study of how "the vision of an agitated kosmos — achieved with the aid of scientific inquiry and information — is related to an ecological ethos and logos — an effort to participate in the pulses of nature in deed and word" (xv), Eric Wilson includes an excellent chapter on Whitman. And there has been a flurry of ecocritical interest in Whitman's prose work *Specimen Days* (see chapter 6).

5. See, for example, Karla Armbruster and Kathleen R. Wallace, eds., *Beyond Nature Writing: Expanding the Boundaries of Ecocriticism*; Steven Rosendale, ed., *The Greening of Literary Scholarship: Literature, Theory, and the Environment*; John

Tallmadge and Henry Harrington, eds., *Reading Under the Sign of Nature: New Essays in Ecocriticism*; and Norbert Platz, "Rediscovering the Forgotten Space of Nature: A Plea for Ecocriticism in the New Literatures in English."

6. See, in addition to *Farther Afield*, the collection he co-edited with Greta Gaard, *Ecofeminist Literary Criticism*.

7. While I admire the overall thrust of Murphy's concern with genre, I would question his decision to keep the old categories of "writing" and "literature" unproblematically intact.

8. A readable yet subtle account of the growing theoretical complexity of the field appears in Jonathan Levin's review essay "Beyond Nature? Recent Work in Ecocriticism," to which I am indebted in this discussion. See also Laurence Coupe's cautionary remarks in his introduction to *The Green Studies Reader*. Ecology, he says, "is committed to resisting the global theme park which we call 'postmodernity,' and so must be especially careful to distinguish this condition from that complex body of ideas, potentially more favourable to ecology than to consumerist capitalism, which we call 'postmodernism'" (7). On the current theoretical challenge to ecocriticism, I share Lawrence Buell's views: "How hard it is in the present climate of critical opinion to think 'mimesis' without going to one extreme or another! — whether it be to overprotect ecocriticism against textuality or social construction theory by exaggerating literature's capacity to render factual environments or environmental phenomena, or whether it be to warn us off from trying to reopen such an unfashionable subject, or whether it be to want to play down or finesse the issue . . . by placing primary emphasis on artifact, culture, environment as the product of simultaneously interpenetrating technologies" ("The Ecocritical Insurgency" 705–706).

9. For good treatments of the phenomenology of nature and the problem of language from the perspective of environmental philosophy, see the works of Neil Evernden; see also David Abram, *The Spell of the Sensuous: Perception and Language in a More-than-Human World*.

10. Even this position, though, leaves me with an uncomfortable recognition. Though Mazel energetically exposes the "covert" political positions of environmentalists, he seems to have missed a connection of his own kind of thinking with reactionary politics. His reasoning sometimes reminds me of the position taken by the arch antienvironmentalist James Watt, President Reagan's secretary of the interior, who said in a 1983 interview that the environmentalists' "real thrust is not clean air, or clean water, or parks, or wildlife but the form of government under which America will live. The environment is a good vehicle to achieve their objectives. That is why you see the hard-line left drifting toward that position." See the discussion in Killingsworth and Palmer, *Ecospeak*, 36–40, and M. Jimmie Killingsworth, "Can an English Teacher Contribute to the Energy Debate?"

11. My interests in the pragmatic and dramatic qualities of nature writing parallel Aaron Dunckel's interest in the deictic qualities. See his essay "'Mont Blanc': Shelley's Sublime Allegory of the Real," which questions the ultimate usefulness of the preoccupation with mimesis and representation. I also realize that not all ecocritics are thrilled with the new theoretical complexities. Many entered the field to escape the profession's current preoccupation with abstract theory.

Understandably, they grow weary over the endless debates of the same old issues and frustrated with the pompous style, which writers like Bate and Murphy, to their credit, work hard to avoid. In the desire to open my work to the widest possible audience, I am sympathetic with the complaint of writers such as Frederick Waage, a pioneer in the field. Our conceptual writing suffers from a stylistic paradox, he argues; it "pleads for experiential content in opaque, audience-limited abstract language" (143). In "Seeking the Language of Solid Ground: Reflections on Ecocriticism and Narrative," another pioneer, Scott Slovic (one of the first three self-proclaimed ecocritics I ever met, along with his friends Cheryll Glotfelty and Michael Branch), writes, "Language without context, without grounding in the world means next to nothing" (34), and he argues that university professors "might be able to contribute to society's understanding of nature if we remember to pay attention to nature itself, if we don't lose ourselves in words, theories, texts, laboratories" (38). In a suggestion that I find very attractive (witness the opening of this chapter), Slovic also offers an insight that hints that the realistic pole of the ecocritical continuum, which seems most "naive" to recent theorists, might be viewed not as a stopping place or end point or point of departure but in fact a place at which criticism opens out into personal nature narrative, the telling of encounters with the resistant earth: "To the extent that our scholarship emerges from our experiences in and concern for the physical world of nature, we must seek an appropriately grounded language. The language of stories, charged with emotion and sensation, may be our best bet." Slovic's essay is a fine example of the kind of work he advocates. The concept is developed at greater length and with equal eloquence in John Tallmadge's "Toward a Natural History of Reading," which urges ecocritics to balance "erudition" with "engagement."

12. See Levin's remarks on Buell and Murphy, for example, in "Beyond Nature?" Interestingly, there was more attention to single authors and close reading in the first wave of books on ecocriticism. Bate's treatment of Wordsworth and Buell's of Thoreau come immediately to mind, as well as Waddell's edited collection on Rachel Carson. For an excellent example of an insightful second-wave monograph on a poet not automatically associated with "nature writing," see Gyorgyi Voros's *Notations of the Wild: Ecology in the Poetry of Wallace Stevens*.

13. On the ties of environmentalism to cold war rhetoric, see Killingsworth and Palmer, *Ecospeak* and "Millennial Ecology: The Apocalyptic Narrative from *Silent Spring* to *Global Warming*"; Kroeber, *Ecological Literary Criticism*; and Waddell, *"And No Birds Sing."*

14. For an account of the standard view that the war ruined Whitman, see the chapter on biographical and historical criticism in M. Jimmie Killingsworth, *The Growth of Leaves of Grass: The Organic Tradition in Whitman Studies*. For the alternative, see especially Roy Morris Jr., who says that "the Civil War saved Walt Whitman" in the very first sentence of his book *The Better Angel: Walt Whitman and the Civil War* (3). The same view is developed more subtly in Robert Leigh Davis's *Whitman and the Romance of Medicine* and Jerome Loving's *Walt Whitman: The Song of Himself*.

1. THINGS OF THE EARTH

1. The best treatment of the problem of personifying abstractions comes from Mark Maslan, who writes in *Whitman Possessed: Poetry, Sexuality and Popular Authority*: "In his 1802 preface to the *Lyrical Ballads* . . . Wordsworth warns his readers that 'personification of abstract ideas rarely occurs in these volumes' because 'I have proposed to myself to imitate and, as far as possible, to adopt the very language of men; and assuredly such personifications do not make any natural or regular part of that language.' And Wordsworth's wish to 'keep [his] reader in the company of flesh and blood' is endorsed by Whitman in his 1855 preface to *Leaves of Grass* when he calls art 'which distorts honest shapes or which creates unearthly beings . . . a nuisance and a revolt'" (6). Certainly Whitman shared Wordsworth's interest in what Maslan calls the "naturalization of poetics" (6), though there are limits to Whitman's debt, the best treatment of which remains that of the poet's friend John Burroughs in his 1867 book *Notes on Walt Whitman as Poet and Person*. See James Perrin Warren, "Whitman Land: John Burroughs's Pastoral Criticism." Burroughs claims, among other things, that Wordsworth wrote about nature but that Whitman wrote from the perspective of nature, embodying it in himself. I follow Burroughs (and Warren) in seeking to discover how Whitman redefined the subject-object relationship for ecopoetics.

2. The connections of Whitman's poetry with Taoism made him an important influence in Chinese modernism, as several of the essays point out in Ed Folsom's collection *Whitman East and West: New Contexts for Reading Walt Whitman*. On the ecological strains of ancient Chinese thought, see Mary Evelyn Tucker and John Berthrong, eds., *Confucianism and Ecology: The Interrelation of Heaven, Earth and Humans*, and Mary Evelyn Tucker and Duncan Ryuken Williams, eds., *Buddhism and Ecology: The Interconnection of Dharma and Deeds*.

3. Literally "that horrible sin not to be named among Christians." See my discussion in *Whitman's Poetry of the Body: Sexuality, Politics, and the Text*, 99–100; see also Loving, *Walt Whitman*, 184–185.

4. Gary Schmidgall develops this thesis in *Walt Whitman: A Gay Life*.

5. For a further treatment, see Gary Schmidgall, ed., *Intimate with Walt: Selections from Whitman's Conversations with Horace Traubel 1888-1892*, 84–86; and Killingsworth, *Whitman's Poetry of the Body*, 166–173.

6. Ecocritics, as well as the cultural and historical scholars Richard Poirier addresses directly, would do well to heed the warning that Whitman was "among the most elusive and easily the foxiest and most manipulative of American writers" (34).

7. Christopher Hitt's essay "Toward an Ecological Sublime" offers a history of the term and a definitive treatment of how the concept of the sublime regains much of the power it lost in modern times within the context of environmental crisis.

8. On deep ecology as a conjunction of mysticism, science, and activism, see Killingsworth and Palmer, *Ecospeak*, especially the introduction and chapter 1. For key texts, see Bill Devall and George Sessions, *Deep Ecology: Living as if Nature Mattered*, and Thomas Berry, *The Dream of the Earth*.

9. See Beth Jensen's *Leaving the M/Other: Whitman, Kristeva, and Leaves of Grass*, especially 53–54. Jensen misses the direct reference to the mother in the manuscript but still picks up the connection through the relationship of this poem to "Out of the

Cradle Endlessly Rocking," in which the mother/ocean "laves" the body of the son/poet just as here the sea is allowed finally "to lick my naked body all over with its tongues." See chapter 4 below for an ecopoetical reading of "Out of the Cradle."

10. The difference between Whitman and Thoreau here is illuminated by Gretchen Legler's somewhat overstated but poignant commentary on Thoreau in her essay "Body Politics in American Nature Writing: 'Who May Contest for What the Body of Nature Will Be?'" "Thoreau was in part constructing a certain white, masculine aesthetic of the body in nature," she writes, "a disembodied body that transcends its own materiality. Nature in Thoreau's work is constructed as a place that nurtures this white masculine aesthetic . . . . Thoreau regards the body as a site for battle between purity and danger. He argues that to have a relationship with the landscape, one has to transcend one's body. His writing reflects this disdain for the messiness of nature, his disgust for his own bodily needs and desires" (75).

11. My thanks to Matthew Miller of the University of Iowa for challenging me to account for this bizarre and difficult but highly rewarding poem.

12. A good summary of the key issues appears in Burton Hatlen's entry on the poem in the Whitman encyclopedia. Hatlen draws especially upon the work of Bauerlein, Larson, and Nathanson. My reading is most strongly influenced by Mark Bauerlein's *Whitman and the American Idiom*. I also draw upon Jerome Loving's reading in *Emerson, Whitman, and the American Muse*.

13. For a look at the roots of this tradition in the intrepretation of signs, see Stephan H. Daniel, *The Philosophy of Jonathan Edwards: A Study in Divine Semiotics*. My own use of the term "incapacities" in this chapter is intended as an allusion to the different but related phenomena discussed in Peirce's famous essay "Some Consequences of Four Incapacities" (*Peirce on Signs* 54–84). The pragmatists' frank acknowledgment of human fallibility makes an excellent commentary on the treatment of mental limits in thing theory. On Whitman's relationship to pragmatism, Stephen Mack's *The Pragmatic Whitman* provides an excellent starting point. See also Frances Dickey and M. Jimmie Killingsworth, "Love of Comrades: The Urbanization of Community in Walt Whitman's Poetry and Pragmatist Philosophy."

14. The fullest critical treatment of these themes appears in Maslan's *Whitman Possessed*, though his reading of the conjoined concepts of possession, inspiration, and sexual power in Whitman is not as original as he himself suggests it is. See also the work of Lewis Hyde (*The Gift*), Byrne Fone, and especially George Hutchinson. I am indebted in my reading to all of these scholars but take particular inspiration from Hutchinson's identification of the parallel to shamanistic practice in Whitman's work. "In some cases," Hutchinson writes, "the shaman's own soul may serve as a 'helper' or a possessing agent of sorts. Ake Hultkrantz tells us that among the Naskapi Indians of Labrador the spirits may be replaced by 'the shaman's power-filled free-soul. . . . [A] free-soul distanced from its owner may take on the same functions as a guardian spirit. That is, the extraordinary ecstatic powers of the shaman may be interpreted as flowing from his own semi-detached soul or acquired spirit potency.'" In Whitman's poems, Hutchinson continues, "[t]he invitation of the soul often sets the groundwork for the spiritual adventure" (*Ecstatic Whitman* xv–xvi).

15. Thanks to my friend Sally Moreman for showing me this outstanding example of spider mythology in modern writing.

16. In "Whitmanian Cybernetics," an essay in cultural criticism (and a sort of virtual geography) growing out of dissatisfaction with current spatial metaphors for computer-mediated communication, Paul H. Outka argues that "Whitman's complex understanding of subjectivity"—which emerged during the nineteenth-century version of the information revolution, to which the poet was a witness and contributor—"offers a sorely needed way to understand cyberspace's own tangled negotiations of identity, textuality, landscape, and democratic politics." On the notion of "writing environments," see Marilyn Cooper, "An Ecology of Writing," and David Barton, *Literacy: An Introduction to the Ecology of Written Language.* For an interesting take on computer environments, consider Jean-François Lyotard's claim that computers are the new nature.

17. The editor of NUPM, Edward Grier, dates the note 1856. Paul Diehl, in the fullest treatment of the manuscript and publication history of the poem, "'A Noiseless Patient Spider': Whitman's Beauty — Blood and Brain," is more circumspect, dating the composition of the note "sometime between 1855 and 1863" (119). The note's thematic similarity to "A Song of the Rolling Earth" argues for an early date, such as the one suggested by Grier. On the other hand, it would also make sense to see this note coming between the composition of the draft manuscript and the final poem. The mention of the worm hints at conversations Whitman had with John Burroughs around the time the final version of the poem was composed. I'm accepting the predominant critical opinion that dates the note before the first draft of the poem, but it could just as well intervened between the early draft and the magazine version of 1868. In such a case, Whitman would not have connected it with the spider poem till later when he saw an opportunity to make the *Calamus*-like draft into more of a soul poem, replacing "worm" with spider, and making the predatory spider more of a soul-searcher.

18. A full treatment of Luhmann's complex theory is well beyond the scope of this book and for that matter, well beyond my own ability. Luhmann's work is not well known in the United States, certainly not as well known as that of his colleague Jürgen Habermas. My hope here is to do as little damage as possible to his theory while borrowing what we might call a highly resonant concept that deserves more attention among ecopoetical theorists. I have long hoped other scholars whose expertise in cognitive studies and systems theory is considerably more sophisticated than my own will go further. In a book that appeared just as I was finishing the revisions for this study, Andrew McMurry's intriguing study *Environmental Renaissance: Emerson, Thoreau, & the Systems of Nature*, my hopes seem to have been realized. Unfortunately, it arrived too late for me to make full use of its many insights in my work.

19. In this sense, the concept of resonance anticipates Julia Kristeva's concept of pulsations arising from the semiotic *chora*, a theory of the origins of poetic language that has been fruitfully applied to Whitman's poetry by both Beth Jensen and Daneen Wardrop.

20. On the troubled definition of *nature*, see, for starts, Raymond Williams's treatment in *Keywords: A Vocabulary of Culture and Society.*

2. THE FALL OF THE REDWOOD TREE

1. In a famous appendix to *A Grammar of Motives*, Kenneth Burke argues for four master tropes — metaphor, metonymy, synecdoche, and irony. Several scholars have followed Burke's lead in reducing the number of tropes — Hayden White, for example, in his *Tropics of Discourse: Essays in Cultural Criticism* — while Lakoff and Johnson in their influential work have reduced the field to metaphor alone, arguing that the other tropes are primarily variations of metaphor. Some scholars in rhetoric — notably Brian Vickers — have objected to this trend, arguing that we lose the subtlety of classical rhetoric, which numbered hundreds of tropes. My position is that while there is a lot of redundancy and confusion in the classical canon, the modern position is a bit too reductive. My inclination is to reduce the field even further — using the term trope as a general tool — in order to open it up: to look at each trope as an individual language experiment, using the categories of ancient rhetoric and poetics as guides to possible effects but not as hard and fast sets of rules.

2. In Burke's scheme, while metaphor is the figure of perspective, metonymy and synecdoche involve reduction and representation, respectively. Personification can address all three motives depending upon the context.

3. Lawrence Buell gives full coverage to these trends in an excellent chapter on personification in *The Environmental Imagination*, 180–218.

4. The complexity of Whitman's tropic engagement with nature, in particular the weather, is argued brilliantly in M. Wynn Thomas's essay "Weathering the Storm: Whitman and the Civil War." Of particular interest is Thomas's claim that Whitman drew upon the changing concept of weather during his day — capitalizing on the "crossover from the real science of his time to the older, pre-scientific modes of thinking" — to create a vocabulary for representing in language the agonizing progression of the war (87). The rhetorical and conceptual functions that Thomas identifies for the weather in Whitman's prose works and poetry (notably "When Lilacs Last in the Dooryard Bloom'd") are truly far ranging and fascinating: "The weather as a mnemonic device, designed to fix the inner meaning of an event in national memory; the weather employed as a symbolic means of creating a climate of sympathy in the civilian world for the conditions of living and dying at the front as in the hospitals; the weather as somehow mysteriously sympathizing with the Union cause, and signifying, in its own terms, the uniqueness of a democratic society; the weather as symbolically legitimizing and consecrating the Northern effort through portents; the weather as a means of turning a socio-political struggle into a cosmically significant conflict, and in the process 'naturalizing' Northern, democratic society" (101–102).

5. Contrast, on the one hand, the mildness of the present-day concept of the nature lover as a "tree hugger," and, on the other hand, the macho put-down, "He'd fuck a hole in the ground if it winked at him," which eroticizes in the same direction as Whitman but reinforces the separation of human beings and the earth.

6. On Whitman's use of the "spermatic economy" of nineteenth-century phrenology and eclectic medical science, see M. Jimmie Killingsworth, "Whitman's Love-Spendings," and Harold Aspiz's fine book *Walt Whitman and the Body Beautiful*. The idea of wilderness as a region of excess was first suggested to me by my stu-

dent Cephas Sekhar. Dillard's idea is that, by human standards, nature is fearsome in its abundance, its wastefulness, producing a thousand insects rather than one, so that the few that survive may replicate their kind.

7. Annette Kolodny, *The Lay of the Land: Metaphor as Experience and History in American Life and Letters.* For more recent and self-consciously ecocritical treatments, see Legler's "Body Politics in American Nature Writing" and the essays in Greta Gaard and Patrick D. Murphy's collection, *Ecofeminist Literary Criticism: Theory, Interpretation, Pedagogy.*

8. See Kirkpatrick Sale, *The Green Revolution: The American Environmental Movement 1962–1992*; Killingsworth and Palmer, *Ecospeak*; and Waddell, *"And No Birds Sing."*

9. Thanks to my colleague Paul Parrish for directing me to the poems of Vaughan as examples within this tradition.

10. I have no idea how scientifically reliable this photograph could possibly be. Web sites by people who strike me as verging on unscrupulous offer more recent photographs claiming to be authentic shots of the animal in the wild, but some go on to explain for tourists and photographers how the nautilus can be baited and trapped and thus brought up to manageable depths in waters that the creature is known to frequent. Web sources also explain how South Sea natives would fish for the chambered nautilus on the deep banks of coral reefs at night. In light of the value of the shell among collectors, such information, resonating along the links of the electronic web, seems calculated to produce specific predatory results.

11. Qtd. in the text notes for Oliver Wendell Holmes, "The Chambered Nautilus," *Representative Poetry On-line.*

12. See Morris Berman's fascinating account of progress and its discontents in his *The Reenchantment of the World.*

13. Qtd. in the text notes for Holmes, "The Chambered Nautilus."

14. Other writers in the genteel tradition retain a stronger Christian focus in their approach to nature. Contrast, for example, Longfellow's lovely poem "The Cross of Snow" (in Ellmann 97), which imposes human grief and Christian symbolism upon what seems the most accidental of natural objects, the shape of snow accumulations on a rocky cliffside.

15. I thank my colleague Margaret Ezell for calling my attention to Traherne's prose works.

16. See Diane Kirk, "Landscapes of Old Age in Walt Whitman's Later Poetry," 8–12. I thank my former colleague Kenneth Price, who directed Kirk's dissertation, for calling my attention to it. For another essay that contemplates the meaning of the poem's various contexts, including the scientific background that Kirk discusses, as well as the magazine context, see James Perrin Warren, "Contexts for Reading 'Song of the Redwood-Tree.'"

17. For a brief introduction to the notion of environmental justice and the protest against environmental racism in contemporary American literature, see M. Jimmie Killingsworth and Jacqueline S. Palmer, "Ecopolitics and the Literature of the Borderlands: The Frontiers of Environmental Justice in Latina and Native American Writing." See also two essays by Jim Tarter: "'Dreams of Earth': Place, Multiethnicity, and Environmental Justice in Linda Hogan's *Solar*

Storms" and "Locating the Uranium Mine: Place, Multiethnicity, and Environmental Justice in Leslie Marmon Silko's *Ceremony*."

18. For this reading of the poem and the biographical details, I am indebted to Jerome Loving, *Walt Whitman* (356–357). Loving's treatment builds upon the earlier work of Gay Wilson Allen in *The Solitary Singer*.

3. GLOBAL AND LOCAL, NATURE AND EARTH

1. The transcription is that of Kenneth Price, which differs slightly from the one given by Edward Grier in NUPM 3:969. I am grateful to Kenneth Price and to Ed Folsom for bringing this work to my attention as they prepared it for inclusion in the Walt Whitman electronic archive.

2. See James T. Lemon, *Liberal Dreams and Nature's Limits*, 87–99. See also Edwin G. Burrows and Mike Wallace, *Gotham: A History of New York City to 1898*. On the ways that Whitman's immersion in the print culture of his day influenced his poetry, see especially Ezra Greenspan's *Walt Whitman and the American Reader*.

3. In light of his rather backward views on enfranchisement of the freed slaves, the point over which Whitman quarreled with his liberal friend William Douglas O'Connor, the hint about interracial marriage here is rather surprising. The poet could have been introduced to the idea (albeit in a satirical form) by his associate in the world of New York publishing, David Goodman Croly, who coined the word *miscegenation* and published a pamphlet by that title in 1864. Unfortunately, there is no evidence that Whitman read *Miscegenation*. See Loving, *Walt Whitman*, 346, 352–354.

4. On the reference to Cuba in this passage and Whitman's troubled interest in Latin America, see Kirsten Silva Gruesz's insightful chapter on Whitman in *Ambassadors of Culture: The Transamerican Origins of Latino Writing*.

5. Compare the response of the *Drum-Taps* poet to the stars in "When I Heard the Learn'd Astronomer." Growing weary during a scientific lecture, the poet glides out into the "mystical moist night air" and greets the stars with "perfect silence," standing reverent before the mystery of nature in good Romantic fashion. See chapter 5 for a discussion.

6. Cecil John Rhodes, "Guardians" — Matopo Hills. Qtd. on the Web site Cecil John Rhodes: Rhodesword. http://www.cecilrhodes.net/sword.html.

7. On the importance of knowing what is *enough* when it comes to the human manipulation of nature, see Bill McKibben's *Enough: Staying Human in an Engineered Age*.

8. Whitman goes public with his practice of outdoor note taking and list making in his prose work *Specimen Days*. The manuscripts for the poems often build upon the practice. He was in the habit of carrying small homemade notebooks in his large pockets whenever he went out walking. See chapter 6 for a discussion of Whitman's return to the earth in *Specimen Days*.

9. See chapter 2. As for the local quality of the experience, Leopold tells of his time as a forest ranger in the Southwest and dwells with loving care on his place of settlement in Wisconsin's Sand County, and while Carson repeats reports from many sites around the country, she shows a special fondness for and gives closest attention to her beloved homeland in New England. For a treatment of

Leopold's sensitivity to a kind of alternating consciousness — in his case, between humanist subjectivity and scientific objectivity — see Killingsworth and Palmer, *Ecospeak*, especially 63.

10. Nearly every critic sympathetic to the gay reading of Whitman's poems (including me: see *Whitman's Poetry of the Body*, 35–39) has agreed with Robert K. Martin that Section 28 recounts (or fantasizes) a homosexual encounter, either group sex or a gang rape. See Martin, "Whitman's 'Song of Myself': Homosexual Dream and Vision," 80, and his influential chapter on Whitman in *The Homosexual Tradition in American Poetry*.

11. Of course, in the case of "Bunch Poem," the universality is undercut by the maleness of the image. Whitman's extension of the same principle to women in this passage from the 1855 Preface and in poems like "I Sing the Body Electric" and "A Woman Waits for Me" has never seemed very convincing to his feminist critics.

12. See Jared Diamond, *Guns, Germs, and Steel: The Fates of Human Societies*.

4. THE ISLAND POET AND THE SACRED SHORE

1. Loving, my colleague at Texas A&M, told me that he once considered calling his Whitman biography "Paumanok," which was not only the name that Whitman preferred for Long Island but also one that he sometimes used as a pen name in his journalism. In addition to Loving's excellent chapter on Whitman's early life on Long Island, see Bertha H. Funnell's *Walt Whitman on Long Island*, which provides a useful compendium of most of what we know about Whitman's island experience. In *A New Theory for American Poetry*, Angus Fletcher cites Whitman's personal connection with the ocean and his corresponding reliance on wave patterns in versification and poetic structure.

2. Whitman shares the seashore as a sacred site of mystical illumination and poetic inspiration — as well as the experience related in "When I Heard the Learn'd Astronomer" of growing impatient with charts and graphs of nature and preferring something more thingish and ineffable, the "perfect silence" and "the mystical moist night air" (see chapter 5) — with Fritjof Capra, who begins his highly popular work of New Age metaphysics, *The Tao of Physics: An Exploration of the Parallels between Modern Physics and Eastern Mysticism*, with the following account: "Five years ago, I had a beautiful experience which set me on a road that has led to the writing of this book. I was sitting by the ocean one late summer afternoon, watching the waves rolling in and feeling the rhythm of my breathing, when I suddenly became aware of my whole environment as being engaged in a gigantic cosmic dance. Being a physicist, I knew that the sand, rocks, water and air around me were made of vibrating molecules and atoms, and that these consisted of particles which interacted with one another by creating and destroying other particles. I knew also that the Earth's atmosphere was continually bombarded by showers of 'cosmic rays,' particles of high energy undergoing multiple collisions as they penetrated the air. All this was familiar to me from my research in high-energy physics, but until that moment I had only experienced it through graphs, diagrams and mathematical theories. As I sat on the beach my former experiences came to life; I 'saw' cascades of energy coming down from outer space, in which particles were created and destroyed in rhythmic pulses; I 'saw' the atoms

of the elements and those of my body participating in this cosmic dance of energy; I felt its rhythm and I 'heard' its sound, and at that moment I *knew* that this was the Dance of Shiva, the Lord of Dancers worshipped by the Hindus" (11).

3. See Snyder's essay "The Rediscovery of Turtle Island" (*Place in Space* 236–251); see also Buell's *Writing for an Endangered World*, which develops the idea of reinhabitation at length, especially as it applies to an ecopoetical view of urban landscapes.

4. For more on double (or multiple) appeals in environmentalist rhetoric, see the introduction to Killingsworth and Palmer, *Ecospeak*.

5. The environmental historian William Cronon, in his tour de force *Nature's Metropolis: Chicago and the Great West*, uses the island trope in this manner: "Convinced of our human omnipotence, we can imagine nature retreating to small islands — 'preserves' — in the midst of a landscape which otherwise belongs to us" (18). As a corrective, he draws upon the web metaphor: "Just as our own lives continue to be embedded in a web of *natural* relationships, nothing in nature remains untouched by the web of *human* relationships that constitute our common history" (19).

6. My main source for the study of sacred spaces is, again, Vine Deloria Jr., *God Is Red: A Native View of Religion*, especially 271–282; but see also Mircea Eliade's widely cited treatment in *The Sacred and the Profane: The Nature of Religion*, chapter 1.

7. "Out of the Cradle" is, in my view, an exception to the trend of Whitman's magazine poems to conform more strongly to the expectations of conventional readers than the poems written exclusively for *Leaves of Grass* in the 1850s. The reason has to do with the particular venue, Henry Clapp's infamous Bohemian journal, the *Saturday Press*. See Loving, *Walt Whitman*; see also M. Jimmie Killingsworth, "*The Saturday Press*." On the other hand, the poem fits the pattern of magazine publication in drawing heavily upon poetic convention. As Michael Vande Berg shows in "'Taking All Hints to Use Them': The Sources of 'Out of the Cradle Endlessly Rocking,'" it is perhaps the most richly derivative poem in the Whitman corpus.

8. See especially Bauerlein's *Whitman and the American Idiom*; see also Kerry Larson's *Whitman's Drama of Consensus*. I gratefully acknowledge the special influence of Bauerlein on my reading of the poem. A good if necessarily sketchy summary of the major approaches and readings of the poem appears in Bauerlein's entry in *Walt Whitman: An Encyclopedia*. See also Donald Barlow Stauffer's entry on "Opera and Opera Singers." Leo Spitzer's "'Explication de Texte' Applied to Walt Whitman's 'Out of the Cradle Endlessly Rocking'" is a widely recognized classic of formalist criticism, to which I have returned many times for insights. I follow Betsy Erkkila in reading "Out of the Cradle" as a poem of crisis: "The transformation of the bird from a joyous singer of light and union to an elegiac singer of darkness and separation is similar to the transformation that Whitman himself underwent during the period of heightening schism in the nation between 1855 and 1860" (171–172).

9. In his impressive study of Whitman's many and varied sources for the poem, Michael Vande Berg argues that Whitman imitated the mockingbird's tendency (which he learned about from ornithological studies of northeastern birds) to

intertwine fragments of other birds' (poets') songs into his own trilling and chirping series of varied notes. In tracing Whitman's borrowings, Vande Berg cleverly argues that the autobiographical core event symbolically transformed and narrated in the poem is Whitman's habit of reading other writers out on lonely stretches of the shoreline, where he subsumed other poets' habits of expression into his own unique poetic practices. I might add to this reading that the poet's aggressive denial of having made poems from other poems and his territorial defense of his own originality fit with the mockingbird analog as well. Though none of Whitman's sources appear to suggest it, the mockingbird is notoriously territorial and aggressive. In American literature from Phillip Freneau to Harper Lee, the bird appears as a blameless singer, but such a characterization is out of kilter with ornithological observation. With no urging from me (indeed, somewhat to my dismay), my daughter wrote a high school term paper that took issue with the symbolic use to which Lee put the bird in *To Kill a Mockingbird*. She drew upon the ornithological literature to demonstrate the bird's pugnacious tendencies. As I might have predicted, the teacher's sense of poetic license was deeply offended by our budding ecocritic who, without having the background to make the argument complete, was on the way to a revision of the pathetic fallacy demanded by ecopoetics. Whitman's friend the naturalist John Burroughs wrote of Whitman's mockingbird, "The poet's treatment of the bird is entirely ideal and eminently characteristic. That is to say, it is altogether poetical and not at all ornithological; yet it contains a rendering or free translation of a birdsong . . . that I consider quite unmatched in our literature" (*Birds and Poets with Other Papers*, 12–13). He goes on to say, "The poets are the best natural historians, only you must know how to read them. They translate the facts largely and freely" (18). Work in progress by the ecocritic Tom Gannon, a protégé of Ed Folsom, promises a fuller treatment of the "avian other" in English poetry, contrasting the Romantics with Native American writers.

10. I take up the theme of possession briefly in my earlier reading of the poem in *Whitman's Poetry of the Body* (92–96) and hint at Whitman's adaptation of the gothic and sentimental traditions of treating the intertwined themes of love and death as well as his anticipation of the feminist poetics of openness. The concept of inspiration as possession, also prominent in the work of Hyde and Hutchinson, receives its fullest treatment in Maslan's *Whitman Possessed*.

11. On Whitman's use of sentimental conventions in dealing with love and death, particularly in the 1860 poems, see Killingsworth, *Whitman's Poetry of the Body*; see also Aspiz's *Walt Whitman and the Body Beautiful* and the Whitman chapter in David S. Reynolds's *Beneath the American Renaissance: The Subversive Imagination in the Age of Emerson and Melville*. For more on Whitman and Bryant, see chapter 2; see also Loving, *Walt Whitman*.

12. Jonathan Smith, among others, suggests that poetics and the "spiritual" approach to nature belong outside the sphere of science, a view to which Jacqueline Palmer and I assent in *Ecospeak*. But the question is not cut and dry. It would be useful to study more closely the interaction of objective and spiritual language in nineteenth-century science, beginning with Darwin's use of Nature as a god term. Despite his efforts at demystification, the author of *Origin of Species* is constantly

betrayed by his metaphors, most clearly perhaps in the concept of natural selection, in which nature substitutes for God or humankind as the agent of creation or change. When I point this problem out to my scientist colleagues, they tell me that I should do what they do and ignore the subtext. "It's only a metaphor." But I continue to wonder how thoroughly we have exorcised the metaphysical element when we find ourselves unable to develop new language.

13. The sociopolitical significance of the difference is suggested by Deloria, who argues that monotheism "is usually the product of the political unification of a diverse society" (66).

14. Whitman may well be drawing on his Quaker background here as well. See Susan Dean, "Seeds of Quakerism at the Roots of *Leaves of Grass.*"

15. For two more outstanding readings of the poem within its historical context, see Allen Grossmen, "The Poetics of Union in Lincoln and Whitman: An Inquiry toward the Relationship of Art and Policy," and Helen Vendler, "Poetry and the Mediation of Value: Whitman on Lincoln." I mention these both for their influence on me and as supplements to my rather brief and narrowly focused reading.

16. I thank Professor James Throgmorton of the University of Iowa for calling my attention to this passage.

17. Recall that in the 1856 poem "Spontaneous Me," Whitman says that "real poems" are the ones "that all men carry," the penis "drooping shy and unseen," and that "what we call poems" are "merely pictures" (CRE 103).

18. Significantly, according to his own account, Whitman and his mother stopped their daily routine when they heard the news of Lincoln's assassination, going a full day without their regular meals (French 770).

19. For the insight into the meaning of "summ'd," I'm particularly indebted to Ed Folsom.

20. Ed Folsom, who generously helped me write this section, also pointed out the revision of "This Compost."

21. As Mark Maslan points out, Whitman followed Wordsworth in expressly ruling out this kind of trope in the 1855 Preface. I am not saying that the personification isn't powerful or effective; on the contrary, it strongly communicates the sense of presence that the grieving person feels for the thoughts of death. I'm only saying that it represents a retreat from earlier principles.

5. URBANIZATION AND WAR

1. Of all Whitman's biographers, Gay Wilson Allen still captures this sense of movement the best in *The Solitary Singer,* which begins with Whitman's early memory of moving from the farm to Brooklyn.

2. The concept of maturity figures similarly in Stephen Mack's treatment of Whitman's changing philosophy of democracy. See Mack's *The Pragmatic Whitman.*

3. See chapter 6 for more on *Specimen Days.* For a similar treatment of Whitman's relation to modernity, but with an emphasis on his attitudes toward technological development, see the highly suggestive *Romantic Cyborgs: Authorship and Technology in the American Renaissance* by Klaus Benesch.

4. An early version of the "urban" section of this chapter was originally developed for the essay "Love of Comrades: The Urbanization of Community in Walt⸱

Whitman's Poetry and Pragmatist Philosophy," which I coauthored with Frances Dickey. I gratefully acknowledge Dickey's influence on the whole of this work. In my view, the best treatment of Whitman and the city remains that of M. Wynn Thomas in *The Lunar Light of Whitman's Poetry*, especially chapters 5, 6, and 7, which nicely summarize and subsume many previous contributions. See also the biographies by Allen, Kaplan, and Loving and the history of New York, *Gotham*, by Burrows and Wallace (especially 705–711). Other important studies that have appeared since Thomas's work include Christopher Beach, *The Politics of Distinction: Whitman and the Discourses of Nineteenth-Century America*; Dana Brand, *The Spectator and the City in Nineteenth-Century American Literature*; James Dougherty, *Walt Whitman and the Citizen's Eye*; William Chapman Sharpe, *Unreal Cities: Urban Figuration in Wordsworth, Baudelaire, Whitman, Eliot and Williams*; and Alan Trachtenberg, "Whitman's Lesson of the City." The general trend of these studies is to focus on Whitman's varying representation of the cityscape as it relates to themes associated with the tension between the individual and the social collective. The first deeply ecocritical study of Whitman's urban themes appears in Buell's *Writing for an Endangered World*. Buell's book adds significantly to the range of ecocriticism both by considering the relationship of the city to the surrounding natural environment and the flow between the two spaces (following the lead of the environmental historian William Cronon) and by including a strong reading of Whitman, whom he links with Frederick Law Olmstead because of the two men's interest in applying Romantic aesthetic values to city life. My readings are indebted to Buell's study. For a more general treatment of the issue of urban ecocriticism, see the introduction to Michael Bennett and David W. Teague's collection, *The Nature of Cities: Ecocriticism and Urban Environments*. See also the essay in that book by Adam W. Sweeting, "Writers and Dilettantes: Central Park and the Literary Origins of Urban Nature," which mentions Whitman's journalism, as well as Bryant's, in arguing that Central Park can be interpreted as a work of literature.

5. Burrows and Wallace, as well as Buell in the Whitman chapter of *Writing for an Endangered World*, comment on the troublesome old topic of the difference between Whitman's journalism and his poetry. As a journalistic reformer, Whitman had to acknowledge the bad on the way to advocating the good. In his idealistic poems of the 1850s, however, he was free to dwell upon the promise of the good. From this perspective, the 1860 poem "I Sit and Look Out," in which the poet acknowledges "the meanness and agony without end" but steadfastly remains the observer committed not to reform but silence, represents a retrospective poetics of his urban poetry of the 1850s. As a journalist, he could hardly say with the poet, "I [...] See, hear, and am silent" (CRE 273).

6. As Ed Folsom has suggested to me, the "lover" here might also be construed as the reader, so that the poem becomes a lament over the loss of the ideal reader, the poet's audience that, by 1860, he feared would never materialize. On the interplay between love and art and the substitution of "poetry" for "community," see Dickey and Killingsworth, "Love of Comrades."

7. Though she does not discuss this particular echo, Daneen Wardrop develops a strong case for the intellectual and poetic kinship of Poe with Whitman and

Dickinson in *Word, Birth, and Culture: The Poetry of Poe, Whitman, and Dickinson*. Wardrop is especially concerned with the issue of language and its representational incapacities in the work of the three poets. Her treatments of Kristeva's concept of the *chora* and the special appeals of poetic language make an interesting alternative to my treatment of resonance in chapter 1.

8. I hope it is not unfair to suggest that this poem seems an embarrassment to those scholars who make great claims for the artistic quality and "maturity" of the Civil War poems. Both Robert Leigh Davis and Roy Morris Jr. neglect to mention it in their books.

9. In *The Metaphysical Club: A Story of Ideas in America*, Louis Menand strongly demonstrates how the Civil War became a point of division between the generation of intellectuals represented by William James and Oliver Wendell Holmes Jr. and that represented by their famous fathers.

6. LIFE REVIEW

1. One of the best examples of this tendency, I'm sorry to say, can be found in my own book, *Whitman's Poetry of the Body*.

2. I am grateful to Ed Folsom for suggesting these themes to me and for challenging me to take another look at the late poems. Again, the individualist rhetoric of contemporary criticism, driven by the demands of career advancement and competitive publication in an academic economy, often obscures the essentially communal nature of our work. It seems to me consistent with the goals of ecocriticism that we restore our connections, our influences, and even our dependencies whenever we can.

3. Ecocriticism joins recent studies in autobiography in appreciation of *Specimen Days*. In addition to the fine essay by Philippon cited here, see William Major's "'Some Vital Unseen Presence': The Practice of Nature in Walt Whitman's *Specimen Days*," which discusses the "melding of the natural with the ideological" in Whitman's autobiographical reports of his "personal health practices and vision of nature during the 1870s" (79–80). In his essay on *Specimen Days* in the Whitman encyclopedia, Hutchinson writes, "Whitman emphasizes that his personal history has been shaped by geography and history, which in turn are the results of cosmic, natural processes," and argues that "*Specimen Days* presents the formation of a self through participation in communal and even ecological processes; unlike most confessional autobiographies in the Western tradition, Whitman emphasizes the dependence of individual identity upon communal identity, and thus historical placement" (679). Howard Nelson includes the passage on nakedness from *Specimen Days* (discussed below) in his collection of Whitman's nature writing. A long excerpt also appears in *The Norton Book of American Autobiography*, edited by Jay Parini (1999). My own reading of the book is not as enthusiastic, as this chapter suggests. Unlike the moving *Memoranda During the War*, *Specimen Days* reveals flashes of brilliance but could not stand on its own, in my view, were it not known to have been written by the author of *Leaves of Grass*. Overall, I follow Glenn Cummings, who offers a moderating view in his essay "Whitman's *Specimen Days* and the Theatricality of 'Semirenewal.'" The recovery Whitman seeks is only partially successful, Cummings argues,

largely because the poet observes nature as a theatrical event rather than metaphorically uniting with it as he did in his earlier work.

4. For a gay critical perspective on this episode of Whitman's life, see especially Charley Shively's reading in *Calamus Lovers* with its hints about Whitman's "codes" in *Specimen Days*. See also Schmidgall's *Walt Whitman*.

5. This passage is in fact an extraordinary prose poem. Set up in lines, it would rank with the poet's best.

6. On the Romantic foundations of modern environmentalism, see, among others, Nash, Buell, Bate, and Jonathan Smith. For a lively recent invocation of the division of ecosphere and technosphere, see Bill McKibben's fascinating *The Age of Missing Information*, in which the author contrasts the information gained from spending twenty-four hours outdoors near his home in upstate New York to watching twenty-four hours of cable television on ninety-three channels — a viewing via video tape that takes nearly a month — and his latest book, *Enough: Staying Human in an Engineered Age*, in which the question of humanity's own nature is posed against the background of advances in genetic engineering.

7. For an alternative view, the best philosophical and secular defense of Whitman's alignment of democracy with nature, see Mack's *The Pragmatic Whitman*.

8. See the detailed readings of Whitman's prairie poems and references to the Great Plains in two essays by Ed Folsom, "Paradise on the Prairies: Walt Whitman, Frederick Jackson Turner, and the American West" and especially "Walt Whitman's Prairie Paradise."

9. Thanks to Ed Folsom for pointing out this metrical feature, along with the odd enjambment in lines 3–4 of "To the Sun-Set Breeze," discussed below, a very rare device in *Leaves of Grass*, an ample indication of the poet's sustained experimentation with verse techniques.

10. In a fine essay on the poem, "Whitman and the Correspondent Breeze," Dwight Kalita argues that while Whitman draws upon English Romantic typology in his depiction of the breeze as spirit, he adds a sensuous element that distinguishes him from Wordsworth and others who speak of the breeze as the spirit of God.

Bibliography

Abram, David. *The Spell of the Sensuous: Perception and Language in a More-than-Human World.* New York: Pantheon, 1996.

Agassiz, Louis, and Augustus A. Gould. *Principles of Zoology. Part I: Comparative Physiology.* Boston: Gould, Kendall & Lincoln, 1848.

Allen, Gay Wilson. "How Emerson, Thoreau, and Whitman Viewed the Frontier." In *Toward a New American Literary History: Essays in Honor of Arlin Turner,* ed. Louis J. Budd, Edwin H. Cady, and Carl L. Anderson, 111–128. Durham, N.C.: Duke University Press, 1980.

———. *The Solitary Singer.* New York: Macmillan, 1955.

Allen, Paula Gunn. *The Sacred Hoop: Recovering the Feminine in American Indian Traditions.* Boston: Beacon, 1986.

Amburn, Ellis. *Subterranean Kerouac: The Hidden Life of Jack Kerouac.* New York: St. Martin's, 1998.

Anderson, Quentin. *The Imperial Self: An Essay in American Literary and Cultural History.* New York: Knopf, 1971.

Armbruster, Karla, and Kathleen R. Wallace, eds. *Beyond Nature Writing: Expanding the Boundaries of Ecocriticism.* Charlottesville: University Press of Virginia, 2001.

Arms, George. *The Fields Were Green: A New View of Bryant, Whittier, Holmes, Lowell, and Longfellow, with a Selection of Their Poems.* Stanford, Calif.: Stanford University Press, 1953.

Aspiz, Harold. *Walt Whitman and the Body Beautiful.* Urbana: University of Illinois Press, 1980.

Asselineau, Roger. *The Evolution of Walt Whitman.* Expanded ed. Iowa City: University of Iowa Press, 1999.

———. "Grass and Liquid Trees: The Cosmic Vision of Walt Whitman." In Folsom, *Whitman East and West,* 221–227.

Awiakta, Marilou. *Selu: Seeking the Corn-Mother's Wisdom.* Golden, Colo.: Fulcrum, 1994.

Barrett, Betty. "'Cavalry Crossing a Ford': Walt Whitman's Alabama Connection." *Alabama Heritage* 54 (Fall 1999): 6–17.

Barthes, Roland. *Mythologies.* Trans. Annette Lavers. New York: Hill, 1974.

Barton, David. *Literacy: An Introduction to the Ecology of Written Language.* Oxford: Blackwell, 1994.

Bate, Jonathan. *Romantic Ecology: Wordsworth and the Environmental Tradition.* London: Routledge, 1991.

———. *The Song of the Earth.* Cambridge, Mass.: Harvard University Press, 2000.

Battalio, John T. *The Rhetoric of Science in the Evolution of American Ornithological Discourse.* Stamford, Conn.: Ablex, 1998.

Bauerlein, Mark. "'Out of the Cradle Endlessly Rocking' (1859)." In LeMaster and Kummings, *Walt Whitman,* 495–497.

————. *Whitman and the American Idiom*. Baton Rouge: Louisiana State University Press, 1991.

Beach, Christopher. *The Politics of Distinction: Whitman and the Discourses of Nineteenth-Century America*. Athens: University of Georgia Press, 1996.

Beaver, Joseph. *Walt Whitman: Poet of Science*. New York: Octagon, 1974.

Beckert, Sven. *The Monied Metropolis: New York City and the Consolidation of the American Bourgeoisie, 1850–1896*. Cambridge: Cambridge University Press, 2001.

Benesch, Klaus. *Romantic Cyborgs: Authorship and Technology in the American Renaissance*. Amherst: University of Massachusetts Press, 2002.

Bennett, Michael, and David W. Teague, eds. *The Nature of Cities: Ecocriticism and Urban Environments*. Tuscon: University of Arizona Press, 1999.

Benveniste, Emile. *Problems in General Linguistics*. Trans. Mary Elizabeth Meek. Coral Gables, Fla.: University of Miami Press, 1971.

Bergland, Renée L. *The National Uncanny: Indian Ghosts and American Subjects*. Hanover, N.H.: University Press of New England, 2000.

Berman, Morris. *The Reenchantment of the World*. Ithaca, N. Y.: Cornell University Press, 1981.

Berry, Thomas. *The Dream of the Earth*. San Francisco: Sierra Club, 1988.

Bloom, Harold. "The Real Me." *New York Review of Books*, April 26, 1984, 3–7.

Bowers, Fredson. *Textual and Literary Criticism*. Cambridge: Cambridge University Press, 1966.

Brand, Dana. *The Spectator and the City in Nineteenth-Century American Literature*. New York: Cambridge University Press, 1991.

Brown, Bill. "Thing Theory." *Critical Inquiry* 28 (Autumn 2001): 1–22.

Buell, Lawrence. "The Ecocritical Insurgency." *New Literary History* 30 (1999): 699–712.

————. *The Environmental Imagination: Thoreau, Nature Writing, and the Formation of American Culture*. Cambridge, Mass.: Harvard University Press, 1995.

————. *Writing for an Endangered World: Literature, Culture, and Environment in the U.S. and Beyond*. Cambridge, Mass.: Harvard University Press, 2001.

Burke, Kenneth. *Counter-Statement*. Berkeley: University of California Press, 1968.

————. *A Grammar of Motives*. Berkeley: University of California Press, 1969.

————. *A Rhetoric of Motives*. Berkeley: University of California Press, 1969.

Burroughs, John. *Birds and Poets with Other Papers. The Writings of John Burroughs, Volume III*. New York: Russell and Russell, 1904.

————. *Notes on Walt Whitman as Poet and Person*. 1867. Reprint, New York: Haskell House, 1971.

Burrows, Edwin G., and Mike Wallace. *Gotham: A History of New York City to 1898*. New York: Oxford University Press, 1999.

Cantrill, James G., and Christine Oravec, eds. *The Symbolic Earth: Discourse and Our Creation of the Environment*. Lexington: University Press of Kentucky, 1996.

Capra, Fritjof. *The Tao of Physics: An Exploration of the Parallels between Modern Physics and Eastern Mysticism*. Berkeley, Calif.: Shambhala, 1975.

Carson, Rachel. *Silent Spring*. New York: Fawcett Crest, 1962.

Cavitch, David. *My Soul and I: The Inner Life of Walt Whitman*. Boston: Beacon, 1985.

Chauncey, George. *Gay New York: Gender, Urban Culture, and the Making of the Gay Male World 1890–1940*. New York: Basic, 1994.

Commoner, Barry. *Making Peace with the Planet*. New York: Pantheon, 1990.

Cooper, Marilyn. "An Ecology of Writing." *College English* 48 (1986): 364–375.

Coupe, Laurence, ed. *The Green Studies Reader: From Romanticism to Ecocriticism*. London: Routledge, 2000.

Cousteau, Jacques. *The Ocean World of Jacques Cousteau. Part I: Oasis in Space*. Danbury, Conn.: Danbury, 1973.

Coviello, Peter. "Intimate Nationality: Anonymity and Attachment in Whitman." *American Literature* 73 (2001): 85–119.

Cronon, William. *Nature's Metropolis: Chicago and the Great West*. New York: Norton, 1991.

Crowlcy, John. *Little, Big*. New York: Harper, 1981.

Cummings, Glenn N. "Whitman's *Specimen Days* and the Theatricality of 'Semirenewal.'" *ATQ* n.s. 6 (September 1992): 177–187.

Daniel, Stephan H. *The Philosophy of Jonathan Edwards: A Study in Divine Semiotics*. Bloomington: Indiana University Press, 1994.

Davis, Robert Leigh. *Whitman and the Romance of Medicine*. Berkeley: University of California Press, 1997.

Dean, Susan. "Seeds of Quakerism at the Roots of *Leaves of Grass*." *WWQR* 16: 191–201.

Deloria, Vine, Jr. *God Is Red: A Native View of Religion*. 2nd ed. Golden, Colo.: Fulcrum, 1992.

Devall, Bill, and George Sessions. *Deep Ecology: Living as if Nature Mattered*. Salt Lake City: Peregrine Smith, 1985.

Dewey, John. *Experience and Nature*. New York: Dover, 1958.

Diamond, Jared. *Guns, Germs, and Steel: The Fates of Human Societies*. New York: Norton, 1999.

Dickey, Frances, and M. Jimmie Killingsworth. "Love of Comrades: The Urbanization of Community in Walt Whitman's Poetry and Pragmatist Philosophy." *WWQR* (forthcoming).

Diehl, Paul. "'A Noiseless Patient Spider': Whitman's Beauty — Blood and Brain." *WWQR* 6 (1989): 117–132.

Dillard, Annie. *Pilgrim at Tinker Creek*. New York: Harper's Magazine Press, 1974.

Dobrin, Sidney I. "Writing Takes Place." In Weisser and Dobrin, *Ecocomposition*, 11–25.

Dobrin, Sidney I., and Christian R. Weisser. *Natural Discourse: Toward Ecocomposition*. Albany, N.Y.: SUNY Press, 2002.

Dodge, Jim. "Living by Life: Some Bioregional Theory and Practice." In *Home!: A Bioregional Reader*, ed. Van Andruss, Christopher Plant, Judith Plant, and Eleanor Wright, 5–12. Philadelphia: New Society, 1990.

Donne, John. *Poetry and Prose*. Ed. Frank J. Warnke. New York: Modern Library, 1967.

Doudna, Martin K. "Nature." In LeMaster and Kummings, *Walt Whitman*, 451–454.

Dougherty, James. *Walt Whitman and the Citizen's Eye*. Baton Rouge: Louisiana State University Press, 1993.

Dubos, Rene. "The Limits of Adaptability." In *The Environmental Handbook*, ed. Garrett De Bell, 27–30. New York: Ballantine, 1970.

Dunckel, Aaron. "'Mont Blanc': Shelley's Sublime Allegory of the Real." In Rosendale, *The Greening of Literary Scholarship*, 207–223.

Eastman, Charles A. (Ohiyesa). *The Soul of the Indian: An Interpretation*. 1911. Reprint, Lincoln: University of Nebraska Press, 1980.

Edwards, Grace Toney, Mary Margaret Thompson, and M. Lynda Ely. "Our Mothers' Voices: Narratives of Generational Transformation." *Journal of Appalachian Studies* 2 (1996): 131–139.

Elder, John. *Imagining the Earth: Poetry and the Vision of Nature*. Urbana: University of Illinois Press, 1985.

Eliade, Mircea. *The Sacred and the Profane: The Nature of Religion*. San Diego, Calif.: Harcourt, 1987.

Ellmann, Richard, ed. *The New Oxford Book of American Verse*. New York: Oxford University Press, 1976.

Emerson, Ralph Waldo. *Essays and Lectures*. Washington, D.C.: Library of America, 1983.

Erkkila, Betsy. *Whitman the Political Poet*. New York: Oxford University Press, 1989.

Erodes, Richard, and Alfonzo Ortiz. "Grandmother Spider Steals the Sun (Cherokee)." In *American Indian Myths and Legends*, 154–155. New York: Pantheon, 1984.

Evernden, Neil. *The Natural Alien: Humankind and Environment*. Toronto: University of Toronto Press, 1985.

———. *The Social Construction of Nature*. Baltimore: Johns Hopkins University Press, 1992.

Fleck, Ludwik. *Genesis and Development of a Scientific Fact*. Chicago: University of Chicago Press, 1979.

Fletcher, Angus. *A New Theory for American Poetry: Democracy, the Environment, and the Future of Imagination*. Cambridge, Mass.: Harvard University Press, 2004.

Folsom, Ed. "Paradise on the Prairies: Walt Whitman, Frederick Jackson Turner, and the American West." In *Utopian Visions of Work and Community*, ed. Jay Semel and Annie Tremmel Wilcox, 101–113. Iowa City, Iowa: Obermann Center for Advanced Studies, 1996.

———. *Walt Whitman's Native Representations*. Cambridge: Cambridge University Press, 1994.

———. "Walt Whitman's Prairie Paradise." In *Recovering the Prairie*, ed. Robert F. Sayre, 47–60. Madison: University of Wisconsin Press, 1999.

———. "'When I Heard the Learn'd Astronomer' (1865)." In LeMaster and Kummings, *Walt Whitman*, 769.

———, ed. *Whitman East and West: New Contexts for Reading Walt Whitman*. Iowa City: University of Iowa Press, 2002.

Fone, Byrne R. S. *Masculine Landscapes: Walt Whitman and the Homoerotic Text*. Carbondale: Southern Illinois University Press, 1992.

French, R. W. "When Lilacs Last in the Dooryard Bloom'd (1865)." In LeMaster and Kummings, *Walt Whitman*, 770–773.

Funnell, Bertha H. *Walt Whitman on Long Island.* Port Washington, N.Y.: Kennikat, 1971.

Gaard, Greta, and Patrick D. Murphy, eds. *Ecofeminist Literary Criticism: Theory, Interpretation, Pedagogy.* Urbana: University of Illinois Press, 1998.

Garman, Bryan K. *A Race of Singers: Whitman's Working-Class Hero from Guthrie to Springsteen.* Chapel Hill: University of North Carolina Press, 2000.

Geffen, Arthur. "Silence and Denial: Walt Whitman and the Brooklyn Bridge." *Walt Whitman Quarterly Review* 1 (1984): 1–11.

Gilbert, David W. *Greening the Lyre: Environmental Poetics and Ethics.* Reno: University of Nevada Press, 2002.

Glotfelty, Cheryll, and Harold Fromm, eds. *The Ecocriticism Reader: Landmarks in Literary Ecology.* Athens: University of Georgia Press, 1996.

Graber, Linda. *Wilderness as Sacred Space.* Washington, D.C.: Association of American Geologists, 1976.

Greenspan, Ezra. *Walt Whitman and the American Reader.* Cambridge: Cambridge University Press, 1990.

Grossmen, Allen. "The Poetics of Union in Lincoln and Whitman: An Inquiry toward the Relationship of Art and Policy." In *The American Renaissance Reconsidered,* ed. Donald S. Pease and Walter Benn Michaels, 183–208. Baltimore: Johns Hopkins University Press, 1985.

Gruesz, Kirsten Silva. *Ambassadors of Culture: The Transamerican Origins of Latino Writing.* Princeton, N.J.: Princeton University Press, 2001.

Grünzweig, Walter. "Noble Ethics and Loving Aggressiveness: The Imperialist Walt Whitman." In *An American Empire: Expansionist Cultures and Policies 1881–1917,* ed. Serge Ricard, 151–165. Aix-en Provence: Université de Provence, 1990.

Harrison, Jim. *The Beast God Forgot to Invent.* New York: Grove, 2000.

Hatlen, Burton. "'A Song of the Rolling Earth' (1856)." In LeMaster and Kummings, *Walt Whitman,* 665–666.

Hausman, Gerald. *Turtle Island Alphabet: A Lexicon of Native American Symbols and Culture.* New York: St. Martin's, 1992.

Heidegger, Martin. *Basic Writings.* Ed. D. F. Krell. New York: Harper, 1977.

Helms, Alan. "'Hints . . . Faint Clews and Indirections': Whitman's Homosexual Disguises." In *Walt Whitman: Here and Now,* ed. Joann P. Krieg, 61–67. Westport, Conn.: Greenwood, 1985.

———. "Whitman's 'Live Oak with Moss.'" In *The Continuing Presence of Walt Whitman,* ed. Robert K. Martin, 185–205. Iowa City: University of Iowa Press, 1992.

Herndl, Carl, and Stuart Brown, eds. *Green Culture: Environmental Rhetoric in Contemporary America.* Madison: University of Wisconsin Press, 1996.

Hindus, Milton, ed. *Walt Whitman: The Critical Heritage.* New York: Barnes and Noble, 1971.

Hitt, Christopher. "Toward an Ecological Sublime." *New Literary History* 30 (1999): 603–623.

Hollis, C. Carroll. *Language and Style in Leaves of Grass.* Baton Rouge: Louisiana State University Press, 1983.

Holmes, Oliver Wendell. "The Chambered Nautilus" (text with notes). *Representative Poetry On-line*, ed. I. Lancashire. Toronto: University of Toronto, 1998. <http://www.library.utoronto.ca/utel/rp/poems/holmes6.html>.

Hutchinson, George. *The Ecstatic Whitman: Literary Shamanism and the Crisis of the Union*. Columbus: Ohio State University Press, 1986.

———. "*Specimen Days* (1882)." In LeMaster and Kummings, *Walt Whitman*, 678–681.

Huxley, Aldous. *The Perennial Philosophy*. New York: Harper and Row, 1945.

Hyde, Lewis. *The Gift: Imagination and the Erotic Life of Property*. New York: Vintage, 1979.

———. *Trickster Makes This World: Mischief, Myth, and Art*. New York: Farrar, Straus and Giroux, 1998.

Jakobson, Roman. "Shifters, Verbal Categories, and the Russian Verb." In *Selected Writings*, 2:130–147. The Hague: Mouton, 1971.

James, William. "The Moral Equivalent of War." In *The Writings of William James: A Comprehensive Edition*. Ed. John J. McDermott, 660–671. Chicago: University of Chicago Press, 1977.

Jensen, Beth. *Leaving the M/Other: Whitman, Kristeva, and Leaves of Grass*. Madison, Va.: Fairleigh Dickinson University Press, 2002.

Johnson, Linck C. "The Design of Walt Whitman's *Specimen Days*." *Walt Whitman Review* 21 (1975): 3–14.

Kalita, Dwight. "Whitman and the Correspondent Breeze." *Walt Whitman Review* 21 (1975): 125–130.

Kaplan, Justin. *Walt Whitman: A Life*. New York: Simon and Schuster, 1980.

Kerridge, Richard. Introduction. In Kerridge and Samuells, *Writing the Environment*, 1–9.

Kerridge, Richard, and Neil Samuells, eds. *Writing the Environment: Ecocriticism and Literature*. London: Zed, 1998.

Kerouac, Jack. *On the Road*. 1957. Reprint, New York: Penguin, 1976.

Killingsworth, M. Jimmie. "Can an English Teacher Contribute to the Energy Debate?" *College English* 43 (1981): 581–586.

———. *The Growth of Leaves of Grass: The Organic Tradition in Whitman Studies*. Columbia, S.C.: Camden House, 1993.

———. "*The Saturday Press*." In *American Literary Magazines: The Eighteenth and Nineteenth Centuries*, ed. Edward Chielens, 357–364. Westport, Conn.: Greenwood, 1986.

———. "Whitman and the Gay American Ethos." In *A Historical Guide to Walt Whitman*, ed. David S. Reynolds, 121–151. New York: Oxford University Press, 2000.

———. "Whitman's Love-Spendings." *Walt Whitman Review* 26 (1980): 145–153.

———. *Whitman's Poetry of the Body: Sexuality, Politics, and the Text*. Chapel Hill: University of North Carolina Press, 1989.

Killingsworth, M. Jimmie, and Jacqueline S. Palmer. "The Discourse of 'Environmentalist Hysteria.'" *Quarterly Journal of Speech* 81 (1995): 1–19.

———. "Ecopolitics and the Literature of the Borderlands: The Frontiers of Environmental Justice in Latina and Native American Writing." In Kerridge and Samuells, *Writing the Environment*, 196–207.

———. *Ecospeak: Rhetoric and Environmental Politics in America.* Carbondale: Southern Illinois University Press, 1992.

———. "Millennial Ecology: The Apocalyptic Narrative from *Silent Spring* to *Global Warming.*" In Herndl and Brown, *Green Culture,* 21–45.

Kirk, Diane. "Landscapes of Old Age in Walt Whitman's Later Poetry." Ph.D. diss., Texas A&M University, 1994.

Kolodny, Annette. *The Lay of the Land: Metaphor as Experience and History in American Life and Letters.* Chapel Hill: University of North Carolina Press, 1975.

Kroeber, Karl. *Ecological Literary Criticism: Romantic Imagining and the Biology of Mind.* New York: Columbia University Press, 1994.

Lakoff, George, and Mark Johnson. *Metaphors We Live By.* Chicago: University of Chicago Press, 1980.

Lao Tzu. *The Way of Life.* Trans. R. B. Blakney. New York: Penguin, 1983.

Larson, Kerry. *Whitman's Drama of Consensus.* Chicago: University of Chicago Press, 1988.

Latour, Bruno. *Science in Action: How to Follow Scientists and Engineers through Society.* Cambridge, Mass.: Harvard University Press, 1987.

Legler, Gretchen. "Body Politics in American Nature Writing: 'Who May Contest for What the Body of Nature Will Be?'" In Kerridge and Samuells, *Writing the Environment,* 71–87.

Leifel, Gregory. *The Day I Met Walt Whitman.* Cary, Ill.: Thriving Moss, 2001.

LeMaster, J. R., and Donald D. Kummings, eds. *Walt Whitman: An Encyclopedia.* New York: Garland, 1998.

Lemon, James T. *Liberal Dreams and Nature's Limits: Great Cities of North America since 1600.* Toronto: Oxford University Press, 1996.

Leopold, Aldo. *Sand County Almanac.* New York: Ballantine, 1966.

Levin, Jonathan. "Beyond Nature? Recent Work in Ecocriticism." *Contemporary Literature* 43 (2002): 171–186.

Loving, Jerome. *Emerson, Whitman, and the American Muse.* Chapel Hill: University of North Carolina Press, 1982.

———. *Walt Whitman: The Song of Himself.* Berkeley: University of California Press, 1999.

Luhmann, Niklas. *Ecological Communication.* Trans. J. Bednarz Jr. Chicago: University of Chicago Press, 1989.

Lyotard, Jean-François. *The Postmodern Condition.* Trans. Geoff Bennington and Brian Massumi. Minneapolis: University of Minnesota Press, 1984.

Mack, Stephen. *The Pragmatic Whitman.* Iowa City: University of Iowa Press, 2002.

Major, William. "'Some Vital Unseen Presence': The Practice of Nature in Walt Whitman's *Specimen Days.*" *ISLE* 7 (2000): 79–96.

Martin, Doug. "Whitman's 'Cavalry Crossing a Ford.'" *Explicator* 60 (2002): 198–200.

Martin, Robert K. *The Homosexual Tradition in American Poetry.* Austin: University of Texas Press, 1979.

———. "Whitman's 'Song of Myself': Homosexual Dream and Vision." *Partisan Review* 42 (1975): 80–96.

Maslan, Mark. *Whitman Possessed: Poetry, Sexuality and Popular Authority.* Baltimore: Johns Hopkins University Press, 2001.

Matthiessen, Peter. "How to Kill a Valley." *New York Review of Books,* February 7, 1980, 31–36.

Mazel, David. *American Literary Environmentalism.* Athens: University of Georgia Press, 2000.

———, ed. *A Century of Early Ecocriticism.* Athens: University of Georgia Press, 2001.

McKibben, Bill. *The Age of Missing Information.* New York: Random House, 1992.

———. *The End of Nature.* New York: Anchor, 1989.

———. *Enough: Staying Human in an Engineered Age.* New York: Times Books, 2003.

McMurry, Andrew. *Environmental Renaissance: Emerson, Thoreau, & the Systems of Nature.* Athens: University of Georgia Press, 2003.

———. "'In Their Own Language': Sarah Orne Jewett and the Question of Non-Human Speaking Subjects." *ISLE* 6 (1999): 51–63.

Menand, Louis. *The Metaphysical Club: A Story of Ideas in America.* New York: Farrar, 2001.

Miller, Edwin Haviland. *Walt Whitman's Poetry: A Psychological Journey.* New York: New York University Press, 1968.

Millner, Michael. "The Fear Passing the Love of Women: Sodomy and Male Sentimental Citizenship in the Antebellum City." *Arizona Quarterly* 58 (Summer 2002): 19–52.

Moon, Michael. *Disseminating Whitman: Revision and Corporeality in Leaves of Grass.* Cambridge, Mass.: Harvard University Press, 1991.

Morris, Roy, Jr. *The Better Angel: Walt Whitman in the Civil War.* New York: Oxford University Press, 2000.

Murphy, Patrick D. *Farther Afield in the Study of Nature-Oriented Literature.* Charlottesville: University of Virginia Press, 2000.

Nash, Roderick. *Wilderness and the American Mind.* 3rd ed. New Haven, Conn.: Yale University Press, 1982.

Nathanson, Tenney. *Whitman's Presence: Body, Voice, and Writing in Leaves of Grass.* New York: New York University Press, 1992.

Nelson, Howard, ed. *Earth, My Likeness: Nature Poems of Walt Whitman.* St. Albans, Vt.: Wood Thrush, 2001.

O'Brien, Susie. "Articulating a World of Difference: Ecocriticism, Postcolonialism and Globalization." *Canadian Literature* 170–171 (2001): 140–158.

O'Grady, John P. *Pilgrims of the Wild: Everett Ruess, Henry David Thoreau, John Muir, Clarence King, Mary Austin.* Salt Lake City: University of Utah Press, 1993.

Outka, Paul H. "Whitmanian Cybernetics." *Mickle Street Review* (on-line journal) 14 (2001), n.p. <www.micklestreet.rutgers.edu>.

Parini, Jay, ed. *The Norton Book of American Autobiography.* New York: Norton, 1999.

Parker, Hershel. "The Real 'Live Oak, with Moss': Straight Talk about Whitman's 'Gay Manifesto.'" *Nineteenth-Century Literature* 51 (1996): 145–160.

Peirce, Charles Sanders. *Peirce on Signs*. Ed. James Hoopes. Chapel Hill: University of North Carolina Press, 1991.

Philippon, Daniel J. "'I Only Seek to Put You in Rapport': Message and Method in Walt Whitman's *Specimen Days*." In *Reading the Earth: New Directions in the Study of Literature and the Environment*, ed. Michael P. Branch, Rochelle Johnson, Daniel Patterson, and Scott Slovic, 179–193. Moscow: University of Idaho Press, 1998.

Platz, Norbert. "Rediscovering the Forgotten Space of Nature: A Plea for Ecocriticism in the New Literatures in English." In *Borderlands: Negotiating Boundaries in Post-Colonial Writing*, ed. Monika Reif-Hülser, 175–188. Amsterdam: Rodopi, 1999.

Poe, Edgar Allan. *Poetry and Tales*. Washington, D.C.: Library of America, 1984.

Poirier, Richard. *Trying It Out in America: Literary and Other Performances*. New York: Farrar, Straus, and Giroux, 1999.

Pollak, Vivian. *The Erotic Whitman*. Berkeley: University of California Press, 2000.

Quammen, David. *The Song of the Dodo: Island Biogeography in an Age of Extinction*. New York: Simon and Schuster, 1996.

Quetchenbach, Bernard W. *Back from the Far Field: American Nature Poetry in the Late Twentieth Century*. Charlottesville: University Press of Virginia, 2000.

Reynolds, David S. *Beneath the American Renaissance: The Subversive Imagination in the Age of Emerson and Melville*. New York: Knopf, 1988.

Rigby, Kate. "Ecocriticism." In *Introducing Criticism at the 21st Century*, ed. Julian Wolfreys, 151–178. Edinburgh: Edinburgh University Press, 2002.

Roorda, Randall. *Dramas of Solitude: Narratives of Retreat in American Nature Writing*. Albany, N.Y.: SUNY Press, 1998.

Rosendale, Steven, ed. *The Greening of Literary Scholarship: Literature, Theory, and the Environment*. Iowa City: University of Iowa Press, 2002.

Sale, Kirkpatrick. *The Green Revolution: The American Environmental Movement 1962–1992*. New York: Hill and Wang, 1993.

Schmidgall, Gary. *Walt Whitman: A Gay Life*. New York: Dutton, 1997.

———, ed. *Intimate with Walt: Selections from Whitman's Conversations with Horace Traubel 1888–1892*. Iowa City: University of Iowa Press, 2001.

Scholnick, Robert. "'The Password Primeval': Whitman's Use of Science in 'Song of Myself.'" In *Studies in the American Renaissance*, ed. Joel Myerson, 385–425. Charlottesville: University Press of Virginia, 1986.

Scigaj, Leonard M. *Sustainable Poetry: Four American Ecopoets*. Lexington: University of Kentucky Press, 1999.

Sharpe, William Chapman. *Unreal Cities: Urban Figuration in Wordsworth, Baudelaire, Whitman, Eliot and Williams*. Baltimore: Johns Hopkins University Press, 1990.

Shively, Charley, ed. *Calamus Lovers: Walt Whitman's Working Class Camerados*. San Francisco: Gay Sunshine Press, 1987.

Silko, Leslie Marmon. *Ceremony*. New York: Viking, 1977.

Simpson, David. "Destiny Made Manifest: The Styles of Whitman's Poetry." In *Nation and Narration*, ed. Homi Bhabba, 177–196. New York: Routledge, 1990.

Sloan, Gary. "Walt Whitman: When Science and Mysticism Collide." *Skeptical Inquirer* 27 (March/April 2003): 51–54.

Slotkin, Richard. *The Fatal Environment: The Myth of the Frontier in the Age of Industrialization.* New York: Atheneum, 1985.

Slovic, Scott. *Seeking Awareness in American Nature Writing: Henry Thoreau, Annie Dillard, Edward Abbey, Wendell Berry, Barry Lopez.* Salt Lake City: University of Utah Press, 1992.

———. "Seeking the Language of Solid Ground: Reflections on Ecocriticism and Narrative." *Fourth Genre* 1, no. 2 (1999): 34–38.

Smith, Jonathan M. "The Place of Nature." In *American Space/American Place: Geographies of the Contemporary United States,* ed. John A. Agnew and J. M. Smith, 21–51. Edinburgh: Edinburgh University Press, 2002.

Snyder, Gary. *A Place in Space: Ethics, Aesthetics, and Watersheds.* Washington, D.C.: Counterpoint, 1995.

———. *Turtle Island.* New York: New Directions, 1974.

Snow, C. P. *The Two Cultures and the Scientific Revolution.* New York: Cambridge University Press, 1959.

Sorisio, Carolyn. *Fleshing Out America: Race, Gender, and the Politics of the Body in American Literature, 1833–1879.* Athens: University of Georgia Press, 2002.

Spann, Edward K. *The New Metropolis: New York City, 1840–1857.* New York: Columbia University Press, 1981.

Spitzer, Leo. "'Explication de Texte' Applied to Walt Whitman's 'Out of the Cradle Endlessly Rocking.'" *ELH* 16 (1949): 229–249.

Stauffer, Donald Barlow. "Opera and Opera Singers." In LeMaster and Kummings, *Walt Whitman,* 484–486.

Sweeting, Adam W. "Writers and Dilettantes: Central Park and the Literary Origins of Urban Nature." In Bennett and Teague, *The Nature of Cities,* 93–110.

Tallmadge, John. "Toward a Natural History of Reading." *ISLE* 7 (2000): 33–45.

Tallmadge, John, and Henry Harrington, eds. *Reading Under the Sign of Nature: New Essays in Ecocriticism.* Salt Lake City: University of Utah Press, 2000.

Tarter, Jim. "'Dreams of Earth': Place, Multiethnicity, and Environmental Justice in Linda Hogan's *Solar Storms.*" In Tallmadge and Harrington, *Reading Under the Sign of Nature,* 128–147.

———. "Locating the Uranium Mine: Place, Multiethnicity, and Environmental Justice in Leslie Marmon Silko's *Ceremony.*" In Rosendale, *The Greening of Literary Scholarship,* 97–110.

Thayer, Robert L., Jr. *LifePlace: Bioregional Thought and Practice.* Berkeley: University of California Press, 2003.

Thomas, M. Wynn. *The Lunar Light of Whitman's Poetry.* Cambridge, Mass.: Harvard University Press, 1987.

———. "Weathering the Storm: Whitman and the Civil War." *WWQR* 15 (1997/98): 87–109.

Thoreau, Henry David. *Walden* and *Resistance to Civil Government.* 2nd ed. Norton Critical Edition. Ed. William Rossi. New York: Norton, 1992.

———. "Walking." In *Walden and Other Writings.* Ed. Brooks Atkinson, 625–663. New York: Modern Library, 2000.

Bibliography

Trachtenberg, Alan. *The Incorporation of America: Culture and Society in the Gilded Age.* New York: Hill and Wang, 1982.

———. "Whitman's Lesson of the City." In *Breaking Bounds: Whitman and American Cultural Studies,* ed. Betsy Erkkila and Jay Grossman, 163–173. New York: Oxford University Press, 1996.

Traherne, Thomas. *The Centuries.* New York: Harper, 1960.

Traubel, Horace. *With Walt Whitman in Camden.* 9 vols. Various publishers, 1906–1996.

Tucker, Mary Evelyn, and Duncan Ryuken Williams, eds. *Buddhism and Ecology: The Interconnection of Dharma and Deeds.* Cambridge, Mass.: Harvard University Press, 1997.

Tucker, Mary Evelyn, and John Berthrong, eds. *Confucianism and Ecology: The Interrelation of Heaven, Earth, and Humans.* Cambridge, Mass.: Harvard University Press, 1998.

Turner, Mark. *Reading Minds: The Study of English in the Age of Cognitive Science.* Princeton, N.J.: Princeton University Press, 1991.

Vande Berg, Michael. "'Taking All Hints to Use Them': The Sources of 'Out of the Cradle Endlessly Rocking.'" *WWQR* 2 (Spring 1985): 1–20.

Vaughan, Henry. *The Complete Poetry of Henry Vaughan.* Ed. French Fogle. Garden City, N.Y.: Anchor, 1964.

Vendler, Helen. "Poetry and the Mediation of Value: Whitman on Lincoln." *Michigan Quarterly Review* 39 (2000): 1–35.

Vickers, Brian. *In Defense of Rhetoric.* New York: Oxford University Press, 1988.

Voros, Gyorgyi. *Notations of the Wild: Ecology in the Poetry of Wallace Stevens.* Iowa City: University of Iowa Press, 1997.

Waage, F[rederick]. "Ecocriticism in Theory and Practice." *Mississippi Quarterly* 53 (1999–2000): 143–150.

Waddell, Craig, ed. *"And No Birds Sing": The Rhetoric of Rachel Carson.* Carbondale: Southern Illinois University Press, 2000.

Wardrop, Daneen. *Word, Birth, and Culture: The Poetry of Poe, Whitman, and Dickinson.* Westport, Conn.: Greenwood, 2002.

Warren, James Perrin. "Contexts for Reading 'Song of the Redwood-Tree.'" In Tallmadge and Harrington, *Reading Under the Sign of Nature,* 165–178.

———. "Whitman Land: John Burroughs's Pastoral Criticism." *ISLE* 8 (2001): 83–96.

Weisser, Christian R., and Sidney I. Dobrin, eds. *Ecocomposition: Theoretical and Pedagogical Approaches.* Albany, N.Y.: SUNY Press, 2001.

White, Hayden. *Tropics of Discourse: Essays in Cultural Criticism.* Baltimore: Johns Hopkins University Press, 1978.

Whitman, Walt. *An American Primer.* Ed. Horace Traubel. 1904. Reprint, Stevens Point, Wis.: Holy Cow! 1987.

———. *Complete Poetry and Collected Prose* (CPCP). Washington, D.C.: Library of America, 1982.

———. *The Correspondence of Walt Whitman.* 6 vols. Ed. Edwin Haviland Miller. New York: New York University Press, 1961–1977.

———. *Drum-Taps (1865) and Sequel to Drum-Taps (1865–66): A Facsimile Reproduction* (D-T). Ed. F. DeWolfe Miller. Gainesville, Fla.: Scholars' Facsimiles and Reprints, 1959.

———. *Faint Clews and Indirections: Manuscripts of Walt Whitman and His Family.* Ed. Clarence Gohdes and Rollo G. Silver. Durham, N.C.: Duke University Press, 1949.

———. *Leaves of Grass: Comprehensive Reader's Edition* (CRE). Ed. Sculley Bradley and Harold W. Blodgett. New York: New York University Press, 1973.

———. *Notebooks and Unpublished Manuscripts* (NUPM). 6 vols. Ed. Edward F. Grier. New York: New York University Press, 1984.

———. *Specimen Days* (SD). In Whitman, *Complete Poetry and Collected Prose*, 689–926.

———. *Uncollected Poetry and Prose of Walt Whitman* (UPP). 2 vols. Ed. Emory Holloway. 1921. Reprint, Gloucester, Mass.: Peter Smith, 1972.

———. *The Walt Whitman Archive* (LG + date). Ed. Kenneth M. Price and Ed Folsom, <http://jefferson.village.Virginia.edu/whitman/>.

———. *Walt Whitman's Blue Book: The 1860–61 Leaves of Grass Containing His Manuscript Additions and Revisions* (Blue Book). Ed. Arthur Golden. 2 vols. New York: New York Public Library, 1968.

Williams, Raymond. *Keywords: A Vocabulary of Culture and Society.* Rev. ed. New York: Oxford University Press, 1983.

Wilson, Eric. *Romantic Turbulence: Chaos, Ecology, and American Space.* New York: St. Martin's, 2000.

Woolf, Virginia. *A Room of One's Own.* New York: Harcourt, 1929.

Wordsworth, William. *Selected Poems and Prefaces.* Ed. Jack Stillinger. Boston: Houghton Mifflin, 1965.

Index

Abbey, Edward, 49

abstraction, 75, 80, 84, 90, 92, 93, 94, 120, 123, 127, 147, 167; nature as, 92, 189n1; problem of, 35, 39, 53–73; in relation to personification, 15

Agassiz, Louis, 55; *Principles of Zoology*, 56

aging, 166, 168, 171, 178, 179, 181, 182, 183

alienation, 35, 49, 57, 94, 123, 139, 147, 157, 170–171

allegory, 15

Allen, Gay Wilson, 88, 89; "How Emerson, Thoreau, and Whitman Viewed the Frontier," 64–66

Allen, Paula Gunn, 37

Alabama, 109

Amburn, Ellis, *Subterranean Kerouac*, 41

American Indians. *See* Native Americans

"America's Characteristic Landscape" (Whitman), 178–179

"Among the Multitude" (Whitman), 45

Anderson, Quentin, 143

Arizona, 57

Arms, George, *The Fields Were Green*, 53

artisanal republicanism, 142–145, 157

"As I Ebb'd with the Ocean of Life" (Whitman), 98–99, 123–129, 149

Aspiz, Harold, 157

Asselineau, Roger, 33, 89, 90

autoeroticism. *See* sexuality

Barrett, Betty, "Cavalry Crossing a Ford: Walt Whitman's Alabama Connection," 158–159

Barthes, Roland, 61

Bate, Jonathan, *The Song of the Earth*, 5–8, 176

"Bathed in War's Perfume" (Whitman), 164

Baudelaire, Charles, 89, 145

Beach, Christopher, *The Politics of Distinction*, 138–139

"Beat! Beat! Drums" (Whitman), 134

Beat poetry, 16

Beaver, Joseph, 156

Bergland, Renée L., 87; *The National Uncanny: Indian Ghosts and American Subjects*, 70

bird, 60, 107, 108, 109, 114, 115, 196–197n9

Bishop, Elizabeth, 56

"Bivouac on a Mountain Side" (Whitman), 159

Blakney, R[aymond] B[ernard], 16–17

"Blood Money" (Whitman), 59

body, 29, 30, 31, 33, 43, 45, 50, 51, 82, 84, 91, 93, 94, 99, 100, 107, 111, 114, 124, 132, 166, 168, 171, 172, 182, 183

Boston, 55, 56

Brer Rabbit, 127

Broadway (street), 141

"Broadway" (Whitman), 181

Broadway Magazine, 53

Brooklyn, 102, 116, 134, 140

Brooklyn Bridge, 142

Brooklyn Daily Eagle, 139

Brown, Bill, 23, 24. *See also* thing theory

Bryant, William Cullen, 15, 53, 123, 137; "Thanatopsis," 111, 113, 114; "To a Waterfowl," 59–60, 158

Bucke, Richard Maurice, 160, 177

Buddhism, 30

Buell, Lawrence, *The Environmental Imagination*, 7, 113

"Bunch Poem" (Whitman). *See* "Spontaneous Me"

Burke, Kenneth, 174; *Counter-Statement*, 123; *A Rhetoric of Motives*, 150

Burroughs, John, 153, 159, 167; *Notes on Walt Whitman as Poet and Person*, 92

Calamus, 18, 41, 45, 85, 89, 90, 101, 111, 123, 135, 147, 148, 150, 152, 168

Camden (New Jersey), 71, 72, 165

Canada, 160, 165, 177

Carlyle, Thomas, 165

Carson, Rachel, 72, 163; *Silent Spring*, 15, 51–52, 83, 170

"Cavalry Crossing a Ford" (Whitman), 158–159

"Cavalry Crossing a Ford: Walt Whitman's Alabama Connection" (Barrett), 158–159

Cavitch, David, *My Soul and I: The Inner Life of Walt Whitman*, 99

"Centenarian, The" (Whitman), 65

"Centennial Edition" (Whitman), 164

Central Park, 173

Centuries, The (Traherne), 63–64

Century of Early Ecocriticism, A (Mazel), 92

Ceremony (Silko), 37

"Chambered Nautilus, The" (Holmes), 17, 53–61, 158

Chauncey, George, *Gay New York*, 147

Children of Adam (Whitman), 44

"Child's Reminiscence, A" (Whitman). *See* "Out of the Cradle Endlessly Rocking"

Chinese mysticism, 16, 189n2

city, 101, 102, 117, 121, 133–140, 143–150, 152, 165, 167–169, 171, 172, 180, 181, 198–199n4

"City of Orgies" (Whitman), 147

Civil War, 39, 42, 52, 65, 75, 92, 93, 99, 107, 116, 120–123, 132, 134–137, 148, 151–153, 156, 160, 163, 165, 166, 167, 169, 178, 188n14

Civilian Conservation Corps, 163

Clemens, Samuel, 69

Columbus, Christopher, 77

Commoner, Barry, *Making Peace with the Planet*, 163, 170

"Continuities" (Whitman), 182

Counter-Statement (Burke), 123

Cousteau, Jacques, 56

Coviello, Peter, 123, 148

Crane, Hart, 137

Crocodile Dundee, 143

Cronon, William, 138, 139, 150

"Crossing Brooklyn Ferry" (Whitman), 89, 98, 99, 125, 128, 130, 131, 135, 140, 150, 172

Crowley, John, *Little, Big*, 101

Custer, George A., 65–66

"Dalliance of the Eagles, The" (Whitman), 159–160, 175

Darwin, Charles, 49, 55, 105

Davis, Robert Leigh, 53, 123; *Whitman and the Romance of Medicine*, 135

Day I Met Walt Whitman, The (Leifel), 176

"Death Sonnet for Custer, A" (Whitman), 65. *See also* "From Far Dakota's Cañons"

Debs, Eugene, 142

Deloria, Vine, Jr., 77–78, 129–130, 135; *God Is Red*, 71. *See also* sacred spaces

democracy, 152, 165, 172, 173, 174, 175, 181

Democratic Vistas (Whitman), 46, 53, 73, 78, 152, 164

depression, 71, 89, 114, 124, 152, 164

"Design of Walt Whitman's *Specimen Days*, The" (Johnson), 166

Dewey, John, *Experience and Nature*, 174

Dickinson, Emily, 15, 93

Dillard, Annie, *Pilgrim at Tinker Creek*, 51

Dodge, Jim, 100

Donne, John, 103

Doudna, Martin K., 92; "Nature," 53

Doyle, Peter, 72

Dresden, 162

Drum-Taps (Whitman), 39, 65, 123, 132, 134, 135, 152, 153, 156, 160, 161, 165, 175

Dubos, Rene, 52

Dylan, Bob, 142

"Each and All" (Emerson), 55, 62–64, 82

Earth Day, 1, 163

"Earth, My Likeness" (Whitman), 41, 44

Earth, My Likeness: Nature Poems of Walt Whitman (Nelson), 65

Eastern mysticism, 16

ecocriticism, 36, 64, 92, 100, 161,
185–186n1, 186n2, 186n4, 187–188n11,
200–201n3
Ecological Communication (Luhmann),
43
ecology, 19, 24, 51–52, 61, 122, 170, 186n8
ecopoetics, 15, 16, 23, 30, 33, 35, 37, 42, 43,
81, 95, 112, 115, 119, 135, 154, 157, 166, 171;
island poetics, 115–131; and metaphor,
48–50
Edwards, Jonathan, 15, 24, 37, 54
Ehrlich, Paul, 163
Eisenhower, Dwight D., 75
Eliot, T[homas] S[tearns], 137
Emerson, Ralph Waldo, 15, 24, 92, 123,
128, 137; concept of self reliance, 142;
critique of travel, 75–76; "Each and
All," 55, 62–64, 82; "Hamatreya," 112,
113, 114, 129; and language theory,
24–26; *Nature*, 24–26; oversoul, 31
End of Nature, The (McKibben), 170
Enfans d'Adam (Whitman), 150, 165
Engels, Friedrich, *The German Ideology*,
61
England, 102, 103
Enlightenment, 137
Environmental Imagination, The (Buell),
113
Erkkila, Betsy, 143
Europe, 103
Evening Post, The, 59
evolution, 105, 106
Experience and Nature (Dewey), 174
extinction, 105, 106

*Fatal Environment: The Myth of the
Frontier in the Age of
Industrialization, The* (Slotkin), 65
"Fear Passing the Love of Women:
Sodomy and Male Sentimental
Citizenship in the Antebellum City,
The" (Milner), 147–148
Ferlinghetti, Lawrence, 137
Fichte, Johann Gottlieb, 167
Fields Were Green, The (Arms), 53
"Fine Afternoon, 4 to 6, A" (Whitman),
172–173, 177

Folsom, Ed, 156–157, 158; *Walt Whitman's
Native Representations*, 26, 71, 176
Fone, Byrne, 133
Foucault, Michel, 89
Freud, Sigmund, 15–16
"From Far Dakota's Cañons"
(Whitman), 65. *See also* "Death
Sonnet for Custer, A"
"From Montauk Point" (Whitman),
180, 181
"From Pent-Up Aching Rivers"
(Whitman), 44
Fulton Ferry, 75
future, 46, 80, 128, 137, 141, 150, 152

Galápagos, 105
Garman, Bryan, 100, 142, 143
Gay New York (Chauncey), 147
Geffen, Arthur, "Silence and Denial:
Walt Whitman and the Brooklyn
Bridge," 75
German Ideology, The (Engels and
Marx), 61
Gilbert, David W., *Greening the Lyre:
Environmental Poetics and Ethics*, 66,
67
Ginsberg, Allen, 137
"Give Me the Splendid Silent Sun"
(Whitman), 132–136, 146, 147
God, 15, 60, 72, 77, 79, 80, 174, 175
God Is Red (Deloria), 71
"Good-Bye, My Fancy" (Whitman), 164,
177, 178, 182
Gould, Augustus A., *Principles of
Zoology*, 56
Grace Church, 141
Grant, Ulysses S., 162
Great Plains, 177, 178, 179
*Greening the Lyre: Environmental Poetics
and Ethics* (Gilbert), 66, 67
Griswold, Rufus, 18
Grünzweig, Walter, 143
Gullah, 127
Guthrie, Woody, 142

"Had I the Choice" (Whitman), 181–182
"Hamatreya" (Emerson), 112, 113, 114, 129

Harper's Magazine, 72
Harris, Joel Chandler, 127
Harrison, Jim, 176
Harvard University, 55
Hausman, Gerald, *Turtle Island Alphabet*, 104
Hawthorne, Nathaniel, "My Kinsman, Major Molineaux," 143
Heidegger, Martin, 5, 7, 176
Helms, Alan, "'Hints . . . Faint Clews and Indirection': Whitman's Homosexual Disguises," 148
Hicks, Elias, 44
Hindu metaphysics, 16
"'Hints . . . Faint Clews and Indirection': Whitman's Homosexual Disguises" (Helms), 148
Hiroshima, 162
Hollis, C. Carroll, 33, 36
Holmes, Oliver Wendell, 15, 156; "The Chambered Nautilus," 17, 53–61, 158
Homer, 181
homoeroticism. *See* sexuality
homosexuality. *See* sexuality
"Hours for the Soul" (Whitman), 171
"How Emerson, Thoreau, and Whitman Viewed the Frontier" (Allen), 65–66
Hughes, Langston, 137
"Human and Heroic New York" (Whitman), 171
Hurston, Zora Neale, 93
Hurt, Mississippi John, "Make Me a Pallet on the Floor," 146
Hutchinson, George, 33, 135, 166
Hyde, Lewis, 32, 33, 135
hysteria, 15, 20

"I Dreamed in a Dream" (Whitman), 152
"I Sing the Body Electric" (Whitman), 31, 81, 84, 86, 123, 124, 143–144
identification, 27, 33, 49, 60, 72, 99, 111, 116, 127, 139, 150, 169
imagism, 147, 158, 159, 160, 175, 176
"In a Station at the Metro" (Pound), 147, 158

indirection 43, 45, 48, 52, 66, 160. *See also* resonance
island poetics, 98, 99, 101, 102–106, 113, 115, 116, 117, 118–131, 137–138, 149, 166, 172, 177, 179, 180, 182, 195n2, 196n3

James, William, "The Moral Equivalent of War," 162–163
Japan, 77
Johnson, Linck, "The Design of Walt Whitman's *Specimen Days*," 166

Kaplan, Justin, 101
Keats, John, "Ode to a Grecian Urn," 63
Kerouac, Jack, 137; *On the Road*, 17
Kirk, Diane, 69
Kolodny, Annette, 51, 161

"Land Ethic, The" (Leopold), 52
language theory, 25–26, 43
Lanier, Sidney, 15
Lankavatara Sutra, 30
Lao Tzu, 16–17
"Laws for Creation" (Whitman), 45
Leaves of Grass (Whitman), different editions: 1855 (first edition), 16, 18, 31, 35, 53, 85, 89, 97, 99, 142, 143; 1856 (second edition), 16, 31, 35, 53, 89, 97, 99, 143; 1860 (third edition), 53, 84, 85, 89, 97, 107, 123, 147, 150, 151; 1867 (fourth edition), 89, 124, 151, 152, 153, 164; 1871–72 (fifth edition), 89; 1876 ("Centennial Edition"), 65, 74, 89, 161, 164; 1881–82 (sixth edition), 89, 164; 1891–92 ("Deathbed Edition"), 88, 89, 164, 177, 179, 182; Comprehensive Reader's Edition, 23, 40
Leifel, Gregory, *The Day I Met Walt Whitman*, 176
Leopold, Aldo, 72; "The Land Ethic," 52; *Sand County Almanac*, 15, 38; "Thinking Like a Mountain," 52, 83
Lincoln, Abraham, 98, 115, 116, 117, 121, 123, 137, 152, 198n18
Little, Big (Crowley), 101
Little Big Horn, 65

"Live Oak, with Moss" (Whitman), 90, 150

"Loafing in the Woods" (Whitman), 177

Long Island, 84, 86, 101–102, 106, 117, 121, 131, 134, 139, 143, 177, 180

Longfellow, Henry Wadsworth, 53

Loving, Jerome, 59, 123; *Walt Whitman*, 121, 136, 141, 147, 160

Lowell, Robert, 53

Lucretius, 156

Luhmann, Niklas, *Ecological Communication*, 43

Lunar Light of Whitman's Poetry, The (Thomas), 31, 61, 66, 115, 135, 142

"Make Me a Pallet on the Floor" (Hurt), 146

Making Peace with the Planet (Commoner), 163, 170

"Maldive Shark, The" (Melville), 158

Manhatttan, 101, 131, 134, 140, 147, 148

manifest destiny, 64, 69–73, 77–78, 84–86, 91–92, 130, 160

"Mannahatta" (Whitman), 179, 180

Marsh, George Perkins, 116

Martin, Doug, 159

Marx, Karl, 15; *The German Ideology*, 61

Maslan, Mark, 123, 133

Mather, Cotton, 54

Mazel, David, 8, 65; *A Century of Early Ecocriticism*, 92

McKibben, Bill, *The End of Nature*, 170

McLuhan, Marshall, 76

McMurray, Andrew, 67

Mediterranean Sea, 77

Melville, Herman, "The Maldive Shark," 158

Memoranda During the War (Whitman), 164, 165

metaphor, 15, 26, 33, 48, 56, 59, 61, 62, 95, 96, 105, 108, 129, 137, 141, 158, 161, 163, 171, 173, 181, 191n16, 192n2; island, 102–106; and personification, 48–51

metaphysical poets, 49, 60

metonymy, 33, 158. *See also* trope

"Million Dead, Too, Summ'd Up" (Whitman), 121–122

Milner, Michael, "The Fear Passing the Love of Women: Sodomy and Male Sentimental Citizenship in the Antebellum City," 147–148

Mississippi River, 75

Montauk, 102

Moon, Michael, 33, 53

Moore, Marianne, 15, 56, 137

"Moral Equivalent of War, The" (James), 162–163

Morris, Roy, Jr., 123

Muir, John, 153

Murphy, Patrick D., 6–7, 19

"My Kinsman, Major Molineaux" (Hawthorne), 143

My Soul and I: The Inner Life of Walt Whitman (Cavitch), 99

mysticism, 111, 156

Nagasaki, 162

narrative, 105, 117

National Uncanny: Indian Ghosts and American Subjects, The (Bergland), 70

Native Americans, 69–71, 85–88, 103, 123, 146, 190n14; Cherokee, 37; and ecopoetics, 30; mythology, 37; Pueblos, 30, 37; Sioux, 65–66; tradition, 38

naturalism, 49

nature: as abstraction, 42, 53, 64, 83, 74, 75, 79, 80, 92, 94, 127, 164; alienation from, 57; appeals to, 172, 174, 181; and the body, 107, 168; and the celebration of the human, 62; and the city, 149, 152, 172; coldness of, 112; communion with, 24, 27, 136; connection to, 79; and death, 115; definition of, 48, 191n20; deified, 126, 133, 137; and democracy, 174, 175; discourse on, 38; distance from, 173; eloquence of, 45; as "environment," 137; as force, 49, 53, 137; as foundation for an organic theory of art, 174; as god term, 114, 174, 175, 197–198n12; "going back to," 166,

nature, as abstraction (*continued*)
169, 170; and human creativity, 95;
and human history, 61, 70, 99, 132;
and humanity, 165; identification
with, 111 (*see also* identification); ideological constructs of, 65; and language, 24, 25, 125–126; as lover, 51;
mastery over, 154; as "mere" anything,
99–100; as mere reference, 147; modernist understanding of, 135; as
mother, 51; as non-human, 48, 49, 59,
61, 150; as object, 53, 58, 64, 114, 153;
objects of, 167; observation of, 60, 61;
as other, 19, 20; out of, 165; pagan
view of, 156; and the pathetic fallacy,
109 (*see also* pathetic fallacy); personification of, 52, 57, 126 (*see also* personification); as place, 132, 165; and
poet, 15, 96, 129, 180; and psychoanalytic criticism, 99; rejection of, 133,
134; as resource, 44, 58, 64, 73, 76, 114;
responsibilities toward, 51; as retreat,
149, 155, 157, 165, 169; returning to, 168;
and Romanticism, 113–114, 155, 167,
171; separation from, 162; and society,
136; and the soul, 31, 94, 96; as spirit,
58, 64, 73, 114, 153; as sublime, 50;
things of, 30, 184; as token, 115; turning away from, 38, 134; views of, 58, 73;
voice of, 66; warfare with, 161, 163;
Whitman's engagement with, 192n4;
wonder of, 64
"Nature" (Doudna), 53
nature poetry, 16, 49, 53, 59, 60, 62, 90,
137, 176
Navesink, 177
Netherlands, 102
negation, poetic act of, 23, 25, 26, 28, 35
Nelson, Howard, *Earth, My Likeness:
Nature Poems of Walt Whitman*, 65
New Jersey, 179
New Orleans, 101, 121
New York, 69, 74, 76, 101–102, 145, 172,
173, 174, 177
New York Criterion, The, 18
New York Tribune, The, 65

Niagara, 176
"Niagara" (Whitman), 177
"Noiseless Patient Spider, A," 36, 38, 41,
42, 43, 48, 53, 54, 60, 81, 133, 153, 191n17
*Notes on Walt Whitman as Poet and
Person* (Burroughs), 92
November Boughs (Whitman), 44

"O Captain, My Captain" (Whitman),
121
"O Magnet-South" (Whitman), 121
O'Connor, Ellen, 72
"Ode on a Grecian Urn" (Keats), 63
"Of That Blithe Throat of Thine"
(Whitman), 181
"On the Beach at Night" (Whitman), 45,
130
"On the Natural History of the Aru
Islands" (Wallace), 105
On the Road (Kerouac), 17
"Once I Pass'd through a Populous
City" (Whitman), 146–147
"Out of the Cradle Endlessly Rocking"
(Whitman), 66–68, 80, 98, 106, 107,
111, 112, 114, 115, 118–124, 149, 152,
196–197n9

Paine, Thomas, 142
"Passage to India" (Whitman), 53,
75–86, 88, 92, 95, 96, 101, 111, 132, 152,
160, 164
"'Password Primeval': Whitman's use of
Science in 'Song of Myself,' The"
(Scholnick), 156
pastoral tradition, 113, 114
pathetic fallacy, 15, 48, 88, 107, 109
Paumanok, 126, 180, 195n1
"Paumanok" (Whitman), 84, 109
Peace Corps, 163
Peirce, Charles Sanders, 24
personification, 15, 21, 33, 35, 48–52, 57,
58, 61, 71, 83, 107–108, 118, 122, 192n2,
198n21
Philadelphia, 69
Philippon, Daniel J., 167
phonocentric fallacy, 67, 68

Pilgrim at Tinker Creek (Dillard), 51
"Pioneers! O Pioneers!" (Whitman),
    135, 160, 161
"Place of Nature, The" (Smith), 113, 154
Plato, 27
Poe, Edgar Allan, 157, 156; "Sonnet—To
    Science," 155, 156
"Poem of the Sayers of The Words of
    The Earth" (Whitman), 24. *See also*
    "Song of the Rolling Earth, A"
"Poem of Wonder at the Resurrection of
    the Wheat" (Whitman), 23. *See also*
    "This Compost"
Politics of Distinction, The (Beach),
    138–139
Pollack, Vivian, 53, 143
Pound, Ezra, 137; "In a Station at the
    Metro," 147, 158
"Prayer of Columbus" (Whitman), 72,
    79, 125, 164
Principles of Zoology (Agassiz and
    Gould), 56
"Proto-Leaf" (Whitman), 84–85. *See
    also* "Starting from Paumanok"
psychoanalysis, 90
psychology, 32

Quammen, David, *Song of the Dodo*, 105

religion, 85, 91, 92, 130
renewal, 34, 100, 101, 114, 116
resistance, 48, 101, 133, 141
resonance, 28, 30, 35, 36, 37, 43, 44, 45,
    66, 96, 119–120, 123, 132, 135, 170
Rhetoric of Motives, A (Burke), 150
Rhodes, Cecil, 81
Rocky Mountains, 166
Roethke, Theodore, 15
*Romantic Turbulence: Chaos, Ecology,
    and American Space* (Wilson), 156
Romanticism, 64, 142, 155, 165, 170, 171
Ruskin, John, 49

sacred places, sacred sites, 75, 101, 106,
    107, 114, 115, 116, 123, 130, 131, 132, 136,
    177, 179, 196n6

San Francisco Bay, 77
Sand County Almanac (Leopold), 15, 38
Sandburg, Carl, 137
"Sands at Seventy" (Whitman), 179–181
Saturday Press, 107, 196n7
Schelling, Friedrich Willhelm, 167
Scholnick, Robert, "'The Password
    Primeval': Whitman's Use of Science
    in 'Song of Myself,'" 156
science, 48, 49, 52, 55, 56, 57, 58, 59, 104,
    153, 154, 155, 156, 157
"Science and Art" (Whitman), 155
Scigaj, Leonard M., 19
Sea Drift (Whitman), 106, 107, 135
"Seeing Niagara to Advantage"
    (Whitman), 175–177
semiotics, 24, 26, 28. *See also* thing
    theory
sexuality, 30, 41, 50, 51, 89, 90, 91, 93, 94,
    96, 98, 99, 100, 106, 107, 133, 160; auto-
    eroticism, 31, 94; homoeroticism, 40,
    41, 88, 89, 90; homosexuality, 18, 99,
    147, 148, 150
Shakespeare, William, 38, 181
shamanism, 32, 114, 190n14
Sherman, William Tecumseh, 162
"Silence and Denial: Walt Whitman and
    the Brooklyn Bridge" (Geffen), 75
Silent Spring (Carson), 15, 51–52, 83, 170
Silko, Leslie Marmon, *Ceremony*, 37
Simpson, David, 143
sites, distinction from sights, 177
"Sleepers, The" (Whitman), 39, 98, 106,
    144–145
Slotkin, Richard, *The Fatal Environ-
    ment: The Myth of the Frontier in the
    Age of Industrialization*, 65
Smith, Jonathan, "The Place of Nature,"
    113, 154
Snow, C[harles] P[ercy], 154
Snyder, Gary, *Turtle Island*, 103–106
"So Long!" (Whitman), 26
social Darwinism, 70–73
"Song of Myself" (Whitman), 17,
    18, 22, 23, 24, 28, 31, 33, 35, 39, 41,
    48, 50, 52, 62, 71, 79, 80, 89, 93, 94,

"Song of Myself" (*continued*)
98, 106, 110, 112, 114, 119, 125, 128, 135, 137, 140, 148, 150, 157, 160, 168, 170
"Song of Occupations" (Whitman), 140
"Song of the Broad-Axe" (Whitman), 161
Song of the Dodo (Quammen), 105
The Song of the Earth (Bate), 5–8, 176
"Song of the Open Road" (Whitman), 39
"Song of the Redwood-Tree" (Whitman), 64–73, 75–79, 85–86, 101, 122, 156, 160, 164, 170
"Song of the Rolling Earth, A" (Whitman), 24, 25, 26, 28, 29, 30, 35, 43, 44, 48, 132
"Sonnet—To Science" (Poe), 155–156
Sorisio, Carolyn, 143
soul, 27, 28, 29, 30, 31, 32, 33, 34, 35, 36, 38, 42, 43, 45, 48, 59, 61, 75, 76, 77, 79, 80–81, 84, 86, 91, 94, 96, 99, 108, 110, 114, 119, 124, 128, 130, 131, 132, 135, 155, 164, 170, 171, 172, 190n14
Specimen Days (Whitman), 101, 102, 106, 121, 136, 165, 166–180, 184, 200–201n3
spider, 37, 38, 39, 40, 41, 43, 60, 61, 62, 81, 90–91, 106, 114, 124, 153. *See also* "Noiseless Patient Spider, A" *and* web
"Spontaneous Me" (Whitman), 93, 94, 95, 98
Springfield, Illinois, 116–117
Springsteen, Bruce, 142
St. Louis, Missouri, 75
Stafford, Harry, 168
"Starting from Paumanok" (Whitman), 84–88, 89, 92
strangers, 42, 135, 146, 152
stroke, 75, 79, 165
sublime, 19, 22, 58, 76
Subterranean Kerouac (Amburn), 37
Suez Canal, 76
"Sun-Bath—Nakedness, A" (Whitman), 168
sympathy, sympathetic imagination, 35, 138, 140, 141, 145, 147, 184
synecdoche, 105–106, 133, 147, 171

Taylor, Edward, 54
technology, 137, 153; communication, 76–78, 88, 100; photography, 176, 178; transportation, 75–78, 88, 141, 165, 176
Tennyson, Alfred Lord, 123
"Thanatopsis" (Bryant), 111, 113, 114
Thayer, Robert L., Jr., 100
thing theory: 15–19, 89, 154, 182; in Whitman, 19–47
"Thinking Like a Mountain" (Leopold), 52, 83
"This Compost" (Whitman), 19, 23, 24, 34, 35, 48, 81, 83–84, 93, 94–95, 98, 111, 113, 114, 121, 122, 127, 132, 154, 182, 183. *See also* "Poem of Wonder at the Resurrection of the Wheat"
Thomas, Dylan, 111
Thomas, M. Wynn, 100; *The Lunar Light of Whitman's Poetry*, 31, 61, 66, 115, 135, 142
Thoreau, Henry David, 51, 75–76, 153, 190n10; *Walden*, 23; "Walking," 116, 117
"Thou Orb Aloft Full-Dazzling" (Whitman), 88, 89
Timber Creek, 165, 168, 171–172
time, 129–130, 131, 132, 141, 150, 152, 166, 177, 178
"To a Waterfowl" (Bryant), 59–60, 158
"To the Sun-Set Breeze" (Whitman), 182–183
Tokyo, 162
Trachtenberg, Alan, 142
Traherne, Thomas, *The Centuries*, 63–64
transcendentalism, 23, 24; and language theory, 25, 75
Traubel, Horace, 18, 142
travel writing, 175–178
trope, 15, 21, 30, 33, 34, 35, 45, 48, 49, 50, 59, 62, 71, 80, 82, 83, 97, 99, 105, 108, 107, 128, 134, 141, 145, 173, 192n1
Turtle Island, 103–106
Turtle Island (Snyder), 103–106
Turtle Island Alphabet (Hausman), 104

urbanization, 129, 132–133, 135–139, 142–148, 150, 152, 165, 198–199n4

Vaughan, Henry, 15, "The Waterfall," 54
Vestiges of Creation, 157
Vietnam, 163
Virginia, 121
"Voice of the Rain, The" (Whitman), 181

Walden (Thoreau), 23
"Walking" (Thoreau), 116, 117
Wallace, Alfred Russell, "On the Natural
    History of the Aru Islands," 105
Walt Whitman (Loving), 121, 136, 141,
    147, 160
Walt Whitman's Native Representations
    (Folsom), 26, 71, 176
war, 101, 102, 132, 133, 135, 161. *See also*
    Civil War
Warren, James Perrin, 53
Washington, D.C., 71, 72, 101, 117
"Waterfall, The" (Vaughn), 54
web, informational, 76–77; poem as, 95;
    as symbol, 37, 38; World Wide, 38. *See
    also* spider
West, the, 87–88
"When I Heard at the Close of the Day"
    (Whitman), 148–150
"When I Heard the Learn'd
    Astronomer" (Whitman), 136, 153,
    154, 156, 157–158, 160, 161
"When Lilacs Last in the Dooryard
    Bloom'd" (Whitman), 66–68, 98, 99,
    101, 112, 115–123
"When the Full-Grown Poet Came"
    (Whitman), 164, 165, 180
"Whispers of Heavenly Death"
    (Whitman), 43
Whitman and the Romance of Medicine
    (Davis), 135
Whitman, George, 39, 72
Whitman, Walt: 1855 Preface, 46, 95;
    "America's Characteristic Landscape,"
    178–179; "Among the Multitude," 45;
    "As I Ebb'd with the Ocean of Life,"
    98, 99, 123, 124, 125, 126, 127, 128, 129,
    149; "Bathed in War's Perfume," 164;
    "Beat! Beat! Drums," 134; "Bivouac on
    a Mountain Side," 159; "Blood
    Money," 59; "Broadway," 181;

Calamus, 18, 41, 45, 85, 89, 90, 101, 111,
    123, 135, 147, 148, 150, 152, 168; "Cavalry
    Crossing a Ford," 158–159;
    "Centenarian, The," 65; *Children of
    Adam,* 44; "City of Orgies," 147; Civil
    War, 39; "Continuities," 182; "Crossing
    Brooklyn Ferry," 89, 98, 99, 128,
    130–131, 140, 150; "Dalliance of the
    Eagles, The," 159–160, 175; "Death
    Sonnet for Custer," 65 (*see also* "From
    Far Dakota's Cañons"); *Democratic
    Vistas,* 46, 53, 73, 152, 164; depression,
    71; *Drum-Taps,* 39, 65, 123, 134, 135, 152,
    153, 156, 158, 160, 161, 165, 175; "Earth,
    My Likeness," 41, 44; "Election Day,
    November, 1884," 181; "From Far
    Dakota's Cañons," 65; "From
    Montauk Point," 180, 181; "From
    Pent-Up Aching Rivers," 44; "Give Me
    the Splendid Silent Sun," 132, 146, 147;
    "Had I the Choice," 181–182; "Hours
    for the Soul," 171; "I Dreamed in a
    Dream," 152; "I Sing the Body
    Electric," 31, 81, 84, 86, 123, 124; "Laws
    of Creation," 45; *Leaves of Grass,* 15,
    23, 31, 33, 35, 36, 37, 39, 40, 41, 43, 49,
    52, 53, 65, 84, 85, 86, 88, 89, 92, 97, 98,
    99, 106, 107, 111, 112, 113, 114, 115, 123,
    124, 137, 139, 142, 143, 147, 148, 150, 151,
    152, 153, 157, 160, 161, 164, 165, 177, 179;
    "Live Oak, with Moss," 90;
    "Mannahatta," 179, 180; *Memoranda
    During the War,* 164, 165; "Noiseless
    Patient Spider, A," 36, 38, 39, 41, 42, 43,
    48, 53, 54, 60, 81, 133, 153; *November
    Boughs,* 44; "Of That Blithe Throat of
    Thine," 181; "On the Beach at Night,"
    45, 130; "Once I Pass'd through a
    Populous City," 146–147; "Out of the
    Cradle Endlessly Rocking," 66–68, 80,
    149, 152; "Passage to India," 53, 75–86,
    88, 92, 95–96, 101, 111, 132, 152, 160, 164;
    "Pioneers! O Pioneers!" 136, 160, 161;
    "Poem of the Sayers of the Words of
    The Earth," 24 (*see also* "Song of the
    Rolling Earth, A"); "Poem of Wonder
    at the Resurrection of the

Whitman, Walt (*continued*)
Wheat," 23 (*see also* "This Compost");
"Prayer of Columbus," 72, 79, 125, 164;
"Proto-Leaf," 84–85, 94 (*see also*
"Starting from Paumanok"); "Sands
at Seventy," 179–181; *Sea Drift*, 106,
107, 135; "Seeing Niagara to
Advantage," 175, 176, 177; "Science and
Art," 155; "Sleepers, The," 39, 144–145;
"So Long!," 26; "Song of Myself," 17,
22, 23, 24, 31, 33, 35, 39, 41, 48, 50, 52,
62, 71, 79, 80, 89, 93–94, 98, 110, 112,
114, 125, 128, 131, 135, 137, 140, 148, 150,
157, 160, 168, 170; "Song of
Occupations," 140; "Song of the
Broad-Axe," 161; "Song of the Open
Road," 39; "Song of the Redwood-
Tree," 64–73, 75–79, 85–86, 101, 122,
156, 160, 164, 170; "Song of the Rolling
Earth, A," 24, 25, 26, 28, 29, 30, 35, 43,
44, 48, 132; *Specimen Days*, 101, 121,
136, 165, 166–180; "Spontaneous Me,"
93, 94, 95, 98; "Starting from
Paumanok," 84–88, 89, 92; "Sun-
Bath—Nakedness," 168; thing theory,
15; "This Compost," 19, 23, 24, 34, 35,
48, 82, 83–84, 93, 94–95, 97, 113, 114,
121, 122, 127, 132, 154, 182, 183; "Thou
Orb Aloft Full-Dazzling," 88, 89; "To
the Sun-Set Breeze," 182–183; "Voice
of the Rain, The," 181; "When I Heard
at the Close of the Day," 148–149, 150;
"When I Heard the Learn'd
Astronomer," 135, 153, 154, 156,
157–158, 160, 161; "When Lilacs Last in
the Dooryard Bloom'd," 66–68, 98,
99, 101, 112, 115–123, 128, 152, 164, 165;

"When the Full-grown Poet Came,"
164–165, 180; "Whispers of Heavenly
Death," 43; "With Husky-Haughty
Lips, O Sea!," 181; "Woman Waits for
Me, A," 160; "You Tides of Ceaseless
Swell," 45

Whittier, John Greenleaf, 53
wilderness, 116–117
Williams, Raymond, 61
Williams, William Carlos, 158, 176
Wilson, Eric, *Romantic Turbulence:
Chaos, Ecology, and American Space*,
156
"With Husky-Haughty Lips, O Sea!"
(Whitman), 181
"Woman Waits for Me, A" (Whitman),
160
Woolf, Virginia, 38
"Word Out of the Sea, A" (Whitman),
107. *See also* "Out of the Cradle
Endlessly Rocking"
Wordsworth, William, 15; "I Wandered
Lonely as a Cloud," 54; "The Tables
Turned," 154–155, 157, 170, 171; "The
World Is Too Much with Us," 57–62,
88, 150, 156, 170
World War I, 162
World War II, 75, 92, 162
Wright, Frances, 142

Yellowstone National Park, 178
yoga, 32
Yosemite National Park, 178
"You Tides with Ceaseless Swell"
(Whitman), 45, 181

Zen, 17, 49

The
Iowa
Whitman
Series

Intimate with Walt: Selections from
   Whitman's Conversations with Horace Traubel, 1888–1892,
   edited by Gary Schmidgall

The Pragmatic Whitman:
   Reimagining American Democracy,
   by Stephen John Mack

Visiting Walt:
   Poems Inspired by the Life and Work of Walt Whitman,
   edited by Sheila Coghill and Thom Tammaro

Walt Whitman and the Earth: A Study in Ecopoetics,
   by M. Jimmie Killingsworth

Walt Whitman: The Correspondence,
   Volume VII, edited by Ted Genoways

Whitman East and West:
   New Contexts for Reading Walt Whitman,
   edited by Ed Folsom